FOOD SERVICES AND CATERING MANAGEMENT

FOOD SERVICES AND CATERING MANAGEMENT

R.P. Saxena

CENTRUM PRESS
NEW DELHI-110002 (INDIA)

CENTRUM PRESS
H.O.: 4360/4, Ansari Road, Daryaganj,
New Delhi-110002 (India)
Tel: 23278000, 23261597, 23255577, 23286875
B.O.: No. 1015, Ist Main Road, BSK IIIrd Stage,
IIIrd Phase, IIIrd Block, Bangalore-560085 (INDIA)
Tel: 080-41723429
Email: centrumpress@gmail.com
Visit us at: www.centrumpress.com

Food Services and Catering Management

First Edition, 2010

ISBN 978-93-80540-84-9

PRINTED IN INDIA

Printed at Balaji Offset, Delhi.

Contents

Preface

Food service or catering industry defines those businesses, institutions, and companies responsible for any meal prepared outside the home. This industry includes restaurants, school and hospital cafeterias, catering operations, and many other formats.

The companies that supply food service operators are called food service distributors. Food service distributors sell goods like small wares (kitchen utensils) and bulk foods. Some companies manufacture products in both consumer and food service versions. The consumer version usually comes in individual-sized packages with elaborate label design for retail sale. The food service version is packaged in a much larger industrial size and often lacks the colourful label designs of the consumer version.

Food service sales to restaurants and institutions are estimated to be approximately $400 Billion, about equal with consumer sales of foods through grocery outlets. Major food service providers include Aramark, Brinker International, Compass Group, the Crown Group, Darden Restaurants, Sysco, McLane Company, US Food service and 3663 First for Food service.

Catering is the business of providing food (and often, service) for events. According to the National Restaurant Associations 2010 Restaurant Industry Forecast, social caterers are one of the fastest-growing segments of the restaurant industry.

The book provides a clear understanding of the fundamental aspects of food and catering services and the very best strategies for its management. It serves as a reference for such people: individuals who have affinity for food and cooking – culinary enthusiasts, entrepreneurs, teachers, demonstrators, students as well as chefs and cooks who need to refresh their memories with some principles and procedures.

—R.P. Saxena

1

Introduction to Food

Food is essential for human survival. The cooking of food began thousand of years ago. Initially it was roasting the meat through open fire and since then cooking has become the oldest and the most common method of processing food. Although some of our methods of food preparation originated thousands of years ago, the understanding of exactly what the cooking process does to food is relatively new. Many factors and principles related to food preparation have been identified, but there is still much to be learned. Since food is so important, its preparation has become both science and art. The science of food is concerned with the specific components of food, their interaction, and the influence of temperature, light, and air on palatability. The art of food preparation gives recognition to the aesthetic and cultural aspects of food.

Artistic talents with foods can be expressed through pleasing colour combinations and variety in size and shape. Seasonings and food combinations may be used to accent flavour, and a combination of textures adds interest. Outstanding food-preparation and service skills can be developed so that one becomes an artist with food. Culture patterns of food are very near and dear to the hearts of all of us. Culture influences food choices, food combinations, service, and food traditions. Each culture gives it's our unique value to food, its use, and its service. Foods are evaluated according to their appearance, texture and flavour. Words which are often used to describe these qualities include; *Appearance*-bright, clear, creamy, dull, dry, fine, frothy, curdled; *Texture*-crisp, brittle, chewy, coarse, compact, flaky, stringy, fizzy, light, grainy, gritty, hard, smooth; *Flavour*-acid (lemon), bitter, bland, mild, tangy, burnt, strong, dull, eggy, fishy, spicy, tart, sour, sweet. It is difficult to adequately evaluate food if one or more these senses is lacking. Sight, which is the most important sense with food, influences the feedback received from other sensory receptors.

Through ages food continued to retain its importance and has actually, grown to become more popular in the society. Food through varieties of cooking has become universal in its appeal. The cooking itself has become an art to be gained through training and practice. It has become a specialty that is being imparted through famous institutes all over the world. Those who master it can 'never fail to grow professionally and in stature. In all the hospitality organisations, establishments and even in offices and homes it has become an important component. The variety has developed to such an extent that every village, city, country now boast of its own special type of cuisine. There is no dearth of appreciation for good cuisine. The appeal that cuisine has needs to be understood region by region.

International Cuisine & Their Appreciation

A brief introduction to varieties of cuisine all over the world is as follows: Every country in the world has its gastronomic specialties, its excellent national dishes, but the high art of cooking is essentially French. It is said that eating to the French is not merely a physical function, but it is an intellectual and aesthetic pleasure. France is famous for its haute cuisine and number of regional, traditional specialties. Items like bouillabaisse (a soup) pot-au-feu, lobster soup, Chicken Marengo besides varieties of salads, souffles and mouses are all well known for their taste, class and satisfaction.

Britain is another country that is famous for its strong and robust food items. It English roast beef, Irish stew, roast Turkey, fish and chips, varieties of other regional specialties from Scotland, Ireland, Wales all are tasty and are well known to the people. Italy is another country that is traditionally famous for Pizza and Spaghetti. But it is also famous for varieties of seafood, quality wines and ice creams/sorbets. Greece is another country that is famous for variety and taste. Whether it is moussaka or salad or souvlaki, the country has all the items consisting mostly beef, lamb meat, pork & chicken. Seafood is also very popular to the visitors frequenting its tabernas.

Coming to Asia, Chinese cuisine is internationally famous. Its cuisine consisting of Chinese pork, Pecking duck, Mushrooms, Chinese veal, or items belonging to Szechwan or Cantonese regions are so well known that do not need any introduction.

USA is one continent that is truly cosmopolitan. It has every cuisine. Indian, Chinese, Continental, Jewish, Greek, French and many more. Of course its Kentucky chicken, hamburgers, all American pie are all very popular with tourists as well as its own people.

Besides all the above it is also well known that India has its own prominent place in the art of cooking. Moghulai, South Indian tiffins/ snacks, tandoor dishes are popular all over the world. While one can go on describing about varieties of cooking and the greatness of the taste, it needs to be mentioned that these have become an integral part of tourism. Since every tourist spends 40% of his budget on accommodation and food, needless to mention its potential and importance for tourism development. Besides the contribution of food to the overall satisfaction, health and prosperity of the societies is immense in addition to its role in the development of hospitality industry.

National Cuisine and its Role in Promoting International Tourism

Indian cuisine is as diverse as its regions. Styles of cooking and commonly used ingredients differ not only from region to region but from are household to another. Internationally Indian curry is famous. The curry consists of spices, pieces of vegetarian or non-vegetarian items all go to make a sauce based variously on onions, tomatoes, yoghurt or coconut milk etc. Some of India's best-loved dishes are homely favourites: Panjabi Sarson Ka Saag, Mustard greens simmered ail night long on a coal fire, is a seasonal favourite, being available only for a month or so in winter. Accompanied by thick unleavened bread made from cornmeal, its fullbodied flavour delights the peasant and the urban sophisticate alike. Pau bhaji is a passion in Mumbai and Gujarat, where roadside stalls have a cauldron of simmering vegetables which are served with a bun. Bhelpuri in Mumbai and chaat in Delhi are roadside snacks of crunchy morsels, tempered with piquant seasonings. The coastal states like Goa, Kerala and Bengal have culinary traditions with a preponderance of fish, those of Goa and Kerala making profuse use of coconuts. Goa seafood delights include crab, lobsters, tiger prawns and shellfish, all accompanied by rice and washed down with excellent wine and vermouth of local manufacture. Kerala, in common with the other Southern states is noted for its variety of crisp pancakes and steamed rice cakes made from pounded rice and are locally known as "Dosa". Gujarat and Tamilnadu have important vegetarian traditions, meat eaten only by less number of people. However, because of the seemingly endless array of imaginatively cooked vegetables, lentils and the succession of enticing accompaniments, even confirmed non-vegetarians relish the cuisine.

To Western tastes, the range of Indian sweets is normally found too sweet, but it is precisely because of this quality that they make marvellous digestives after a heavy Indian meal. Sweet traditions in Kolkota, Bikaner and Delhi are famed throughout the country. In the state of Andhra Pradesh too the sweets like "Kakinada Kaja", "Ravva Laddu" and "Pootha rekulu" etc. are well known and are mouth watering.

Nonalcoholic beverages include the countrywide favourite Nimbupaani "a squeeze of sour lime over sugar or salt served in water or soda". Yoghurt and water are vigorously churned to make buttermilk, a delicious accompaniment to Indian meals. Bottled fizzy drinks include various brands of indigenous lime, orange and cola. Other fruit based drinks like guava, mango and tomato are available in tetra packs and tins. Soda, mineral water and fresh coconut water are also widely available. Indian's alcoholic beverages include gin, rum, as well as whisky that are comparable to the finest international brands. Out of numerous brands of wine, good choices are the dry white and rose ones; sparkling wine being made in the country is available in limited quantities for the domestic market. India also produces dozens of brands of beer both very good pilsners and lagers.

Food Science Concepts

Basic Si Units of Length, Area, Volume, and Weight

The SI or International System of measurement is used universally for measurement of matter. In this system, prefixes such as 'deci', 'centi', and 'milli', and units such as `litre', `gram', `metre', and derived units such as `joule' and `pascal' are used.

Prefixes represent numbers or numerical quantities symbolized by letters.

mega = M = 1,000,000 = one million

kilo = k = 1,000 = one thousand

deci = d = 1/10 = one tenth

centi = c = 1/100 = one hundredth

milli = m = 1/1,000 = one thousandth

micro = μ = 1/1,000,000 = one millionth.

Measurement of Length

The unit for measuring length is the metre (m).

Length is measured using a measuring tape or ruler.

One thousand metres (1,000 m) = one kilometre (km).

A metre is divided into hundred parts. Each part is called a centimetre (cm) or

one metre (m) = 100 centimetres (cm).

Each centimetre is made up of ten smaller parts called millimetre (mm) one centimetre = 10 millimetres (mm).

The simplest instrument for measuring length is a scale or ruler measuring one metre, or a measuring tape.

Measurement of Volume

Volume and capacity is measured in litres. A litre is made up of 10 decilitres (dl). Each decilitre is made up of 10 centilitres (cl). A centilitre is made up of 10 millilitres (ml), which means that a litre is made up of one thousand millilitres (1,000 ml).

Most measuring cups and jugs are marked in millilitres and litres. The capacity of cups and spoons is listed below.

1 tablespoon = 15 ml

1 teaspoon = 5 ml

1 breakfast cup = 240 ml

1 coffee cup = 100-120 ml 1 teacup = 150-180 ml

1 water glass = 280-300 ml.

The volume of solids that is not greatly affected by water can be measured by the water displacement method. Solids are immersed in the displacement can and the volume of water displaced, equal to the volume of the solid, is noted.

The seed method is used to measure the volume of cake and bread. A large tin box is filled to the brim with seeds and the volume of seeds required to fill the box is measured in a measuring cylinder.

The cake of which the volume is to be measured is placed in the empty tin and covered with seeds. The volume of seeds remaining after covering the cake is equal to the volume of the cake.

Measurement of Weight or Mass

Weight is the pull experienced on the body by the earth's force of gravity. Mass is the amount of matter contained in a known volume of substance. Mass always remains constant but weight may change in different parts of the world because the force of gravity varies from place to place.

Weight is measured on a weighing scale. The kilogram is the unit for measuring weight and is made up of one thousand smaller parts called grams.

1 kilogram (kg) = 1,000 grams (g)

Each gram is further divided into one thousand smaller parts called milligrams (mg).

1 g = 1,000 mg

Each milligram is further divided into 1,000 micrograms (μg).

1 mg = 1,000 gg From the above we conclude that

1 kg = 1,000,000 mg and a measure of 1 ppm means 1 mg in 1 kg of a substance.

Density

Density is the relationship between the weight and volume of a substance expressed as:

$$\text{Density} = \frac{\text{weight in kg}}{\text{volume in m}^3}$$

It is expressed in kilograms per cubic metre and is used to compare the heaviness or. lightness of different foods.

A fruit cake has a greater density as compared to a sponge cake. The density of liquids is measured in g/cm. Water has a density of 1 g/cm.

Relative Density

Relative density (R.D.) is the ratio of the mass of a known volume of a substance to the mass of the same volume of water. It tells us the number of times the volume of a substance is heavier or lighter than an equal volume of water. If the R.D. of a volume of lead is 11, it means that it is eleven times as heavy as an equal volume of water.

A hydrometer is used to measure the relative density of different liquids. It is made up of a weighted bulb with a graduated stem calibrated to measure the relative density of the liquid directly. The liquid to be tested should be at room temperature and the hydrometer is allowed to float in the liquid. The depth to which it sinks is read on the graduated stem. Hydrometers are specifically calibrated to measure the R.D. of different liquids used in the catering industry.

Saccharometers are used to determine the concentration of sugar solutions, denoted in degrees. A 75% sugar solution is called 75 degrees Brix.

Salinometers are used to determine the R.D. of brine or sodium chloride solutions used for canning vegetables or pickling ham.

Lactometers are used for checking the purity of milk. Addition of water or removal of cream affects the R.D. and is depicted on the graduated scale on the stem. The scale is marked 1.00 to 1.04. 'W' denotes R.D. of water, 'M' denotes pure milk, and 'S' denotes skim milk.

Alcoholometers are used to test the R.D. of alcoholic beverages. It is used to check the number of degrees proof or ethanol content of wines, beers, and spirits, and whether it has been diluted.

Refractometers are used to measure the sugar or total solids in solution (TSS) while preparing jam, syrups, etc. They measure the refractive index of light reflected through the solution.

Besides checking the purity of milk, ethanol content of alcoholic beverages, strength of salt solution, and concentration or stage of 'doneness' for sugar syrups and preserves like jam, sauce, and candied fruit, the other applications of R.D. are

- testing eggs for freshness when eggs are dipped in a 10% salt solution, fresh eggs sink and stale eggs float because of a large air space caused by staling;

- determining the lightness of cakes; and
- choosing potatoes for boiling and frying. Potatoes that have a low R.D. should be boiled, while those that have a high R.D. should be baked or fried.

Temperature

Heat is a form of energy needed to carry out work. Energy is the capacity for doing work. Energy is present in two forms: (1) potential energy or stored energy, such as the energy stored in a bar of chocolate; and (2) kinetic energy or active energy in motion, such as when a person is walking. Energy is present in many forms. Heat is one form of energy. Solar energy, electrical energy, and chemical energy are some of the others.

Heat energy is measured in units called joules and the energy present in food is measured in kilocalories. One kilocalorie is made up of 1,000 calories.

1 kilocalorie (kcal) = 4.2 kilojoules (kJ)

1 calorie = 4.2 joules.

Temperature refers to the relative hotness or coldness of a substance compared with melting ice at 0°C and boiling water at 100°C. Thermometers are used to measure temperature. Temperature is measured either in the Celsius or centigrade scale (°C) or in the Farenheit scale (°F). Each scale has two fixed points:

1. Melting point of ice (0°C or 32°F)
2. Boiling point of water (100°C or 212°F).

The Celsius scale is divided into 100 degrees and the Farenheit scale into 180 degrees. The Celsius scale is the international scale.

Types of Thermometers

Most thermometers are mercury in glass thermometers with different temperature ranges depending on their purpose. Some common thermometers are:

1. Sugar or confectionery thermometers (40°C to 180°C)
2. Dough testing thermometers (10°C to 43°C)
3. Meat thermometers with a special spike which can be pierced into meat and a round dial to record temperature
4. Refrigeration thermometers filled with red coloured ethanol (-30°C to-100°C).

pH or Potential Hydrogen

When an acid is diluted with water it dissociates into hydrogen ions and acid radical ions.

HCl	=	H+	+	Cl^-
Hydrochloric acid		Hydrogen ion		Chloride ion (acid radical)

The term pH (hydrogen ion concentration) is used to express the degree of acidity or alkalinity of a food. It is defined as the negative logarithm to base 10 of the hydrogen ion concentration, i.e., higher the hydrogen ion concentration, lower will be the pH and vice versa. Some foods like fruits contain organic acids and have an acid reaction while others such as milk are neutral. Bakery products leavened with baking powder, have an alkaline reaction. Pure water is pH 7 or neutral. The pH scale of pH 0 to pH 14, i.e., from extremely strong acids to extremely strong alkali is used to describe the acidity or alkalinity of food.

A reading between pH 1 to pH 6.5 indicates acidic food while pH 7.5 to pH 14 indicates alkaline food. The pH of a solution can be measured electrically using the pH meter or it may be measured colorimetrically using pH papers which change colours according to the pH.

Buffers

They are defined as solutions that can resist a change of pH on addition of acids or alkalis but within limits. These solutions are made up of a weak acid and one of its salts or a weak base and one of its salts.

Table : pH values of some common foods

pH	*pH value*	*Food*
Strongly acidic	2.0	Vinegar
	2.3	Lime juice
	2.7	Pickles
	3.0	Apples
	3.7	Orange juice
	4.0	Fruit cake
	4.3	Tomato
	4.6	Banana
	5.0	Bread

Mildly acidic	5.4	Spinach
	5.5	Potatoes
	6.0	Peas
	6.2	Butter chicken
	6.4	Salmon
	6.5	Milk
Neutral	7.0	Chocolate
Mildly	8.0	Egg white
Alkaline	9.0	Soda bread

When hydrogen ions (H+) or hydroxide ions (OH^-) are added, they can be absorbed by these systems without altering the pH of the resulting solution. Common buffers are:

1. Acetic acid and sodium acetate mixture
2. Citric acid and sodium citrate mixture.

Buffering action is very important in the human body and in food. The salts of calcium, phosphorus, sodium, and potassium function as buffers and maintain the pH of milk at a constant level of 6.5.

Applications of pH

1. Preparation of jam-The pectin in jam and marmalade does not form a gel until the pH is lowered to 3.5. If fruit used for making these preserves does not contain sufficient acid, small amounts of citric acid should be added.
2. Retaining bright green colour in green vegetables-Green vegetables tend to get discoloured when cooked. Green colour can be retained by adding a pinch of sodium bicarbonate to the cooking liquor but B complex vitamins and vitamin C gets destroyed in an alkaline medium.
3. Food digestion-pH of the gastrointestinal juices affects our digestive process. The pH of gastric juice is strongly acidic, between 1 and 2, and aids in digestion of food in the stomach while a mildly alkaline pH, between pH 7 and 8 is needed, to complete digestion in the intestine.
4. Texture of cakes-A significant change in texture is observed with a change in pH while baking cakes. Low pH gives a fine texture and high pH gives a coarse texture to the cake crumb.

5. pH of dough-In bread making, compressed yeast is used for fermentation. During fermentation, yeasts convert simple sugars to ethyl alcohol and carbon dioxide.
   (a) Ethyl alcohol takes up oxygen and forms acetic acid
   (b) Carbon dioxide dissolves partially in water to form carbonic acid
   (c) Chemical yeast food, i.e., ammonium sulfate and ammonium chloride if used, produce sulphuric acid and hydrochloric acid respectively.

All these acids lower the pH of the dough from pH 6.0 to pH 4.5. This change in pH makes the dough less sticky and more elastic.

Important Terminologies, Their Definition and Relevance

Boiling Point

Boiling is the use of heat to change a substance from a liquid to a gas. The change takes place throughout the body of the liquid at a definite temperature. Like the melting point, the boiling point of a pure substance is always constant. It changes if impurities or dissolved substances are present or by changes in atmospheric pressure. Pure water boils at 100°C.

Applications of boiling point:

1. Boiling vegetables in salted water increases the boiling point above 100°C.
2. In sugar cookery, the boiling points of sugar solutions is noted at various stages so that fondant, fudge, toffee, and caramel can be prepared.

Boiling Under Pressure

When atmospheric pressure is lowered, water boils at a lower temperature of 70°C. At hill stations, the atmospheric pressure is low so temperature is also lower and food takes longer time to cook. When pressure is increased, e.g., below sea level or boiling in a pressure cooker, water boils at higher temperatures and food cooks faster.

Applications of boiling under pressure:

1. Food is cooked in pressure cookers to reduce cooking time to one-fourth of ordinary cooking time as water boils at a higher temperature under pressure.

2. Autoclaves are used for sterilization by moist heat under pressure at 121°C and 15 lb pressure for 20 minutes.

Evaporation

Evaporation is a change of state from liquid to gas which takes place continuously from the surface of a liquid.

Volatile liquids vaporize easily e.g., petrol and acetone.

Nonvolatile liquids like oils evaporate very gradually. Evaporation is faster when there is breeze and low humidity in the air as well as a large surface area and high temperature.

Applications of evaporation:

1. Bread and cake if left uncovered, hardens and becomes stale because of loss of moisture. This can be prevented by storing food in covered tins.
2. Cooking in shallow uncovered pans will cause greater evaporation and is used for preparing mawa from milk.
3. Milk powder is prepared by dehydration or spray drying in which water from milk is removed by circulating hot air.

Melting Point

Melting or fusion is the change of state from a solid to a liquid.

The temperature at which a solid melts and turns into a liquid is called its melting point. The melting point of fats depends on the percentage of saturated long chain fatty acids present in it.

The melting point for any chemical is fixed and is used to measure the purity of a substance. It is lowered by adding other substances. Melting point of fats:

Vanaspati	37-39°C
Butter	36°C
Lard	44°C
Tallow	48°C
Coconut oil	26°C

Applications of melting point:

1. Ice has a melting point of 0°C. If adequate sodium chloride is added to ice, the melting point falls to-18°C. This lowering of melting point is made use of in the setting of ice cream.

2. Fat is removed from adipose tissue of animals by a process called rendering which is based on the melting point. Boiling water or dry heat is used to liberate the oil from the fat cells.

Corn oil temperatures:

1. Frying	180-195°C
2. Smoke point	232°C
3. Flash point	330°C
4. Fire point	363°C

Smoke point: When fats and oils are heated strongly above frying temperature, they decompose and a stage is reached at which visible thin bluish smoke is given off. This temperature is called the smoke point. The temperature varies with different fats and ranges between 160 and 260°C. The bluish vapour is because of formation of acrolein from overheated glycerol. Acrolein has an acrid odour and is irritating to the eyes. The smoking point is lowered by the following factors:

1. Presence of large quantities of free fatty acids
2. Exposure of large surface area while heating
3. Presence of suspended food particles.

Flash point: This is the temperature at which the decomposition products of fats and oils can be ignited, but will not support combustion. The flash point varies with different fats and ranges between 290 and 330°C.

Fire point: This is the temperature at which the decomposition products of fats and oils support combustion. It ranges between 340 and 360°C for different fats. The oil or fat may catch fire and burn. The smoke point, flash point, and fire point are lowered by the presence of free fatty acids.

Table : Smoke point of some common fats

Oil	*Smoke point (°C)*
Corn oil	232
Cotton seed	236
Soya bean	243
Ground nut	243
Butter	201
Lard	222
Beef dripping	163

Normal frying temperature for most oils is 180-195°C. The smoke point is 25-40°C above normal frying temperature. The application of smoke point is in frying foods. Fats and oils used for deep fat frying should have a high smoke point. Moist foods should be coated well before frying as moisture present in food tends to hydrolyse the fat and increase the free fatty acids present.

Surface Tension

Surface tension is a force experienced on the surface of a liquid. It is caused by cohesion, i.e., a force that causes the molecules of a substance to be attracted to one another.

The molecules of a liquid that are below the surface are pulled by cohesive forces from all directions. But the molecules at the surface behave differently because they are only pulled downwards or sideways. This downward or sideways attraction causes a constant pull on the surface molecules which makes the liquid behave as if it is covered by a thin elastic film. For example, the surface of water can support needles if they are placed carefully.

Because of surface tension, drops of liquid take a spherical shape, which has the smallest possible surface area, e.g., dew drops.

Surface tension causes liquids to rise in a thin tube (capillary tube) when the tube is dipped in liquid. This property of liquids is important in many food systems and in the action of detergents.

Surface tension is also defined as the force of attraction which exists between liquid and solid surfaces.

Applications of surface tension:

1. Addition of detergent to liquids reduces the surface tension of water and the surface attraction between the fibre and greasy stain, and allows the soil to be removed from the fabric.
2. Release agents help prevent the paper lining the tin from sticking to the cake. They contain silicone compounds.
3. Silicones have a property of lowering the surface tension and is added to wood polishes to allow the polish to spread easily.
4. Non-stick cookware is coated with polytetrafluoroethane plastic or silicone to prevent attraction between the food and pan.

Osmosis

Osmosis is the passage of water from a weak solution to a stronger solution through a semipermeable membrane.

When raisins are soaked in a cup of water for sometime, the raisins swell because water from the cup enters the raisins. Similarly, if raisins are placed in a concentrated sugar solution, they shrivel up after sometime because water from the raisins passes into the sugar solution because of osmosis.

Plant and animal cell membranes act as semipermeable membranes and selectively permit water and electrolytes to enter or leave the cell. Applications of osmosis:

1. Osmosis plays an important role in food processing and preservation to retain the original shape and size of canned fruits in syrup and of vegetables in pickles.
2. The freshness of fruits and vegetables depends on the osmotic pressure in the cells. Salads lose their crisp crunchy texture and become limp if salt and sugar is sprinkled much in advance. Lettuce leaves can be revived by immersing then in chilled water.

Humidity

Humidity refers to the presence of water vapour in the air. Water vapour is produced by respiration of plants and animals, evaporation from food during cooking and from water bodies, from rain during the monsoons, etc.

In catering establishments, moisture in the air is quite high because of large volumes of steam from boilers, from cooking food, from dishwashers and laundry processes, and respiration and perspiration of people in a confined area. A humid atmosphere causes discomfort, headache, and tiredness.

The humidity of the air is measured with the help of a hygrometer. This instrument depicts the percentage of water vapour in the air. It is a ratio between the amount of water vapour which air could hold and what it actually holds at the same temperature. Humidity of 60-70% is considered normal and does not cause discomfort or undue spoilage of food.

Applications of humidity:

1. Spoilage organisms multiply and spores germinate at high moisture levels in the atmosphere.

2. Humidity needs to be controlled in air-conditioned rooms along with ventilation and heating which is done by humidifier water sprays which maintain 60-70% humidity.
3. Processed foods are prevented from drying up by adding substances with hygroscopic properties called humectants. Glycerine and sorbitol are used as humectants in jam.

Food Rheology

It is the science of measuring forces which are needed to deform food materials or to study the flow properties of liquid foods. It deals with the viscous behaviour of a system.

Solid food can be chopped up, ground, minced, sliced, torn apart, or broken while it is being prepared or eaten. The texture is determined when we chew food and it is described as crisp, tough, chewy, creamy, sticky, spongy, etc.

Liquid foods are fluid or viscous. Viscosity is defined as the resistance of a liquid to flow. It is measured by an instrument called a viscometer. This property of a liquid is seen in batters, sauces, syrups, etc.

Compression: It is the pressure needed to squash foam or spongy foods to find out their freshness or tenderness. The compressimeter or tenderometer is used to measure the lightness of a product.

Adhesion: Adhesive gumlike properties give stickiness to food which sticks to the teeth when chewed, like toffee. Breaking strength of dry foods, such as spaghetti, biscuits, and potato wafers, are measured by applying a load till the product breaks.

Shearing: It is the force needed to cut or slice through meat, vegetables, fruits, etc., and indicates the toughness of a food. Penetrometers measure the force needed to penetrate a food, such as jelly, cooking fat, canned and fresh fruits, and vegetables.

Rigidity: It is the property of those substances which do not flow, e.g., baked custard and cake. Rigid substances show either elastic property or plastic property.

Elastic substances. These substances do not flow, but flow when force is applied. However, when the force is removed it regains its original shape, e.g., sponge cake.

Elasticity: It is the property which permits a substance to change its shape when a force is applied to it and to come back to its original shape once the force is removed, provided the force applied is within elastic limits.

Applications of elasticity:

1. The stretching power of the dough can be tested before baking. The extensibility of flour is due to gluten formed in flour. Over-kneading of dough results in decreased elasticity.
2. Dough improvers are chemicals added to improve or strengthen the elasticity of bread dough.
3. Addition of malt flour gives a softer-textured dough because of enzymes present in malt.

Plastic substances: These substances resist flow to a certain point, but beyond that point they flow, i.e., they become plastic in nature.

Plasticity is an important property of margarine. A plastic fat is one which can be creamed as well as forms a thin sheet or layer in dough when the dough is rolled out, e.g., flaky pastry.

Summary

A knowledge of basic physical, chemical, and biological sciences are needed by all students studying catering. Today, the SI or International System of measurement is used universally for measuring matter. The unit for measuring length is the metre and for volume it is the litre. Weight is measured in kilograms and may change from place to place because of the force of gravity or pull of the earth. Density is the relationship between weight and volume of a substance while relative density is the mass of a known volume of a substance divided by the mass of the same volume of water. The hydrometer is used to measure the relative density of different liquids and are specifically calibrated to measure the relative density of different sub-stances. The lactometer is used to test the purity of milk, the saccharometer is used to measure the concentration of sugar solutions, alcoholometers are used to check the degrees proof, and salinometers to check the relative density of brine.

Energy is present in many forms, such as heat, solar, electrical, and chemical. Heat is measured in joules. Temperature is measured in degrees Farenheit and degrees Celsius, the potential hydrogen (pH) is used to express the degree of acidity or alkalinity of a food.

A pH between 1 and 6.5 is acidic and above 7.5 it is called basic or alkaline. Pure water has a pH of 7, which is neutral.

Buffers help in maintaining the pH of foods at a constant level.

Many other terminologies are relevant and need to be known and their applications understood by the caterer.

Colloidal Systems in Foods

Food served in catering establishments can be divided into two broad categories namely intact edible tissues and food dispersions. Sliced pineapple, diced vegetables, and fish fillets are examples of intact tissues. However, most food preparations have been subjected to different processes before they are brought to the table. Large masses of food may be subdivided into smaller particles by processes like mincing, grinding, pulping, and homogenizing, and ingredients may be mixed in different ways like beating, cutting and folding, blending, whipping, stirring, emulsifying, etc., converting the intact tissue into complex dispersions. The kind of process food is subjected to will have a bearing on the final quality of the product.

A well baked cake, where ingredients have been mixed correctly and a heavy collapsed cake may have the same chemical composition and nutritive value, but the latter will have no market because its physical qualities, i.e., its volume, texture, and appearance do not meet acceptable standards. These standards are of utmost importance to both the caterer and the consumer, and an understanding of the principles underling food dispersions is necessary for caterers to prepare high quality products.

Constituents of Food

Apart from water, food is mainly composed of three main groups of constituents namely carbohydrates, proteins, fats, and their derivatives. Along with these constituents, minerals, vitamins, organic acids, pigments, enzymes, flavouring substances, and other organic constituents are present in varying amounts in different foods. These constituents give food their structure, texture, colour, flavour, and nutritive value. To the caterer and consumer, the physical appearance is as significant as its chemical composition.

Foods are mixtures or dispersions of two or more types of substances. These sub-stances are present as particles of various sizes. Depending on the particle size or size of the molecule in the mixture, these substances may be classified as a true solution, a colloidal dispersion, or a coarse suspension.

True Solution

It is composed of two parts: the solute which is the dissolved substance and the sol-vent which is the substance in which the solute is dissolved. In a true solution, ions or molecules smaller than one millimicron are dissolved in a liquid. They contain varying amounts of ions or molecules of dissolved substances depending on the temperature of the solvent and on the solute. Solutions may be unsaturated, saturated, or supersaturated. They have the smallest particle size of the three types of dispersions. A solution is homogenous, i.e., alike in all parts, e.g., sugar syrup and brine.

Suspension

Suspensions are dispersions of coarse particles in a liquid. The particles are large and require continuous agitation to keep them dispersed. When agitation ceases, these coarse suspended particles settle down because of force of gravity. When the mixture is stirred, the suspension is formed again. In a suspension the particle size is larger than one micrometre or micron, e.g., starch and cold water paste. Many dispersions in food contain substances which are larger than one micron in size.

Colloidal Systems

Between the particle sizes of the solutions and those of suspensions, lies the area of colloidal systems. The particles are large enough to impart to the system some properties different from those found in true solutions, but small enough so that they do not separate out on standing. Colloidal systems deal with dispersions of a definite size, since it is the size of the particles in the colloidal range that impart the specific and characteristic properties to the system.

Colloidal dispersions are characterized by particles ranging between one millimicron (0.001 'μm) and 100 millimicrons (0.1 gm) with maximum size of up to one micrometre (gm) in diameter.

One micrometre (micron) (gm) = 10^{-3} mm or 1/1,000 mm
10^{-4} cm or
10^{-6} m

One millimicron (mg) = 10^{-3} gm or 1/1,000 gm.

There is no distinct line of demarcation. Particles approaching the limits of the size of one zone may show properties of two zones. For example, sugar exhibits both crystalloid and colloidal properties in food systems. The properties exhibited by colloidal particles around 1 mg in size are different from those of particles around 0.1 gm in size, e.g., crystalline candies have an organized crystalline structure while amorphous candies such as fondant lack an organized crystalline structure.

The gluten particles of hydrated flour proteins have colloidal dimensions but gluten particles of cake and pastry flours are more dispersed or of smaller size than those of bread flours. This is one reason for the different results obtained in cakes when bread flour is used instead of cake flour. All colloidal dispersions or colloidal systems have two phases: a continuous phase and a discontinuous or dispersed phase. The continuous phase extends throughout the system and surrounds the dispersed phase completely. Proteins, carbohydrates, and fats exist in foods as particles of colloidal dimensions. The system is a colloidal system as long as the particle size of the dispersed phase is within colloidal dimensions. Colloidal systems may be a combination of solid, liquid, or gas as the continuous or dispersed phase.

Table : Size of dispersed particle

Sr. No.	*Type of system*	*Size of particle*
1.	True solution	Up to one millimicron
2.	Colloidal dispersion	One millimicron upto one micrometre
3.	Coarse suspension	More than onemicrometre

In food, the following colloidal systems are of importance.

1. *Sol*-Colloidal dispersion of a solid dispersed in a liquid.
2. *Gel*-Colloidal dispersion of a liquid dispersed in a solid.
3. *Emulsion*-Colloidal dispersion of a liquid dispersed in a liquid.
4. *Foam*-Colloidal dispersion of a gas dispersed in a liquid.
5. *Solid foam or suspensoid*-Colloidal dispersion of a gas dispersed in a solid.

Dispersions may be simple or complex. In a simple dispersion a colloid may con-sist of a solid dispersed in a liquid, e.g., when gelatin is dissolved in warm water, a simple dispersion called a sol is formed. Mayonnaise is an example of a complex dispersion since it is an emulsion, a sol, and foam combined in one. Milk is another example of a complex dispersion, i.e., more than one phase is dispersed in a liquid. Milk is a solution of lactose in water, an emulsion of fat in water, and a sol as milk protein is dispersed in water.

Colloidal particles have different characteristics. Some are attracted to water and are called *hydrophilic* or water loving. They get hydrated easily. Others repel water and are called *hydrophobic* or water hating. These different characteristics are seen because of the difference in chemical composition of the' compounds. In certain substances, a part of their structure is hydrophobic while other parts are hydrophilic. Those parts or functional groups that are attracted to water are called *polar groups*. Examples of polar groups are the organic acid group or COOH group in proteins, the aldehyde or CHO group in carbohydrates, etc. *Non polar groups* are hydrophobic, e.g., carbon chains-C-C-C-C-and cyclic structures, which are seen in organic compounds.

Organic substances which have both polar and nonpolar groups are useful as emulsifying agents in food emulsions as part of their molecule is attracted towards the dispersed phase and part towards the continuous phase.

Stability of Colloidal Systems

The stability of a colloidal system depends on two factors.

1. The charge on the colloidal particle
2. A layer of water that is tightly bound to the molecule

Charge on the colloidal particle As the surface charge on the colloidal particle is similar, like charges repel and the particles do not get attracted or join together. This helps in keeping the system stable. When the charge is neutralized, the colloidal particles flocculate and separate out.

Layer on water Water is present in food in two distinct physical states: free water and bound water. Part of the water present in food is free water which can act as a solvent and has flow properties. The rest of the water is bound water which is closely combined with starch or protein by hydrogen bonding and influences the physical properties of food. Many colloidal systems are hydrophilic and attract a layer of water around them. The layer of water acts as an insulation and keep the colloidal system stable.

Types of Colloidal Systems in Food

Sol In this system, solids of colloidal dimensions are dispersed throughout a liquid. Solids form the dispersed phase and liquids the continuous phase. The viscosity of sols may range from liquid, e.g., skim milk to extremely viscous, e.g., tomato ketchup which barely flows. The viscosity of the sol will depend on the con-centration of solid and the temperature of the sol. The higher the concentration of solid in a sol, the more viscous the sol. The viscosity of a sol can be adjusted by adding more liquid.

Irrespective of the viscosity, in a sol the solid is always distributed throughout the sol and does not settle at the bottom. Protein in milk remains dispersed because of the like electrical charges on the surface of the protein molecule, which repel each other. When the charge on the dispersed protein molecules is neutralized by addition of acid, protein flocculates and separates out as is seen while preparing paneer.

Pectin remains dispersed because of its hydrophilic nature. It attracts a layer of water that is tightly bound to the pectin molecule by hydrogen bonding. All sols have flow properties. They flow more readily at higher temperatures than at a lower one. Sometimes a sol may change into a gel when the system is viscous and there is a drop in energy level, e.g., during cooling. The solids start associating with one another and form a three dimensional meshwork in which the liquid is trapped. Milk, cream soups, pouring custard, bechamel sauce, and gravy are commonly used sols in the kitchen.

Gel A gel is a colloidal system in which liquid forms the dispersed phase and solid forms the continuous phase. It is also called a reverse sol. A gel does not flow. Some of the liquid is adsorbed on the surface of the solid molecules and is called bound water. Because of this bound liquid, the gel has structure. The remaining liquid is trapped in the solid three-dimensional meshwork of the gel. As compared to a sol, the concentration of solid is higher in a gel.

A food gel consists of a continuous phase of interconnected particles or macro-molecules in which liquid is dispersed. The rigidity, elasticity, and brittleness of the gel depends on the type and concentration of the solid or gelling agent, the pH, salt content, and temperature, e.g., pectin does not form a gel unless the pH is acidic. The gelling agent may be a polysaccharide like cornflour in blancmange, a protein like albumin in caramel custard or complex colloidal particles like calcium caseinate in curds. Gums, pectins, and gelatin can form gels even at low concentrations.

When a gel is stored for sometime or becomes stale, there is a reduction in gel volume. The liquid which was entrapped in the three-dimensional meshwork of the gel is expelled from the interstitial spaces and the gel shrinks. This condition is called syneresis or weeping gel. Syneresis is seen in baked custards, moulded desserts, and curds. Free liquid may also be released if the gel structure is cut, e.g., in curds, whey separates out when the set gel is cut or disturbed. Sols and gels are reverse colloidal systems and many can be changed from one type to another. Many gels are first sols which on cooling form gels provided the concentration of solids is adequate.

When a sol is converted into a gel, the energy levels fall. This is seen during the cooling process. The solids in the dispersed phase move with difficulty through the continuous phase and ultimately associate with one another by forming secondary bonds. When the dispersion is cold enough, permanent bonds form, which can hold the liquid in the solid meshwork. A gel is formed which differs from a sol because it is apparently solid and is capable of holding its shape when served.

Emulsion An emulsion is a colloidal dispersion of tiny droplets of one liquid suspended in another. In this colloidal system, liquids form the dispersed as well as the continuous phase. One liquid is dispersed as droplets in another liquid. For an emulsion to form, agitation or shaking the two liquids is necessary till they are well mixed. Emulsions form, only when the two liquids are immiscible in each other, e.g., oil and water. The liquid with the higher surface tension forms small droplets or the dispersed phase. When an emulsion is formed the dispersed liquid has a much larger surface area as compared to the two liquids as separate layers.

Food emulsions are of two types:

(a) Oil in water emulsion or O/W emulsion in which the droplets of oil are dispersed in water, for example, mayonnaise and milk.

(b) Water in oil emulsion or W/O emulsion in which droplets of water are dispersed.

Emulsions may also be classified on the basis of stability as follows:

1. Temporary emulsions, e.g., French dressing
2. Semipermanent emulsions, e.g., milk
3. Permanent emulsions, e.g., mayonnaise, homogenized milk.

An emulsion is more viscous than the liquids that form the emulsion. Vinegar and oil when seen individually are very fluid, but when they are agitated together to make the emulsion mayonnaise the mixture becomes viscous.

In a temporary emulsion, the droplets that form the dispersed phase tend to coalesce as they bump into one another and form larger droplets till the emulsion breaks or separates into oil and water.

In food emulsions, the water phase may also contain water soluble constituents of milk, fruit juice, cooked starch paste, whole egg, vinegar, or lime juice as well as salts and other water soluble compounds. The oil phase may contain a blend of different fats and oils and fat soluble compounds.

Theory of Emulsification

1. During the process of emulsification, the main step is to break down the bulk liquid into small droplets and then stabilize the emulsion.
2. In a stable emulsion the droplets remain dispersed. But due to interfacial tension, there is a tendency for droplets to coalesce and separate out. The inter-facial tension is lowered by the addition of emulsifiers. Emulsifiers or emulsifying agents are surface active agents which lower the interfacial tension, i.e., the tension at the interface of two immiscible liquids.
3. The dispersed droplets which are of colloidal dimensions tend to form spherical structures in the continuous phase.
4. To prepare a stable emulsion, it is necessary to reduce the size of the droplets, prevent their coalescing, and increase their surface area.
5. Mechanical aids such as beaters, stirrers, homogenizers, and colloid mills help to reduce the size of the dispersed

droplets, thereby increasing surface area. Energy is required to work against the interfacial tension and allow the continuous phase to stretch out and cover the dispersed droplets.

6. Emulsifiers are used to reduce interfacial tension. They get adsorbed at the interface.
7. In an O/W emulsion, e.g., mayonnaise, the nonpolar group of the emulsifier is oriented towards the oil droplet (salad oil) and is adsorbed in the outermost layer of the droplet.
8. The polar group of the emulsifier is oriented towards the continuous phase of water (vinegar, lime juice, water from egg) surrounding the oil droplet.
9. The molecules of emulsifier surround the droplet completely forming a monomolecular layer of emulsifier (lecithin) around the droplet.
10. The oil droplet is thus protected by a film consisting of 3 layers namely
    (a) the outermost layer of oil molecules
    (b) a layer of emulsifier
    (c) the innermost layer of water.
11. Emulsions are further stabilized by the electric charge.
12. The ingredients used should not be chilled. Warm ingredients emulsify sooner as they are more fluid and spread or split into droplets faster.
13. The consistency of an emulsion ranges from liquid to a plastic solid.

The stability of an emulsion depends on the following factors:

1. The presence and type of emulsifying agent present
2. The amount or concentration of the emulsifying agent 3. The size of the droplets in dispersed phase 4. The ratio of oil and water used 5. The viscosity of the continuous phase.

The presence and type of emulsifying agent present: The most important factor which determines the stability of an emulsion is the presence of an emulsifying agent. The emulsifying agent may be present naturally in one of the ingredients, e.g., lecithin is a natural emulsifying agent present in egg yolk or the emulsifying agent may be added to the emulsion.

An emulsifying agent is a compound containing both polar and nonpolar groups and is thus attracted to both phases of the emulsion at the interface. The polar groups are oriented towards the water phase and the nonpolar groups pull the molecule of the emulsifying agent towards oil. The emulsifier forms a layer at the interface which coats the surfaces of the dispersed droplet completely.

The droplets do not touch each other and coalesce because of the protective layer of the emulsifying agent. The emulsion formed becomes stable and does not separate out into two separate layers because of the presence of the emulsifying agent.

The type of emulsion formed will also depend on the emulsifying agent used, and whether the polar or nonpolar group on the emulsifying agent is stronger.

If the nonpolar group is stronger, the emulsifying agent is more strongly attracted to oil. The surface tension of oil is reduced and water will form droplets or the dispersed phase. The emulsion formed will be a W/O type of emulsion.

The amount or concentration of the emulsifying agent The amount of emulsifier present in the emulsion should be sufficient to coat the dispersed droplets completely. The emulsifier forms a layer at the interface which is monomolecular in thickness. The droplets do not touch each other and coalesce because of the protective layer of emulsifying agent around each droplet. Addition of extra emulsifying agent does not have any beneficial effects. If the emulsifier is insufficient, all droplets will not be coated or protected and stability of the emulsion is affected.

The size of the droplets in dispersed phase: Mechanical aids such as beaters, homogenizers, and colloid mills help to reduce the size of the droplets dispersed, i.e., increase their surface area. The smaller the size of the dispersed droplets, the more stable the emulsion. A large droplet represents a lower energy state than two small droplets and has less stability. Homogenized milk is a stable emulsion as the size of the fat droplets are reduced. The ratio of oil and water used The ratio of oil and water used or the ratio of dispersed phase to the continuous phase is important. The continuous phase should stretch out and cover the dispersed droplets completely. For this proper mixing, shaking, or beating of the emulsion is necessary.

The viscosity of the continuous phase: The viscosity of the continuous phase. A viscous continuous phase will prevent the droplets of the dispersed phase from moving freely, bumping into one another, and coalescing.

Substances that increase the viscosity of a colloidal system are called stabilizers. They do not orient themselves at the interface as an emulsifier, but reduce the speed with which the dispersed droplets move. As viscosity increases the collision between droplets decreases and the droplets remain dispersed for a fairly long time. Examples of stabilizer are starch, sugar, gelatin, gums, finely powered spices, carboxy methyl cellulose, sodium alginate, pectin, etc. The addition of stabilizer alone is not enough to prevent the breakage of an emulsion.

Temporary emulsions have very little emulsifying agent or stabilizer present and are fluid systems. The dispersed droplets move and bump into one another and coalesce. This emulsion separates out on standing in a short while.

Formation of stable emulsions is of utmost importance in the food industry. A broken emulsion loses its viscosity, cannot be spread, and gives the product an unappetizing curdled appearance. Broken emulsions affect the texture and consistency of the final product.

Sometimes stable or permanent emulsions may break due to high changes in temperature like heating and freezing, e.g., Hollandaise sauce curdles at high temperatures and mayonnaise may break if frozen due to ice crystal formation.

Egg yolk contains a phospholipid lecithin which is a good emulsifying agent and forms O/W emulsions. Lecithin contains fatty acids as the hydrophobic group, and phosphate and choline as the hydrophilic group. Caseinogen a protein found in milk acts as a natural emulsifying agent. Glycerly monostearate (GMS) is added as an emulsifier in ice creams. Mayonnaise is a stable emulsion because of lecithin in the egg yolk.

The most widely used natural emulsifiers are lecithins present in egg yolk and extracted from soya beans which is more economical.

Synthetic food emulsifiers most commonly used are mono-and diglycerides. A common example is glyceryl monostearate or GMS. Mono-and diglycerides have one or two fatty acids attached to glycerol. The free groups of glycerol are hydrophilic while fatty acids are hydrophobic giving good emulsifying properties.

Some of the other emulsifying agents are stearyl tartarate, lactic acid monoglyce-ride, polyoxyethylene monostearate, etc.

Some Common Food Emulsions

1. *Milk and cream*-O/W emulsion stabilized by phospholipids and protein caseinogen
2. *Butter and Margarine*-W/O emulsion containing approximately 80% fat. Butter is stabilized by caseinogen and margarine is stabilized by GMS
3. *Egg yolk*-O/W emulsion. It is a good emulsifier as it contains lecithin
4. *Hollandaise sauce*-O/W emulsion stabilized by egg yolk
5. Salad dressings;
   (a) Mayonnaise-O/W emulsion stabilized by egg yolk. Not less than 65% oil by weight. Synthetic emulsifiers may be added like mono-and diglycerides of fatty acids, e.g., GMS.
   (b) French dressing-O/W emulsion may be temporary or permanent emulsion
6. Gravies, sauces, cream soups-O/W emulsions contain high percentage of water stabilized with refined flour
7. Choux pastry-O/W emulsion stabilized by egg
8. Batters-O/W emulsion stabilized by flour and egg
9. Icecream-O/W emulsion stabilized by caseinogen, GMS, alginates, gums/ gelatin.

Foams: A foam is a dispersion of gas bubbles in a liquid or semisolid phase. In this colloidal dispersion, gas forms the dispersed phase and liquid is the continuous phase. Foams are of two types:

1. Gas in liquid
2. Gas in solid.

In food systems, the continuous phase is usually a liquid with added solids or changed to solid by heating, e.g., beaten egg white and sugar foam is a gas in liquid dispersion. When it is baked it becomes a gas in solid dispersion, e.g., meringue. The liquid or semisolid walls are elastic in stable foams and separate the gas bubbles from each other. The gas bubbles range in size from 1 gm to several centimetres.

To form a foam, energy is required to overcome the surface tension of the liquid and stretch it into thin films, which surround bubbles of gas. Liquids which form foams easily have a low vapour pressure and low surface tension.

The presence of solid matter increases the stability of a foam. When egg white, cream, or gelatin is whipped into a foam, the protein which collects at the air-water interface gets denatured or coagulated by the energy used for whipping and helps in making the foam stable.

Whipped cream forms a stable foam because of the following reasons:

1. Proteins get denatured and become firmer
2. Butter fat and other milk solids present in cream increase the viscosity giving the foam a fine texture
3. Cream which has been aged is more concentrated and gives a better foam.

In homogenized cream, the fat is split into very fine particles, reducing its whipping properties. For a stable light textured foam of good volume, adequate mechanical agitation is necessary. At the same time care should be taken to avoid over beating or converting cream into butter.

Foams used in cookery include egg white, egg yolk, gelatin, and cream. They contribute towards lightness, volume, and texture of the product.

The caterer should understand that most of the food materials which are used or prepared in the kitchen are a combination of various colloidal systems. Since the colloidal state depends on particle size, it is important to understand the methods and ingredients used in food preparation that influence degree of dispersion.

1. Mechanical stress to which food has been subjected to before and during pro-duction like grinding, beating, homogenizing, etc., affects dispersion. Grinding of cereals, stirring of custard to prevent clumping and beating of curdled custards reduces the size of the particles and increases dispersion. Homogenization of milk is a

mechanical means of increasing the dispersion of fat globules.

2. Increasing the temperature may bring about greater or lesser dispersion. When milk is heated, dispersion of fat globules in milk increases. When proteins are heated, coagulation takes place, which decreases the degree of dispersion.
3. The addition of acid to milk causes casein to clot and decreases the dispersion. Alkalies bring about greater dispersion of cellulose and pectin in fruits and vegetables during cooking, making them mushy.
4. Amount of water present or the concentration of solids in a sol or gel. If water is present in excess, it will increase dispersion and prevent setting.
5. Enzymes may cause increased or decreased dispersion of foods. The proteinase enzyme in flour increases the dispersion of gluten. Clotting of milk on addition of rennin is an example of decreased dispersion of protein.

Milk, butter, margarine, cream, curd, doughs and batters, souffles and desserts, soups, sauces and gravies, etc., are all examples of colloidal systems. Many of these are multiphase food systems which have two or more discontinuous phases dispersed in a continuous phase.

Summary

Food products are generally multiphase systems in which solids, liquids, and gas are finely distributed during manufacture to give the finished product the desired structure and quality. The physical qualities in terms of volume, texture, appearance, and stability are as important as the chemical constituents present in food. The basic principles underlying food dispersions must be understood by the caterer to prepare high quality products.

Each type of processing or method of mixing and the ingredients used affect the quality of the finished product. Apart from intact tissues of food, the caterer has to deal with solutions, suspensions, and colloidal dispersions such as sols, gels, emulsions, and foams which are of colloidal dimensions. These systems impart special characteristics, to food.

2

Menu Planning and Mass Food Production

In the past few decades, people ate in restaurants occassionally to celebrate a special event such as an anniversary, a birthday, or an achievement. It was an outing to look forward to, and if one indulged, it did not matter as these outings were rare.

Today, the scenario is different. Eating out has become a way of life. Education and employment has taken many of us away from home, and the mother's role now has an added responsibility of contributing to the family income. Modern day compulsions have made eating out a necessity. No longer does one find time for the traditional fare of yesteryears and depends on the caterer for the following:

1. Food for festivals and celebrations
2. Meals at the work place.
3. Ready-to-eat meals picked up on the way home from work
4. Snacks and sweetmeats for daily consumption
5. Preserves, pickles, papads, etc.
6. All meals served in institutions such as hospitals, school/ college cafeteria, mess or dining hall, and boarding schools.

The number of reported cases of diabetes, hypertension, obesity, heart attacks, etc. is on the rise and so is the number of meals consumed away from home. This is not surprising because if one indulges practically everyday, it is bound to result in ill-health because of malnutrition. The caterer's role has become more significant as the responsibility now lies with the caterer for planning nutritionally adequate meals. Menu planning is the key to overcoming this problem.

Definition: Menu planning is defined as a simple process which involves application of the knowledge of food, nutrients, food habits, and likes and dislikes to plan wholesome and attractive meals.

The caterer who is responsible for providing meals has to decide on various aspects, such as:

1. Menu
2. Serving size
3. Food cost
4. Suppliers and quantities to be purchased
5. Standardized recipes to be followed
6. Type of service
7. Meal timings
8. Clientele.

The aim of menu planning is to:

1. Meet the nutritional needs of the individuals who will be consuming the food
2. Plan meals within the food cost
3. Simplify purchase, preparation, and storage of meals
4. Provide attractive, appetizing meals with no monotony
5. Save time and money
6. Minimize overhead expenditure, i.e., fuel, electricity, water, labour.

Menu planning is the most important aspect of planning and organization in the food industry. It is an advance plan of a dietary pattern over a given period of time.

Menus are of the following types.

Banquet menus: These are special menus for banquets or functions.

Institutional menus: Hospital menus, boarding school menus, and industrial can-teen menus.

Menus may be cyclic which means they are compiled to cover a specified period of time. The length of the cycle may vary and is decided upon by the management. A number of menus are set and repeated. They are often modified to take into account variations which may arise for a number of reasons.

Factors Influencing Meal Planning

Many factors influence the acceptability of a meal. Customers select what appeals most to them from a menu card based on individual likes and dislikes, budget, popularity of items, etc. However, while planning meals the following factors need to be considered.

Nutritional Adequacy

The most important consideration in menu planning is to ensure that the meal fulfils the nutrient needs of the individual consuming the meal. For example, if the meal is planned for an industrial worker, it must meet the RDAs for that age group. Foods from all basic food groups should be included in each meal so that the meal is balanced and nutritionally adequate. Nutrient needs may be modified for hospital diets (therapeutic diets).

Economic Considerations

The spending power of the clientele has to be kept in mind and meals have to be planned within the budget. Low cost nutritious substitutes should be included in the menu to keep the costs low. The food cost should be maintained, if the organization has to run profitably.

Type of Food Service

Menus should be planned in relation to the type of food service, whether it is cafeteria, seated service, buffet, etc.

Equipment and Work Space

The menu should be planned keeping the available equipment and work space in mind. Deep freezers, refrigerators, grinders, dough kneaders, deep fat fryers, boilers, etc. should be adequate.

Leftover Food

An effective manager should consider as to how leftovers could be rotated to obtain maximum profit. Adequate storage space and hygienic standards should be ensured to minimize the risk of contamination and spoilage of food.

Food Habits

Food habits of the customer is another important criteria which needs to be considered as food served has to be acceptable to the customer. Special attention should be paid when a particular type of community is catered to. Religious considerations should be known to the meal planner.

Availability

Some fruits and vegetables are seasonal. During the season the cost is reasonable and quality is better. Today, practically all fruits and vegetables are available throughout the year because of advanced preservation technology. However, seasonal fruits and vegetables should be given preference. Regional availability influences menu planning. For example, fish and sea food is fresh and cheaper in coastal areas.

Meat Frequency and Pattern

The meal timings and number of.meals consumed in a day, whether meals are packed or served at the table, also influences the selection of food items on the menu. The age, activity level, physiological state, work schedule, and economic factors need to be known before planning meals for institutional catering.

Variety

This is one of the most important considerations while planning meals. A variety of foods from the different food groups should be included. The term variety means

1. Variety in food ingredients
2. Variety in recipe
3. Method of cooking
4. Colour, texture, and flavour
5. Variety in presentation and garnish.

A meal should look attractive and be appetizing. A judicious blend of flavours, attractive colour combinations, and different textures make food enjoyable and interesting. The method of cooking used for different items on the menu should vary.

All animal proteins Pulses, nuts, and oilseeds.

Protein, vitamin and mineral rich Protein, vitamin, mineral, fibre, oils.

For example, two deep fried items would make the meal heavy. Simple processes such as fermentation and sprouting not only contribute to improved flavour and digestibility, but also enhance the nutritive value of the meal.

A well planned meal which is nutritionally adequate would have a good satiety value and prevent the occurence of hunger-pangs before it is time for the next meal. The nutritional adequacy of a meal in an a la carte service depends on the food choices made by the customer. It is the duty of the caterer to offer adequate, nutrient dense foods to the clients, to choose from.

Planning Balanced Meals

Meal planning involves proper selection of food to ensure balanced meals. We have also read that food can be classified on the basis of its source, the nutrients present in it, or on the basis of its functions into 3-11 food groups. These food groups help us in planning balanced meals which supply all essential nutrients. In this chapter we will study the three basic food groups classified on the basis of functions performed by nutrients as this is the simplest way to ensure adequate nourishment to the body.

The three main functions performed by food are:

1. Providing energy
2. Body building and maintenance
3. Regulation of body processes and protection against infection.

On the basis of functions performed, food is classified into the following three groups.

1. Protective/regulatory foods
2. Body building foods
3. Energy giving foods.

Steps In Planning Balanced Meals

1. Collect information regarding the customer with respect to
    - Age
    - Gender
    - Activity level
    - Religion
    - Socioeconomic background
    - Food habits
2. Check the RDAs for energy and proteins

3. Prepare a food plan, i.e., list number of servings from each food group to meet the RDA
4. Decide on number of meals
5. Distribute servings for each meal
6. Select foods within each group and state their amount
7. Plan a menu
8. Cross check to ensure that all food groups are included in requisite amounts.

Using the above steps, plan a balanced diet for a day.

Example: Planning balanced meals for college students residing in a hostel.

Calculating the Nutritive Value of a Recipe

Using the food composition table, follow the steps given here to calculate nutritive value of a recipe.

1. List the ingredients used and their quantities in the recipe.
2. Prepare a table with the following blank columns, and fill up the ingredient and quantity column from the recipe.
3. Refer to the food composition tables for the nutrients present in 100 g of edible portion of each ingredient.
4. Calculate the nutrients present for the quantities used in the recipe.
5. Weigh the finished product to know the total yeild.
6. Divide these values by the number of portions to know the nutritive value per portion.
7. For general calculations, do not include salt, spices, baking powder, stock, or ingredients which are used in very small quantities (less than 10 g) except for sugar and fat. Baking powder and salt are calculated for their sodium content, and not for their proximate principles, for sodium-restricted diets only.

Special Nutritional Requirements

Pregnancy

Every infant should have the right to begin life with a full-term healthy body and receive the advantage of mother's milk. For this to happen, every would-be mother should take special care of her nutritional needs. Pregnancy is a period of remark-able anabolic activity. A 3.2 kg infant develops in 9 months of pregnancy from the nourishment received from the mother. If the diet is deficient during these months, the foetus draws upon the maternal reserves. A poor diet will ultimately affect both the infant and the mother, and may lead to complications of pregnancy such as pre-mature birth and low birth weight.

Weight gain: A healthy woman is expected to gain 16-24 lbs in the 3 trimesters of pregnancy of which the full-term infant weighs 7 lbs. The remaining weight is due to increase in tissues, an expanding blood volume, and energy stored in the form of fat as a calorie reserve.

Energy: The energy needs increase during the second and third trimesters of pregnancy. An additional 300 kcalories take care of the increased demands of pregnancy. Calorific value of food is adjusted according to the weight gained.

Protein: The protein requirement increases by 15 g for the synthesis of foetal and maternal tissues.

Minerals: The calcium requirement is 1,000 mg and iron is 38 mg for the formation of foetal bones and teeth, and formation of blood respectively. The absorption of minerals improves because of the increased requirement. Iodine in the form of iodized salt, helps in protecting the mother and child against goitre and cretinism.

Vitamins: With an increase in calories, the need for vitamins B_1, B_2, and niacin increases as they are needed for release of energy from carbohydrates, fats, and proteins. The need for folic acid and vitamin D also increases.

Nutrient dense foods should be selected to meet the extra demand for proteins, calcium, iron, and vitamin D and B-complex vitamins.

Lactation

Mother's milk is the most nutritious food designed for an infant. The nutritional needs during lactation are greater than the needs during pregnancy as the mother's body has to supply all nourishment to the rapidly growing infant. The conversion of dietary protein to milk protein is only 50% which means 2 g of good quality pro-tein is converted to 1 g of milk protein.

Energy: Calorie requirements increase by 550 kcal during the first six months of lactation, followed by a marginal decrease during the next six months with 400 kcal being adequate to meet the additional demands.

Proteins: An additional intake of 25 g in the first six months and 18 g in the next six months is adequate.

Minerals: Calcium requirement is 1,000 mg which is necessary for synthesis of milk. Additional iron is not prescribed as milk is a poor source of iron.

Fluid: The intake of fluid increases during lactation.

The diet should be nutritious, easy to digest with restrictions on strongly flavoured vegetables and spicy food.

Human milk is the natural food for the infant. It is safe and convenient as it does not involve sterilizing bottles and preparing formulas throughout the day. At the same time, it is easy to assimilate, has the correct temperature, and gives a safe and secure feeling to the infant, and sense of satisfaction to the mother.

During the first few days after delivery, colostrum is secreted which is not mature milk but a substance richer in protein and vitamin A. Colostrum is secreted in small quantities but is valuable as it increases the resistance to certain infections during the first few months of life.

The intervals of feeding should be fairly flexible instead of following a rigid schedule or a self-demand schedule. For premature and low birth weight (weight less than 2.5 kg) babies a fixed schedule is preferable.

Milk is deficient in iron, vitamin C, and vitamin D. The baby is born with stores of these nutrients which suffice for 3 months. From the third month onwards, supplements should be gradually added to provide those nutrients which are not sup-plied by milk.

From the fifth to ninth month onwards, the infant should be weaned by substituting a cup feeding for a breastfeeding. This change should be gradual and at intervals till the infant is weaned from the breast to the cup before the age of one year.

Nutritional requirements: The next best substitute is cow's milk or modified buffalo milk. Buffalo milk is modified as it con-tains a larger percentage of protein, fat, calcium, and energy as compared to human milk and a lesser percentage of sugar. It is modified by partially skimming it, diluting it with water, and adding little sugar so that its composition resembles human milk.

Supplementary foods during the first year: The age at which supplementary foods should be included depends on a number of factors such as literacy of mother, economic factors, and time available. Supplements if not prepared, stored, and fed to the infant in hygienic conditions is one of the main causes for diarrhoea and gastrointestinal upsets. While introducing a new food the following points should be borne in mind:

1. Introduce one food at a time till the infant's system is used to the new food. Season with salt
2. Give a teaspoonful in the beginning
3. Never force-feed an infant
4. Start with a thin smooth consistency initially
5. Once the infant is used to supplements, introduce variety
6. Follow hygienic practices and do not give any leftover food or drink to an infant.

Choice of food supplements for infants:

1. Egg yolk
2. Strained cereals
3. Strained soup
4. Soft khichdi
5. Rice and dal
6. Pureed vegetables
7. Ready to eat infant cereals
8. Stewed fruit
9. Fruit juice.

Childhood

During these stages rapid growth takes place. There is an increase in height and weight because of increase in the bone and muscle mass. Children use up a lot of energy in playing. They normally carry their lunch, which should be nutritious and interesting, or monotonous, in which case the packed lunch box comes back home unfinished or unopened. Special efforts should be made so that they do not meet their energy needs from junk food.

More energy per kg body weight is required for:

1. Rapid growth which takes place in this age group
2. Enhanced physical activity
3. High BMR as compared to an adult.

Proteins: Good quality proteins should be included to take care of body building and maintenance of tissues. Milk proteins are complete proteins and provide calcium as well.

Carbohydrates and fats: They provide calories, and spare proteins from being oxidized for energy. Refined carbohydrates and poor dental hygiene are the reasons for dental caries in children. The consumption of fruits and vegetables, both cooked and uncooked, should be encouraged. Junk food and aerated beverages should be discouraged.

Vitamins and minerals: If the diet is well planned keeping the principles of menu planning in mind, supplements may not be necessary.

Fluid:Adequate fluid is necessary, specially in active children who play outdoor games and sweat a lot. Fluids should not kill the appetite, which is seen when children are thirsty and drink a lot of liquid just before a meal.

Points to be considered:

1. Regular meal timings
2. No nibbling low nutrient dense snacks between meals
3. Do not force feed, let the normal appetite return
4. Meal timing should be pleasant
5. Food should be appetizing and attractively served. Finger foods should be preferred for children
6. Packed meals should not be messy to eat
7. Attractive colours and shapes appeal to children, and with a little imagination eating green vegetables and drinking milk could become more interesting.

Adolescence

Adolescence is a period of physiological stress for the body because of extremely rapid rate of growth. The appearance of sex characteristic is also accompanied by mental and emotional changes. The diet plays a crucial role in promoting growth, hence the RDAs for all nutrients are high during 13-18 years of age.

Nutrients of particular importance are carbohydrates and fats for energy and proteins, iron and calcium for body building.

During adolescence the basal metabolic rate (BMR) accelerates once again because of the growth spurt and other hormonal changes which take place. The BMR of boys is higher than that of girls because of more muscle tissue.

Food habits change drastically because of peer pressure, maintaining one's figure and weight, skin problems, and the newly found independence.

Energy: Energy needs are high because of higher physical activity and BMR. Sports and aerobic exercises increase the energy requirements for sports people.

Proteins: A generous intake of high quality proteins is necessary for increase in muscles mass and skeletal development. A deficiency of calories and proteins can affect one's optimum height increase and resistance to infections.

Girls grow rapidly between 11-14 years and boys grow rapidly between 13-16 years. Initially, girls are taller than boys between 11-12 years. But later the growth rate is more in boys. Weight gain is a common problem in this age group which is tackled differently by both the sexes. Boys prefer exercise as a means of losing weight and body building while girls prefer going on a diet.

A deficiency of calcium/vitamin D during infancy or childhood results in rickets (deforming of bones). The weak bones cannot withstand the weight of the body and bend causing bow legs or knock knees. Once malformed, bones cannot be straightened. The effect of rickets is seen in adolescents and adults. Along with weight, emotional stress has an adverse effect on health and diet. Friction between parents and adolescents is another area of tension.

Snacks are the all-time favourite food, which often forms a large percentage of energy intake, favourite snacks being burgers, pizzas, pastries, ice creams, french fries, pav wada, pav bhaji, popcorn, and South Indian snacks. Milk is substituted by tea/ coffee (which is more of a social need) or aerated beverages. This trend indicates a high consumption of refined flour, hydrogenated fats, and potato. South Indian snacks are a better option as they are made from a cereal-pulse combination. In general, the diet is deficient in the protein food group and protective food group. Food such as milk, green leafy vegetables, yellow fruits and vegetables, citrus fruits, and whole grain cereals are deficient in the diet of adolescents. Deficiencies during infancy and childhood may leave their scar in adolescence.

Old Age

Anorexia nervosa: This is a disorder seen in adolescent girls concerning figure and weight control. The onset of puberty results in widening of the pelvis and deposition of subcutaneous fat creating a psychological problem in figure conscious young girls. They resort to crash diets for weight loss. This self-induced starvation to attain a slim figure leads to weight loss, loss of muscle tissue, a low BMR, and serious health problems.

Bulimia: It is another disorder in which the appetite increases drastically followed by induced vomiting to throw out whatever has been consumed. Bulimia creates both emotional and physical problems and is also known as the gorging-purging syndrome. Both disorders are mainly seen in adolescent girls from affluent families.

Nutrition in old age or geriatric nutrition is gaining importance as longevity has increased and 65 plus is the fastest growing segment of our population.

Aging is an individual phenomenon depending to a large extent on the health and nutrition status of an individual throughout his life span. People grow old at different rates and in different ways. Aging continues from birth throughout life.

Apart from the biological changes which occur with age, psychological and social changes are also seen. The body functions slow down, there is increasing social stress, and isolation. The elderly are often lonely, restless, and unhappy. They feel they are a burden and cannot contribute physically or monetarily to the family.

The following changes are seen in old age.

Body composition: As age advance, adults lose muscle mass and gain fat. Since active muscle is lost, BMR reduces with age. Bone loss occurs leading to a reduction in height. Collagen content increases giving rise to loss of elasticity in blood vessels, joints, and skin, seen as easy bruises, painful joints, and a wrinkled skin.

Sensory changes: The five senses of sight, hearing, taste, smell, and touch become dim with age. Old people cannot see without bright light, hearing is impaired affecting their social behaviour, and the other senses are less acute.

Digestive functions: Loss of teeth and ill-fitting dentures make it necessary to serve soft well-cooked food. Decreased secretion of saliva makes food difficult to swallow. Heartburn, diarrhoea, or constipation are other complaints.

Metabolic changes: Changes in metabolism, specially glucose tolerance and anaemias, are sometimes seen.

Osteopenia and osteoporosis are seen resulting in excessive bone loss, and fractures due to normal stress is another common finding. Because of age-related disabilities, the elderly should not live alone as they require assistance for all activities and company to overcome psychosocial changes in their life.

Nutritional requirements: The main features of the diet are as follows:

1. A low calorie diet of 1,000-1,500 kCal, as there is a reduction in the basal metabolic rate (BMR).
2. Good quality protein, calcium, and iron. Vitamin A, vitamin C, and folic acid to prevent anaemia.
3. Food should be easy to chew, liquid preparations should be included in each meal as they are light and easy to digest.
4. Hot meals should be served attractively as appetite is low.
5. Five small meals should be preferred to a three meal pattern.
6. Gas forming foods and strongly flavoured vegetables such as bengal gram, cauliflower, cabbage, and onion should be avoided.
7. Fibre rich foods such as whole grains, green leafy vegetables, pulses, and fruits are nutritious and provide fibre necessary for normal elimination. They should be incorporated into the diet gradually to prevent gastric irritation and gas.
8. Fluids: Ample fluids are necessary to flush out toxic wastes. The kidneys function at a slower pace with age, but fluids help in excretion of toxins.
9. Low calorie density and high satiety value foods should be included.

Effect of Quantity Cooking and Processing on Nutrients

Almost all foods consumed today need some form of cooking and processing before it is fit for service and consumption. Fruits and vegetables used in salads or for chutney are consumed uncooked. The nutrients we receive from the meals we consume depend to a large extent on cooking and processing practices which are being used. While some amount of nutrient loss is inevitable, cooking has many benefits which are listed below.

Benefits of Cooking Food

1. Cooking increases palatability
2. Cooking makes food easier to digest by destroying anti-digestive factors such as trypsin inhibitor in soya beans
3. Pathogenic microorganisms are destroyed
4. Shelf life is increased by destruction of spoilage organisms and denaturation of enzymes
5. The appearance of food improves, e.g., cooked meat versus raw meat.

Common Food Processing Techniques

Food prepared in large quantity in Institutional Kitchens or in food processing plants is more prone to loss of nutrients, if adequate care is not taken to retain or preserve the nutrient. This is because if food is cooked in bulk, the pre-preparation begins hours in advance, for example, vegetables have to be cut in advance and if these are not blanched and refrigerated to inactivate enzymes, oxidative losses of labile vitamins will continue at room temperature. Apart from nutritive value, the crisp texture of salads is also lost and phenol containing vegetables will discolour and turn brown, making the dish unattractive and unappetizing.

Effect of heat on nutrients: Cooking has beneficial effects on carbohydrates because of gelatinization of starch, favourable browning reactions such as Maillard reaction and caramelization of sugar which gives colour and flavour to food.

Proteins too take part in Maillard reaction along with sugar. Enzymes which catalyse undesirable enzymatic reactions in fruits such as apple and pears, and vegetables such as potato and brinjal are inactivated on blanching or cooking these foods. Enzymes which hasten oxidative destruction of vitamin C or ascorbic acid are denatured by blanching. Proteins get denatured by heat.

The chemical reactions that take place when oil is heated continuously during deep fat frying bring about hydrolysis, oxidation, and polymerization of the oil.

Triglyceride

The release of moisture, high frying temperatures of 160°-190°C, presence of carbonized crumbs in the oil, and oxygen from the atmosphere during frying brings about oxidation of the oil. Repeated use of the frying medium forms thermal and oxidative products which can cause gastrointestinal irritation and destruction of vitamins. These products undergo polymerization and increase the viscosity of the oil. The oil darkens in colour, has a lower smoke point, and foams when used for frying. Such oil should be discarded. Fat soluble vitamins dissolve in fat used for deep frying specially if food to be fried is not well coated.

Effect of alkali: Alkali is used during cooking and processing to soften vegetables, make pectin soluble, and dissolve hemicellulose. It is also used as lye,sodium hydroxide) to peel vegetables during processing. A pinch of sodium bicarbonate added to green vegetables helps in brightening the green colour. However, B-complex vitamins and ascorbic acid are destroyed in an alkaline medium. The use of alkali to hasten the cooking process for vegetables and pulses should be discouraged. Excessive cooking in an alkaline medium not only destroys vitamins, but makes the texture mushy and gives a soapy taste to the product.

Effect of acid: An acidic medium while cooking helps preserve water soluble vitamins and retards enzymatic browning of certain fruits and vegetables. Vegetables and pulses take a longer time to cook in an acidic medium as acids precipitate pectin and hardens vegetables.

Effect of washing and soaking: While preparing food, water soluble vitamins and minerals leach out into the cooking or washing water. These losses can be minimized by washing the uncut fruit or vegetables and not soaking the cut vegetable in water.

Soaking grains or pulses is beneficial as soaking increases digestibility and reduces cooking time.

Effect of sprouting and fermentation: Soaking whole grains overnight in water and tying them in a muslin cloth to allow them to germinate has many beneficial effects.

1. In sprouted grains, the dormant seed becomes active and synthesizes vitamin C.
2. Partial breakdown of carbohydrates, proteins, and fats begin, making it easier to digest.
3. The bioavailability of nutrients especially calcium and iron increases.
4. The active seeds synthesizes vitamin C or ascorbic acid and thiamine, riboflavin, and niacin content increases.

Exposure to air or oxidation: Exposure of finely divided foods to oxygen of the air reduces the vitamin C content by oxidation. The enzyme ascorbic acid oxidase is released when fruits and vegetables are cut. The enzyme activity is temperature dependant and can be inactivated by blanching, or by storing cut fruits and vegetables at refrigeration temperatures or by adding acid.

Vitamin A is destroyed on exposure to air. The colour of cut carrots (carotene) fades due to oxidation and B-complex vitamins are also affected.

Milling: Whole meal flour contains all nutrients present in the grain. In flour with 100% extraction no nutrients are lost. Low extraction flours (45% extraction) are light in colour and are mainly starch with some protein and fat. Approximately 70°/0 of all B-complex vitamins, minerals, and dietary fibre present in the whole grain are lost during milling.

Polished rice (the form in which rice is consumed) loses 75% vitamin B_1 or thiamine, while parboiling helps in retaining some of the vitamin.

Cooking and processing practices vary widely from one region to another, hence no authentic information on exact losses can be known. While cooking has both adverse and beneficial effects, proper practices can minimize the adverse effects and maximize the benefits so that food can become more whole-some and safe.

3

Recipe Development

The development of recipes was an important part of the Nutrition Education Strategy. The use of horticultural produce added variety, nutrient density and acceptability to the food preparations. Focus group discussions at field sites identified household preferences and food types. Responses were obtained from 41 women farmers in selected villages in different HDTCs on (a) common household cooking methods; (b) common recipes; and (c) knowledge and use of vegetables. These were used in recipe development.

A set of 55 horticultural produce-based recipes were developed including soups, children's snacks, complementary food, main meals, salads, fruit-based beverages, preparations from seldom used vegetable and fruit portions, mushrooms, coconut, spices, besides fruit, vegetable and spice preservation.

The recipes, adapted to local cultural practices and tastes were used to promote consumption of micronutrient-rich vegetables and fruits. Traditional practices that were nutritionally beneficial like roasting and grinding were emphasized. Preservation methods such as fermentation, pickling and drying were used to demonstrate the role of household conservation practices in food security and nutrition.

Acceptability

The acceptability of the recipes was assessed by community-based trials involving district officials and farmers in selected areas, using a five-point score. The sum of all attributes was used to calculate overall acceptability.

The average acceptability for all recipes was 87 percent among district-level participants (non-farmers) and 92 percent among farmers. The community-based acceptability trial found that, in general, *sobuj bhath* and soup were rated the best. Drumstick leaves omelette had a score of 98, but this was attributed to the use of eggs which are generally liked by all households and children.

There were regional differences in acceptability with northern districts like Natore and Chapainawabganj preferring drumstick leaves-based recipes. Older women farmers preferred *sobuj ruti,* everyone liked soup and *sobuj bhath,* and adolescent boys and girls preferred mixed vegetable salad. Both adults and adolescents liked *sobuj bhath* and mixed vegetable *pitha*. All participants were keen to learn more recipes.

Table. Acceptability scores of recipes promoted by project

Recipe	*Acceptability score %*	
	District level	*Farmer level*
Mixed vegetable soup	89	90
Mixed vegetable beans soup	90	92
Mixed vegetable chicken soup	93	95
Mixed vegetable meat soup	89	94
Mixed vegetable fish soup	80	89
Sobuj bhath	90	95
Sobuj ruti	82	90
Drumstick leaves omelette	80	98
Drumstick leaves *pakura*	82	92
Drumstick leaves *bhorta*	60	85
Sweet pumpkin coconut *halwa*	87	90
Coconut egg vegetable curry	82	88
Mixed vegetable egg salad	90	90
Mixed vegetable beans salad	88	89
Colocasia leaves *pitha*	80	85
Mixed vegetable *pitha* (hoppers)	90	92
Mushroom chop	90	90
Mushroom omelette	88	91
Fruit based complementary food	89	90
Carrot based complementary food	91	92
Vegetable based complementary food	88	88
Average score	*87*	92

On average, main meal dishes (*sobuj bhath, sobuj ruti*), soups, preparations from drumstick leaves such as omelette, *pakura* (deep fried in batter) and *bhorta* (steamed or broiled then mashed and spiced) and mushroom-based recipes were rated more than 90 percent by the farmers.

Nutritional Contribution of Recipes

The nutritive values of the recipes, including energy, protein, fat, vitamin A (beta carotene), iron, calcium, and vitamin C, are based on the Indian Food Composition Tables and the HKI Tables of Nutrient Composition of Bangladeshi Foods. The use of sour fruits like Indian gooseberry (*amloki*), tomato, lemon and tamarind with leafy vegetables, increases absorption of iron.

Soups

Mixed vegetable soup is a nutritious preparation of leafy yellow-orange and root vegetables with gourd, cereal (flour), egg, lemon, fresh and dry spices, and oil. Leafy vegetables add micronutrients like beta carotene (vitamin A), folic acid, iron and calcium, while yellow-orange vegetables provide beta carotene (vitamin A). Potatoes, flour and oil give energy while lemon and green chilli add vitamin C and some beta carotene to the dish. Generally, all vegetables used have minerals like sodium and potassium. A small amount of egg adds good quality protein, thickness and palatability. Oil helps absorption of vitamin A from leafy, yellow and orange vegetables such as carrot, yellow pumpkin and yellow sweet potato grown in home gardens or available in village markets.

Table. Nutritive value of soup recipes/serving basis

Recipe	*Energy (kcal)*	*Protein (g)*	*Beta carotene(μg)*	*Iron (mg)*
Mixed vegetable soup	287	10.0	2 634	4.0
Mixed vegetable beans soup	200	9.0	1 600	3.0
Mixed vegetable chicken soup	308	12.0	2 834	7.0
Mixed vegetable meat soup	310	13.0	2 834	8.0
Mixed vegetable fish soup	298	12.0	2 834	7.0

The recipe demonstrates correct cooking practices such as cleaning and washing leafy vegetables before cutting, cutting into large pieces, placing vegetables in boiling water and cooking for minimum time. A mixed vegetable soup is a packaged source of nutrients and fluids, adding bulk and fibre to the diet. It can be a meal in itself or supplement rice, *ruti* or traditional bread for the main lunch, dinner, mid-morning or mid-evening meal.

A serving of soup is estimated to provide much more beta carotene than the recommended dietary allowance (RDA) for vitamin A and about one-sixth of the RDA for iron for a moderately working woman.

Main Meal Dishes

Sobuj bhath is a nutritious main meal of cereals, pulse or beans, leafy vegetables, egg, tomatoes, fresh or dry spices and oil. Leafy vegetables like spinach and drumstick have beta carotene (vitamin A), iron, calcium and folic acid, while tomato adds beta carotene and vitamin C. Rice and oil give energy while pulses or beans and egg are a source of protein and energy. Eggs have some protein, vitamin A and riboflavin. Adding egg and oil promotes absorption of vitamin A from leafy vegetables and tomato.

Leafy vegetables like spinach or drumstick and tomato are grown in home gardens and available in local markets. Fresh coriander contains vitamins A and C while spices such as ginger, garlic and green chilli provide taste, some vitamins and minerals. The recipe shows how different food combinations in appropriate amounts (cereal + pulses or beans + egg + tomato + oil) can improve dietary variety and nutrient availability. It also demonstrates correct cooking methods such as cooking rice in just enough water (by absorption method) to ensure retention of B-complex vitamins.

A "meal-in-a dish" recipe, *sobuj bhath* can be a main meal and a packed school lunch. A culturally appropriate adaptation of the popular *khichuri* (rice and pulse) by adding spinach and other food types, the green rice topped with red tomatoes reminds children and farmers of the national flag, encouraging them to eat green leafy vegetables and fresh tomato. A serving of *sobuj bhath* has more than twice the RDA for vitamin A, a part of the RDA for iron and a little less than one-fourth of the RDA and one-third of the RDA for protein.

Sobuj ruti is a nutritious main meal or breakfast dish of cereals, pulse flour, leafy vegetables, potato (in proportions of 3:1:2:2) and fresh spices like coriander leaves and green chilli. Leafy vegetables have vitamin A, iron, calcium and folic acid, potato has energy and bulk while chickpea and wheat flour add protein. Oil or fat helps in absorption of vitamin A from leafy vegetables. A culturally appropriate adaptation of the popular *ruti* by addition of spinach, drumstick or any leafy vegetable, it can be a nutritious packed school lunch, a main meal or breakfast item.

A serving of *sobuj ruti* has twice the RDA for vitamin A and a part of the RDA for iron. It also furnishes a little less than a fourth of the RDA and a fifth of the RDA for protein.

Drumstick Leaves-based Recipes and Snacks

Drumstick leaves *bhorta* is a good source of energy and micronutrients. Drumstick leaves, locally known as *sajna* or *moringa oleifera,* are an excellent source of vitamin A, riboflavin, folic acid, vitamin C, calcium, iron and protein.

Drumstick leaves have very high contents of beta carotene, calcium and iron (almost eight to nine times that of spinach and amaranth), and only half the quantity of drumstick leaves were used in the recipes. Recipes using drumstick leaves provide vitamin A much above the RDA and a substantial part of the RDA for calcium and iron.

Coconut-based Recipes

Several households in the coastal regions of Khulna, Barisal and Feni in Bangladesh have coconut trees. Coconut contains 35 to 65 percent fat and is a rich source of dietary energy providing 444 kcal per 100 g on a fresh weight basis.

It can be combined with sweet pumpkin or sweet potato, chickpea and jaggery to make a *halwa* which is an energy-and-nutrient-dense dessert. This offers energy from the sweet pumpkin or sweet potato, protein, niacin and some iron from the chickpea, while jaggery provides energy and some iron.

The fat in the coconut helps in the absorption of beta carotene from the sweet pumpkin or sweet potato. The market value of sweet pumpkin can be considerably increased by processing it into sweet pumpkin coconut bars. Sweet pumpkin-coconut *halwa* can be a dessert or dish between meals filling dietary nutrient gaps among vulnerable groups such as adolescents and pregnant or lactating women. One serving provides about half of the RDA for vitamin A, a little less than a fourth of the daily energy requirement and a third of the RDA for iron.

Coconut egg curry is rich in energy with all nutrients except ascorbic acid. Egg protein has the highest quality among all dietary proteins; it also provides riboflavin and vitamin A. Vegetables like carrot, tomato and sweet pumpkin provide vitamin A while potato and coconut give energy, and beans add protein with some iron. Coriander leaves add both beta carotene and vitamin C to the dish. Eggs are easily available to most rural households with poultry while vegetables can be grown in home gardens.

A serving of coconut egg curry contains 590 kcal which is about one-third of the daily RDA for energy and protein, twice the RDA of vitamin A, and a part of the daily RDA for iron.

Salads

A salad of vegetables, beans, potato and egg is a good source of micronutrients (vitamins A and C), protein and energy. Since most vegetables are used in fresh and uncooked form, they serve as good sources of vitamin C. Cabbage, carrot, tomato and egg provide vitamin A while green papaya, radish and cucumber add bulk and variety to the diet.

A lemon dressing adds vitamin C which enhances the absorption of iron from plant sources. Cumin powder in the dressing provides some calcium. The amount of vegetables, potato and egg in the salad make it a packaged source of nutrients and a meal-in-dish. A serving of mixed vegetable egg salad or mixed vegetable beans salad provides much more than the RDA for vitamin C, in addition to nearly the full RDA for vitamin A and other nutrients.

Mushroom-based Recipes

Mushrooms are a low-calorie food having less than 30 kcal/ 100 g with traces of sugar and no cholesterol. Almost free from fat (0.2 g/100 g) mushrooms are highly suitable for overweight people. The low fat content of between 2 to 8 percent is rich in linoleic acid, an essential fatty acid important for growth and cell integrity. Mushrooms contain specific hypocholesterolemic substances. Free of fat and cholesterol, and rich in linoleic acid, mushrooms are a healthy food choice for patients of heart disease. Free of starch and with very low sugar content, mushrooms can be called the "delight of the diabetic". A serving of mushroom chops or mushroom omelette has moderate amounts of energy, small amounts of protein and forms a satisfying meal. Mushrooms have good quality protein, improving the nutritional quality of vegetable-based diets.

Complementary Food (CF)

Complementary feeding supplements breast feeding to meet the nutrient needs of infants starting from the age of six months up till about two years. Complementary food must have adequate energy, protein and micronutrients.

Cereals (grains), pulses and nuts in proportions of 4:1:1 were used to prepare a nutrient-dense complementary food mix (CFM), Mix A for infants and small children. Roasted grains and nuts reduce bulk and are a concentrated source of nutrients. Dehydrated carrot powder is a concentrated source of beta carotene. The two powders can be mixed for food-to-food enrichment.

The consistency of the CF gruel makes it easy for child feeding. The two mixes are nutritious, easy to prepare and household processing methods such as roasting and grinding make it possible to store the CFM for long periods.

Kept in a clean and dry container at room temperature, Mix A has a shelf life of up to two months while carrot powder (Mix B) can be kept for up to three months in a dark glass container at room temperature in a clean and cool place, protected from light. The two mixtures can be prepared at household level using easily available food materials.

Food Preparation Techniques and Cooking Tips

Developing the competence and skills of the farmers to promote horticulture-based food in their diets has been a key component of the nutrition programme. Demonstrations were held on:

a. preparation of horticulture-based foods;

b. processing and preparation of horticulture-based complementary foods.

Specific technologies were developed and transferred to the field emphasizing the use of micronutrient-rich vegetables that are locally available and their combinations with other vegetables and staple food ingredients. Cooking methods to promote maximum retention of the nutritive value along with hygienic handling of vegetables and food were also demonstrated.

Methods to improve the bioavailability of some key micronutrients such as iron in vegetables were emphasised with combinations of sour or vitamin C-rich fruits and vegetables, along with appropriate processing techniques. These food technologies have been well accepted and are now practiced by the farmers. An impact assessment of food preparation demonstrations as validated through a change in farmers' practices has been discussed later.

Cooking partially destroys vitamins C and B1. Raw fruits and vegetables are particularly valuable sources of these vitamins provided they are grown and handled hygienically Peeling of vegetables and fruits can cause significant loss of nutritive value and this was considered while developing the recipes for the Nutrition Education Programme. As the water used for cooking vegetables or fruit contains dissolved minerals and trace elements, the nutrition education programme recommended that this should not be thrown out but used in soups or for preparing other food.

General Composition of Foods

Water:—All foods contain water. Vegetables in their natural condition contain large amounts, often 95 per cent, while in meats there is from 40 to 60 per cent or more. Prepared cereal products, as flour, corn meal, and oatmeal, which are apparently dry, have from 7 to 14 per cent. In general the amount of water in a food varies with the mechanical structure and the conditions under which it has been prepared, and is an important factor in estimating the value, as the nutrients are often greatly decreased because of large amounts of water. The water in substances as flour and meal is mechanically held in combination with the fine particles and varies with the moisture content, or hydroscopicity, of the air. Oftentimes foods gain or lose water to such an extent as to affect their weight; for example, one hundred pounds of flour containing 12 percent of water may be reduced in weight three pounds or more when stored in a dry place, or there may be an increase in weight from being stored in a damp place. In tables of analyses the results, unless otherwise stated, are usually given on the basis of the original material, or the dry substance. Potatoes, for example, contain 2½ per cent of crude protein on the basis of 75 per cent of water; or on a dry matter basis, that is, when the water is entirely eliminated, there is 10 per cent of protein.

The water of foods is determined by drying the weighed material in a water or air oven at a temperature of about 100° C, until all of the moisture has been expelled in the form of steam, leaving the dry matter or material free from water. The determination of dry matter, while theoretically a simple process, is attended with many difficulties. Substances which contain much fat may undergo oxidation during drying; volatile compounds, as essential oils, are expelled along with the moisture; and other changes may occur affecting the accuracy of the work. The last traces of moisture are removed with difficulty from a substance, being mechanically retained by the particles with great tenacity. When very accurate dry matter determinations are desired, the substance is dried in a vacuum oven, or in a desiccator over sulphuric acid, or in an atmosphere of some non-oxidizing gas, as hydrogen.

Dry Matter:—The dry matter of a food is a mechanical mixture of the various compounds, as starch, sugar, fat, protein, cellulose, and mineral matter, and is obtained by drying the material. Succulent vegetable foods with 95 per cent of water contain only 5 per cent of dry matter, while in flour with 12 per cent of water there is 88 percent, and in sugar 99 per cent. The dry matter is obtained by subtracting the per cent of water from 100, and in foods it varies from 5 per cent and less in some vegetables to 99 per cent in sugar.

Ash:—The ash, or mineral matter, is that portion obtained by burning or igniting the dry matter at the lowest temperature necessary for complete combustion. The ash in vegetable foods ranges from 2 to 5 per cent and, together with the nitrogen, represents what was taken from the soil during growth. In animal bodies, the ash is present mainly in the bones, but there is also an appreciable amount, one per cent or more, in all the tissues. Ash is exceedingly variable in composition, being composed of the various salts of potassium, sodium, calcium, magnesium, and iron, as sulphates, phosphates, chlorides, and silicates of these elements. There are also other elements in small amounts. In the plant economy these elements take an essential part and are requisite for the formation of plant tissue and the production in the leaves of the organic compounds which later are stored up in the seeds. Some of the elements appear to be more necessary than others, and whenever withheld plant growth is restricted. The elements most essential for plant growth are potassium, calcium, magnesium, iron, phosphorus, and sulphur.

In the animal body minerals are derived, either directly or indirectly, from the vegetable foods consumed. The part which each of the mineral elements takes in animal nutrition is not well understood. Some of the elements, as phosphorus and sulphur, are in organic combination with the nitrogenous compounds, as the nucleated albuminoids, which are very essential for animal life. In both plant and animal bodies, the mineral matter is present as mineral salts and organic combinations. It is held that the ash elements which are in organic combination are the forms mainly utilized for tissue construction. While it is not known just what part all the mineral elements take in animal nutrition, experiments show that in all ordinary mixed rations the amount of the different mineral elements is in excess of the demands of the body, and it is only in rare instances, as in cases of restricted diet, or convalescence from some disease, that special attention need be given to increasing the mineral content of the ration. An excess of mineral matter in foods is equally as objectionable as a scant amount, elimination of the excess entailing additional work on the body.

The composition of the ash of different food materials varies widely, both in amount, and form of the individual elements. When for any reason it is necessary to increase the phosphates in a ration, milk and eggs do this to a greater extent than almost any other foods. Common salt, or sodium chloride, is one of the most essential of the mineral constituents of the body. It is necessary for giving the blood its normal composition, furnishing acid and basic constituents for the production of the digestive fluids, and for the nutrition of the cells. While salt is a necessary food, in large amounts, as when the attempt is made to use sea water as a beverage, it acts as a poison, suggesting that a material may be both a food and a poison. When sodium chloride is entirely withheld from an animal, death from salt starvation ensues. Many foods contain naturally small amounts of sodium chloride.

Organic Matter:—That portion of a food material which is converted into gaseous or volatile products during combustion is called the organic matter. It is a mechanical mixture of compounds made up of carbon, hydrogen, oxygen, nitrogen, and sulphur, and is composed of various individual organic compounds, as cellulose, starch, sugar, albumin, and fat. The amount in a food is determined by subtracting the ash and water from 100. The organic matter varies widely in composition; in some foods it is largely starch, as in potatoes and rice, while in others, as forage crops consumed by animals, cellulose predominates. The nature of the prevailing organic compound, as sugar or starch, determines the nutritive value of a food. Each has a definite chemical composition capable of being expressed by a formula. Considered collectively, the organic compounds are termed organic matter. When burned, the organic compounds are converted into gases, the carbon uniting with the oxygen of the air to form carbon dioxide, hydrogen to form water, sulphur to form sulphur dioxide, and the nitrogen to form oxides of nitrogen and ammonia.

Classification of Organic Compounds:—All food materials are composed of a large number of organic compounds. For purposes of study these are divided into classes. The element nitrogen is taken as the basis of the division. Compounds which contain this element are called nitrogenous, while those from which it is absent are called non-nitrogenous. The nitrogenous organic compounds are composed of the elements nitrogen, hydrogen, carbon, oxygen, and sulphur, while the non-nitrogenous compounds are composed of carbon, hydrogen, and oxygen. In vegetable foods the non-nitrogenous compounds predominate, there being usually from six to twelve parts of non-nitrogenous to every one part of nitrogenous, while in animal foods the nitrogenous compounds are present in larger amount.

Non-nitrogenous Compounds

Occurrence:—The non nitrogenous compounds of foods consist mainly of cellulose, starch, sugar, and fat. For purposes of study, they are divided into subdivisions, as carbohydrates, pectose substances or jellies, fats, organic acids, essential oils, and mixed compounds. In plants the carbohydrates predominate, while in animal tissue the fats are the chief non-nitrogenous constituents.

Carbohydrates:—This term is applied to a class of compounds similar in general composition, but differing widely in structural composition and physical properties. Carbohydrates make up the bulk of vegetable foods and, except in milk, are found only in traces in animal foods. They are all represented by the general formula CH_2n_2n, there being twice as many hydrogen as oxygen atoms, the hydrogen and oxygen being present in the same proportion as in water. As a class, the carbohydrates are neutral bodies, and, when burned, form carbon dioxide and water.

Cellulose is the basis of the cell structure of plants, and is found in various physical forms in food materials. Sometimes it is hard and dense, resisting digestive action and mechanically inclosing other nutrients and thus preventing their being available as food. In the earlier stages of plant growth a part of the cellulose is in chemical combination with water, forming hydrated cellulose, a portion of which undergoes digestion and produces heat and energy in the body. Ordinarily, however, cellulose adds but little in the way of nutritive value, although it is often beneficial mechanically and imparts bulk to some foods otherwise too concentrated. Cellulose usually makes up a very small part of human food, less than 1 per cent. In refined white fiour there is less than .05 of a per cent; in oatmeal and cereal products from .5 to 1 per cent, depending upon the extent to which the hulls are removed, and in vegetable foods from .1 to 1 per cent. The cellulose content of foods is included in the crude fiber of the chemist's report.

Starch occurs widely distributed in nature, particularly in the seeds, roots, and tubers of some plants. It is formed in the leaves of plants as a result of the joint action of chlorophyll and protoplasm, and is generally held by plant physiologists to be the first carbohydrate produced in the plant cell. Starch is composed of a number of overlapping layers separated by starch cellulose; between these layers the true starch or amylose is found. Starch from the various cereals and vegetables differs widely in mechanical structure; in wheat it is circular, in corn somewhat angular, and in parsnips exceedingly small, while potato starch granules are among the largest.

The nature of starch can be determined largely from its mechanical structure as studied under the microscope. It is insoluble in cold water because of the protecting action of the cellular layer, but on being heated it undergoes both mechanical and chemical changes; the grains are partially ruptured by pressure due to the conversion into steam of the moisture held mechanically. The cooking of foods is beneficial from a mechanical point of view, as it results in partial disintegration of the starch masses, changing the structure so that the starch is more readily acted upon by the ferments of the digestive tract. At a temperature of about 120° C. starch begins to undergo chemical change, resulting in the rearrangement of the atoms in the molecule with the production of dextrine and soluble carbohydrates. Dextrine is formed on the crust of bread, or whenever potatoes or starchy foods are browned.

At a still higher temperature starch is decomposed, with the liberation of water and production of compounds of higher carbon content. When heated in contact with water, it undergoes hydration changes; gelatinous-like products are formed, which are finally converted into a soluble condition. In cooking cereals, the hydration of the starch is one of the main physical and chemical changes that takes place, and it simply results in converting the material into such a form that other chemical changes may more readily occur. Before starch becomes dextrose, hydration is necessary. If this is accomplished by cooking, it saves the body just so much energy in digestion. Many foods owe their value largely to the starch. In cereals it is found to the extent of 72 to 76 per cent; in rice and potatoes in still larger amounts; and it is the chief constituent of many vegetables. When starch is digested, it is first changed to a soluble form and then gradually undergoes oxidation, resulting in the production of heat and energy, the same products—carbon dioxide and water—being formed as when starch is burned. Starch is a valuable heat-producing nutrient; a pound yields 1860 calories.

Sugar:—Sugars are widely distributed in nature, being found principally in the juices of the sugar cane, sugar beet, and sugar maple. They are divided into two large classes: the sucrose group and the dextrose group, the latter being produced from sucrose, starch, and other carbohydrates by inversion and allied chemical changes.

Pectose Substances are jelly-like bodies found in fruits and vegetables. They are closely related in chemical composition to the carbohydrates, into which form they are changed during digestion; and in nutrition they serve practically the same function. In the early stages of growth the pectin bodies are combined with organic acids, forming insoluble compounds, as the pectin in green apples. During the ripening of fruit and the cooking of vegetables, the pectin is changed to a more soluble and digestible condition. In food analysis, the pectin is usually included with the carbohydrates.

Nitrogen-free-extract:—In discussing the composition of foods, the carbohydrates other then cellulose, as starch, sugar, and pectin, are grouped under the name of nitrogen-free-extract. Methods of chemical analysis have not yet been sufficiently perfected to enable accurate and rapid determination to be made of all these individual carbohydrates, and hence they are grouped together as nitrogen-free-extract. As the name indicates, they are compounds which contain no nitrogen, and are extractives in the sense that they are soluble in dilute acid and alkaline solutions. The nitrogen-free-extract is determined indirectly, that is, by the method of difference. All the other constituents of a food, as water, ash, crude fiber (cellulose), crude protein, and ether extract, are determined; the total is subtracted from 100, and the difference is nitrogen-free-extract. In studying the nutritive value of foods, particular attention should be given to the nature of the nitrogen-free-extract, as in some instances it is composed of sugar and in others of starch, pectin, or pentosan (gum sugars). While all these compounds have practically the same fuel value, they differ in composition, structure, and the way in which they are acted upon by chemicals and digestive ferments.

Fat:—Fat is found mainly in the seeds of plants, but to some extent in the leaves and stems. It differs from starch in containing more carbon and less oxygen. In starch there is about 44 per cent of carbon, while in fat there is 75 per cent. Hence it is that when fat is burned or undergoes combustion, it yields a larger amount of the products of combustion—carbon dioxid and water—than does starch. A gram of fat produces 2¼ times as much heat as a gram of starch. Fat is the most concentrated non-nitrogenous nutrient. As found in food materials, it is a mechanical mixture of various fats, among which are stearin, palmitin, and olein. Stearin and palmitin are hard fats, crystalline in structure, and with a high melting point, while olein is a liquid. In addition to these three, there are also small amounts of other fats, as butyrin in butter, which give character or individuality to materials. There are a number of vegetable fats or oils which are used for food purposes and, when properly prepared and refined, have a high nutritive value.

Occasionally one fat of cheaper origin but not necessarily of lower nutritive value is substituted for another. The fats have definite physical and chemical properties which enable them to be readily distinguished, as iodine number, specific gravity, index of refraction, and heat of combustion. By iodine number is meant the percentage of iodine that will unite chemically with the fat. Wheat oil has an iodine number of about 100, meaning that one pound of wheat oil will unite chemically with one pound of iodine. Fats have a lower specific gravity than water, usually ranging from .89 to .94, the specific gravity of a fat being fairly constant. All fats can be separated into glycerol and a fatty acid, glycerol or glycerine being common constituents, while each fat yields its own characteristic acid, as stearin, stearic acid; palmitin, palmitic acid; and olein, oleic acid. The fats are soluble in ether, chloroform, and benzine. In the chemical analysis of foods, they are separated with ether, and along with the fat, variable amounts of other substances are extracted, these extractive products usually being called "ether extract" or "crude fat." The ether extract of plant tissue contains in addition to fat appreciable amounts of cellulose, gums, colouring, and other materials. From cereal products the ether extract is largely fat, but in some instances lecithin and other nitrogenous fatty substances are present, while in animal food products, as milk and meat, the ether extract is nearly pure fat.

Organic Acids:—Many vegetable foods contain small amounts of organic acids, as malic acid found in apples, citric in lemons, and tartaric in grapes. These give characteristic taste to foods, but have no direct nutritive value. They do not yield heat and energy as do starch, fat, and protein; they are, however, useful for imparting flavour and palatability, and it is believed they promote to some extent the digestion of foods with which they are combined by encouraging the secretion of the digestive fluids. Many fruits and vegetables owe their dietetic value to the organic acids which they contain. In plants they are usually in chemical combination with the minerals, forming compounds as salts, or with the organic compounds, producing materials as acid proteins. In the plant economy they take an essential part in promoting growth and aiding the plant to secure by osmotic action its mineral food from the soil. Organic acids are found to some extent in animal foods, as the various lactic acids of meat and milk. They are also formed in food materials as the result of ferment action. When seeds germinate, small amounts of carbohydrates are converted into organic acids. In general the organic acids are not to be considered as nutrients, but as food adjuncts, increasing palatability and promoting digestion.

Essential Oils:—Essential or volatile oils differ from fats, or fixed oils, in chemical composition and physical properties. The essential oils are readily volatilized, leaving no permanent residue, while the fixed fats are practically nonvolatile. Various essential oils are present in small amounts in nearly all vegetable food materials, and the characteristic flavour of many fruits is due to them. The amount in a food material is very small, usually only a few hundredths of a per cent. The essential oils have no direct food value, but indirectly, like the organic acids, they assist in promoting favourable digestive action, and are also valuable because they impart a pleasant taste. Through poor methods of cooking and preparation, the essential oils are readily lost from some foods.

Mixed Compounds:—Food materials frequently contain compounds which do not naturally fall into the five groups mentioned,—carbohydrates, pectose substances, fats, organic acids, and essential oils. The amount of such compounds is small, and they are classed as miscellaneous or mixed non-nitrogenous compounds. Some of them may impart a negative value to the food, and there are others which have all the characteristics, as far as general composition is concerned, of the non-nitrogenous compounds, but contain nitrogen, although as a secondary rather than an essential constituent.

Nutritive Value of Non-nitrogenous Compounds:—The non-nitrogenous compounds, taken as a class, are incapable alone of sustaining life, because they do not contain any nitrogen, and this is necessary for producing proteid material in the animal body. They are valuable for the production of heat and energy, and when associated with the nitrogenous compounds, are capable of forming non-nitrogenous reserve tissue. It is equally impossible to sustain life for any prolonged period with the nitrogenous compounds alone. It is when these two classes are properly blended and naturally united in food materials that their main value is secured. For nutrition purposes they are mutually related and dependent. Some food materials contain the nitrogenous and non-nitrogenous compounds blended in such proportion as to enable one food alone to practically sustain life, while in other cases it is necessary, in order to secure the best results in the feeding of animals and men, to combine different foods varying in their content of these two classes of compounds.

Nitrogenous Compounds

General Composition:—The nitrogenous compounds are more complex in composition than the non-nitrogenous. They are composed of a larger number of elements, united in different ways so as to form a much more complex molecular structure. Foods contain numerous nitrogenous organic compounds, which, for purposes of study, are divided into four divisions,—proteids, albuminoids, amids, and alkaloids. In addition to these, there are other nitrogenous compounds which do not naturally fall into any one of the four divisions.

Protein:—The term "protein" is applied to a large class of nitrogenous compounds resembling each other in general composition, but differing widely in structural composition. As a class, the proteins contain about 16 per cent of nitrogen, 52 per cent of carbon, from 6 to 7 per cent of hydrogen, 22 per cent of oxygen, and less than 2 per cent of sulphur. These elements are combined in a great variety of ways, forming various groups or radicals. In studying the protein molecule a large number of derivative products have been observed, as amid radicals, various hydrocarbons, fatty acids, and carbohydrate-like bodies. It would appear that in the chemical composition of the proteins there are all the constituents, or simpler products, of the non-nitrogenous compounds, and these are in chemical combination with amid radicals and nitrogen in various forms. The nitrogen of many proteids appears to be present in more than one form or radical. The proteids take an important part in life processes. They are found more extensively in animal than in plant bodies. The protoplasm of both the plant and animal cell is composed mainly of protein.

Proteids are divided into various subdivisions, as albumins, globulins, albuminates, proteoses and peptones, and insoluble proteids. In plant and animal foods a large amount of the protein is present as in soluble proteids; that is, they are not dissolved by solvents, as water and dilute salt solution. The albumins are soluble in water and coagulated by heat at a temperature of 157° to 161° F. Whenever a food material is soaked in water, the albumin is removed and can then be coagulated by the action of heat, or of chemicals, as tannic acid, lead acetate, and salts of mercury. The globulins are proteids extracted from food materials by dilute salt solution after the removal of the albumins. Globulins also are coagulated by heat and precipitated by chemicals. The amount of globulins in vegetable foods is small. In animal foods myosin in meat and vitellin, found in the yolk of the egg, and some of the proteids of the blood, are examples of globulins. Albuminates are casein-like proteids found in both animal and vegetable foods. They are supposed to be proteins that are in feeble chemical combination with acid and alkaline compounds, and they are sometimes called acid and alkali proteids. Some are precipitated from their solutions by acids and others by alkalies. Peas and beans contain quite large amounts of a casein-like proteid called legumin. Proteoses and peptones are proteins soluble in water, but not coagulated by heat. They are produced from other proteids by ferment action during the digestion of food and the germination of seeds, and are often due to the changes resulting from the action of the natural ferments or enzymes inherent in the food materials.

As previously stated, the insoluble proteids are present in far the largest amount of any of the nitrogenous materials of foods. Lean meat and the gluten of wheat and other grains are examples of the insoluble proteids. The various insoluble proteids from different food materials each has its own composition and distinctive chemical and physical properties, and from each a different class and percentage amount of derivative products are obtained. While in general it is held that the various proteins have practically the same nutritive value, it is possible that because differences in structural composition and the products formed during digestion there may exist notable differences in nutritive value. During digestion the insoluble proteids undergo an extended series of chemical changes. They are partially oxidized, and the nitrogenous portion of the molecule is eliminated mainly in the form of amids, as urea. The insoluble proteins constitute the main source of the nitrogenous food supply of both humans and animals.

Crude Protein:—In the analysis of foods, the term "crude protein" is used to designate the total nitrogenous compounds considered collectively; it is composed largely of protein, but also includes the amids, alkaloids, and albuminoids. "Crude protein" and "total nitrogenous compounds" are practically synonymous terms. The various proteins all contain about 16 per cent of nitrogen; that is, one part of nitrogen is equivalent to 6.25 parts of protein. In analyzing a food material, the total organic nitrogen is determined and the amount multiplied by 6.25 to obtain the crude protein. In some food materials, as cereals, the crude protein is largely pure protein, while in others, as potatoes, it is less than half pure protein, the larger portion being amids and other compounds. In comparing the crude protein content of one food with that of another, the nature of both proteids should be considered and also the amounts of non-proteid constituents. The factor 6.25 for calculating the protein equivalent of foods is not strictly applicable to all foods. For example, the proteids of wheat—gliadin and glutenin—contain over 18 per cent of nitrogen, making the nitrogen factor about 5.68 instead of 6.25. If wheat contains 2 per cent of nitrogen, it is equivalent to 12.5 per cent of crude protein, using the factor 6.25; or to 11.4, using the factor 5.7. The nitrogen content of foods is absolute; the protein content is only relative.

Food Value of Protein:—Because of its complexity in composition, protein is capable of being used by the body in a greater variety of ways than starch, sugar, or fat. In addition to producing heat and energy, protein serves the unique function of furnishing material for the construction of new muscular tissue and the repair of that which is worn out. It is distinctly a tissue-building nutrient. It also enters into the composition of all the vital fluids of the body, as the blood, chyme, chyle, and the various digestive fluids. Hence it is that protein is required as a nutrient by the animal body, and it cannot be produced from non-nitrogenous compounds. In vegetable bodies, the protein can be produced synthetically from amids, which in turn are formed from ammonium compounds. While protein is necessary in the ration, an excessive amount should be avoided. When there is more than is needed for functional purposes, it is used for heat and energy, and as foods rich in protein are usually the most expensive, an excess adds unnecessarily to the cost of the ration. Excess of protein in the ration may also result in a diseased condition, due to imperfect elimination of the protein residual products from the body.

Albuminoids differ from proteids in general composition and, to some extent, in nutritive value. They are found in animal bodies mainly in the connective tissue and in the skin, hair, and nails. Some of the albuminoids, as nuclein, are equal in food value to protein, while others have a lower food value. In general, albuminoids are capable of conserving the protein of the body, and hence are called "protein sparers," but they cannot in every way enter into the composition of the body, as do the true proteins.

Amids and Amines:—These are nitrogenous compounds of simpler structure than the proteins and albuminoids. They are sometimes called compound ammonia in that they are derived from ammonia by the replacement of one of the hydrogen atoms with an organic radical. In plants, amids are intermediate compounds in the production of the proteids, and in some vegetables a large portion of the nitrogen is amids. In animal bodies amids are formed during oxidation, digestion, and disintegration of proteids. It is not definitely known whether or not a protein in the animal body when broken down into amid form can again be reconstructed into protein. The amids have a lower food value than the proteids and albuminoids. It is generally held that, to a certain extent, they are capable, when combined with proteids, of preventing rapid conversion of the body proteid into soluble form. When they are used in large amounts in a ration, they tend to hasten oxidation rather than conservation of the proteids.

Alkaloids:—In some plant bodies there are small amounts of nitrogenous compounds called alkaloids. They are not found to any appreciable extent in food plants. The alkaloids, like ammonia, are basic in character and unite with acids to form salts. Many medicinal plants owe their value to the alkaloids which they contain. In animal bodies alkaloids are formed when the tissue undergoes fermentation changes, and also during disease, the products being known as ptomaines. Alkaloids have no food value, but act physiologically as irritants on the nerve centers, making them useful from a medicinal rather than from a nutritive point of view. To medical and pharmaceutical students the alkaloids form a very important group of compounds.

General Relationship of the Nitrogenous Compounds:— Among the various subdivisions of the nitrogenous compounds there exists a relationship similar to that among the non-nitrogenous compounds. From proteids, amids and alkaloids may be formed, just as invert sugars and their products are formed from sucrose. Although glucose products are derived from sucrose, it is not possible to reverse the process and obtain sucrose or cane sugar from starch. So it is with proteins, while the amid may be obtained from the proteid in animal nutrition, as far as known the process cannot be reversed and proteids be obtained from amids. In the construction of the protein molecule of plants, nitrogen is absorbed from the soil in soluble forms, as compounds of nitrates and nitrites and ammonium salts. These are converted, first, into amids and then into proteids. In the animal body just the reverse of this process takes place,—the protein of the food undergoes a series of changes, and is finally eliminated from the body as an amid, which in turn undergoes oxidation and nitrification, and is converted into nitrites, nitrates, and ammonium salts. These forms of nitrogen are then ready to begin again in plant and animal bodies the same cycle of changes. Thus it is that nitrogen may enter a number of times into the composition of plant and animal tissues. Nature is very economical in her use of this element.

Comparative Cost and Value of Foods

Cost and Nutrient Content of Foods:—The market price and the nutritive value of foods are often at variance, as those which cost the most frequently contain the least nutrients. It is difficult to make absolute comparisons as to the nutritive value of foods at different prices, because they differ not only in the amounts, but also in the kinds of nutrients. While it is not possible to express definitely the value of one food in terms of another, approximate comparisons may be made as to the amounts of nutrients that can be secured for a given sum of money when foods are at different prices, and tables have been prepared making such comparisons.

Nutrients Procurable for a Given Sum:—To ascertain the nutrients procurable for a given sum first determine the amount in pounds that can be obtained, say, for ten cents, and then multiply by the percentages of fat, protein, carbohydrates, and calories in the food. The results are the amounts, in pounds, of nutrients procurable for that sum of money. For example: if milk is 5 cents per quart, two quarts or approximately four pounds, can be procured for 10 cents. If the milk contains fat, 4 per cent, protein, 3.3 per cent, carbohydrates, 5 per cent, and fuel value, 310 calories per pound, multiplying each of these by 4 gives the nutrients and fuel value in four pounds, or 10 cents worth of milk, as follows:

Protein	0.13 lb.
Fat	0.16 lb.
Carbohydrates	0.2 lb.
Calories	1240

If it is desired to compare milk at 5 cents per quart with round steak at 15 cents per pound, 10 cents will procure 0.66, or two thirds of a pound of round steak containing on an average (edible portion) 19 per cent protein, 12.8 per cent fat, and yielding 890 calories per pound. If 10 per cent is refuse, there is edible about 0.6 of a pound. The amounts of nutrients in the 0.6 of a pound of steak, edible portion, or 0.66 lb. as purchased would be:

Protein	0.11 lb.
Fat	0.08 lb.
Calories	534

It is to be observed that from the 10 cents' worth of milk a little more protein, 0.08 of a pound more fat, and nearly two and one half times as many calories can be secured as from the 10 cents' worth of meat. This is due to the carbohydrates and the larger amount of fat which the milk contains. At these prices, milk should be used liberally in the dietary, as it furnishes more of all the nutrients than does meat. It would not be advisable to exclude meat entirely from the ration, but milk at 5 cents per quart is cheaper food than meat at 15 cents per pound. In making comparisons, preference cannot always be given to one food because of its containing more of any particular nutrient, for often there are other factors that influence the value.

Comparing Foods as to Nutritive Value:—In general, preference should be given to foods which supply the most protein, provided the differences between the carbohydrates and fats are not large. When the protein content of two foods is nearly the same, but the fats and carbohydrates differ materially, the preference may safely be given to the food which supplies the larger amount of total nutrients.

A pound of protein in a ration is more valuable than a pound of either fat or carbohydrates, although it is not possible to establish an absolute scale as to the comparative value of these nutrients, because they serve different functional purposes in the body. It is sometimes necessary to use small amounts of foods rich in protein in order to secure a balanced ration; excessive use of protein, however, is not economical, as that which is not needed for functional purposes is converted into heat and energy which could be supplied as well by the carbohydrates, and they are less expensive nutrients.

Examples

1. Compute the calories and the amounts of protein, fat, and carbohydrates that can be procured for 25 cents in cheese selling for 18 cents per pound; how do these compare with the nutrients in eggs at 20 cents per dozen?
2. Which food furnishes the larger amount of nutrients, potatoes at 50 cents per bushel or flour at $6 per barrel?
3. How do beans at 10 cents per quart compare in nutritive value with beef at 15 Cents per pound?
4. How does salt codfish at 10 cents per pound compare in nutritive value with lamb chops at 15 cents per pound?
5. Compare in nutritive value cream at 25 cents per quart with butter at 30 cents per pound.
6. Calculate the composition and nutritive value of a cake made of sugar, 8 oz.; butter, 4 oz.; eggs, 8 oz.; flour, 8 oz.; and milk, 4 oz.; the baked cake weighs one and three fourths pounds.

Water

Importance:—Water is one of the most essential food materials. It enters into the composition of the body, and without it the nutrients of foods would be unavailable, and life could not be sustained. Water unites chemically with various elements to form plant tissue and supplies hydrogen and oxygen for the production of organic compounds within the leaves of plants. In the animal economy it is not definitely known whether or not water furnishes any of the elements of which the tissues are composed, as the food contains liberal amounts of hydrogen and oxygen; it is necessary mainly as the vehicle for distributing nutrients in suspension and solution, and as a medium in which chemical, physical, and physiological changes essential to life processes take place. From a sanitary point of view, the condition of the water supply is of great importance, as impure water seriously affects the health of the consumer.

Impurities in Water:—Waters are impure because of: (1) excessive amounts of alkaline salts and other mineral compounds; (2) decaying animal and vegetable matters which act chemically as poisons and irritants, and which may serve as food for the development of objectionable bacterial bodies; and

(3) injurious bacteria. The most common forms of impurities are excess of organic matter and bacterial contamination. The sanitary condition of water is greatly influenced by the character of the soil through which it flows and the extent to which it has been polluted by surface drainage.

Mineral Impurities:—-The mineral impurities of water are mainly soluble alkaline and similar compounds dissolved by the water in passing through various layers of soil and rock. When water contains a large amount of sodium chloride, sodium sulphate or carbonate, or other alkaline salts, it is termed an "alkali water." Where water passes through soil that has been largely formed from the decay of rocks containing alkaline minerals, the water dissolves some of these minerals and becomes alkaline. The kind of alkali determines the character of the water; in some cases it is sodium carbonate, which is particularly objectionable. The continued use of strong alkali water causes digestion disorders, because of the irritating action upon the digestive tract. Hard waters are due to the presence of lime compounds. In regions where limestone predominates, the carbon dioxid in water acts as a solvent, producing hard waters. Waters that are hard on account of the presence of calcium carbonate give a deposit when boiled, due to liberation of the carbon dioxid which is the material that renders the lime soluble. Calcium sulphate, or gypsum, on the other hand, imparts permanent hardness. There is no deposit when such waters are boiled. A large number of minerals are found in various waters, often sufficient in amount to impart physiological properties. Water that is highly charged with mineral matter is difficult to improve sufficiently for household purposes. About the only way is by distillation.

Organic Impurities:—Water that flows over the surface of the ground comes in contact with animal and vegetable material in various stages of decay, and as a result some is dissolved and some is mechanically carried along by the water. After becoming soluble, the organic matter undergoes further chemical changes, as oxidation and nitrification caused by bacteria. If the organic matter contain a large amount of nitrogenous material, particularly of proteid origin, a series of chemical changes induced by bacterial action takes place, resulting in the production of nitrites. The nitrifying organisms first produce nitrous acid products (nitrites), and in the further development of the nitrifying process these are changed to nitrates. The ammonia formed as the result of the decomposition of nitrogenous organic matter readily undergoes nitrification changes. Nitrates and nitrites alone are not injurious in water, but they are usually associated with objectionable bacteria and generally indicate previous contamination.

Interpretation of a Water Analysis:—"Total solid matter" represents all the mineral, vegetable, and animal matter which a water contains. It is the residue obtained by evaporating the water to dryness at a temperature of 212° F. Average drinking water contains from 20 to 90 grains per gallon of solid matter. "Free ammonia" is that formed as a result of the decomposition of animal or vegetable matter containing nitrogen. Water of high purity usually contains less than 0.07 parts per million of free ammonia. "Albuminoid ammonia" is derived from the partially decomposed animal or vegetable material in water. The greater the amount of nitrogenous organic impurities, the higher the albuminoid ammonia. A good drinking water ought not to contain more than 0.10 part per million of albuminoid ammonia. An abnormal quantity of chlorine indicates surface drainage or sewage contamination, or an excess of alkaline matter, as common salt. Nitrites should not be present, as they are generally associated with matter not completely oxidized. Nitrites are usually considered more objectionable than nitrates; both are innocuous unless associated with disease-producing nitrorganisms.

Natural Purification of Water:—River waters are sometimes dark coloured because of large amounts of dissolved organic matter, but in contact with the sun and air they gradually undergo natural purification and the organic matter is oxidized. However, absolute reliance cannot be placed upon natural purification of a bad water, as the objectionable organisms often have great resistive power. There is no perfectly pure water except that prepared in the chemical laboratory by distillation. All natural waters come in contact with the soil and air, and necessarily contain impurities proportional to the extent of their contamination.

Water in Relation to Health:—There are many diseases, of which typhoid fever is a type, that are distinctly water-born. The typhoid bacilli, present in countless numbers in the feces of persons suffering or convalescent from typhoid fever, find their way into streams, lakes, and wells. They retain their vitality, and when they enter the digestive tract of an individual, rapidly increase in numbers. Numerous disastrous outbreaks of typhoid fever have been traced to contamination of water. Coupled with the sanitary improvement of a city's water supply, there is diminution of typhoid fever cases, and a noticeable lowering of the death rate. Many cities and villages are dependent for their water upon rivers and lakes into which surface drainage finds its way, with all contaminating substances. Mechanical sedimentation and filtration greatly improve waters of this class, but do not necessarily render them entirely pure. Compounds of iron and aluminium are sometimes added in small amounts, under chemical supervision, to such waters to precipitate the organic impurities. Spring waters are not entirely above suspicion, as oftentimes the soil through which they flow is highly polluted. All water of doubtful purity should be boiled, and there are but few natural waters of undoubted purity.

There is no such thing as absolutely pure water in a state of nature. The mountain streams perhaps approach nearest to it where there are no humans to pollute the banks; but then there are always the beasts and birds, and they, too, are subject to disease. There are very few waters that at some time of the year and under some conditions are not contaminated with disease-producing organisms. No matter how carefully guarded are the banks of lakes furnishing the water supply of cities, more or less objectionable matter will get in. In seasons of heavy rains, large amounts of surface water enter the lakes, carrying along the filth gathered from many acres of land drained by the streams entering the lakes. Some of the most serious outbreaks of typhoid fever have come from temporary contamination of ordinarily fairly good drinking water. In general, too little attention is given to the purity of drinking water. It is just as important that water should be boiled as that food should be cooked. One of the objects of cooking is to destroy the injurious bacteria, and they are frequently more numerous in the drinking water than in the food.

The argument is sometimes advanced that the mineral matter present in water is needed for the construction of the bone and other tissues of the body, and that distilled water fails to supply the necessary mineral matter. This is an erroneous assumption, as the mineral matter in the food is more than sufficient for this purpose. When water is highly charged with mineral salts, additional work for their elimination is called for on the part of the organs of excretion, particularly the kidneys; and furthermore, water nearly saturated with minerals cannot exert its full solvent action.

In discussing the immediate benefits resulting from improvement of water, Fuertes says:

> *"Immediately after the change to the 'four mile intake' at Chicago in 1893, there was a great reduction in typhoid. Lawrence, Mass., showed a great improvement with the setting of the filters in operation in September, 1893; fully half of the deaths in 1894 were among persons known to have used the unfiltered canal water. The conclusion is warranted that for the efficient control of the death rate from typhoid fever it is necessary to have efficient sewerage and drainage, proper methods of living, and pure water. The reason why our large cities, which are all provided with sewerage, have such high death rates is therefore without doubt their continuance of the filthy practice of supplying drinking water which carries in solution and suspension the washings from farms, from the streets, from privies, from pigpens, and the sewage of cities.... And also we should recognize the importance of flies and other winged insects and birds which feed on offal as carriers of bacteria of specific diseases from points of infection to the watersheds, and the consequent washing of newly infected matter into our drinking water by rains."*

There is a very close relationship between the surface water and that of shallow wells. A shallow well is simply a reservoir for surface water accumulations. It is stated that, when an improved system of drainage was introduced into a part of London, many of the shallow wells became dry, indicating the source from which they received their supply. Direct subterranean connection between cesspools and wells is often traced in the following way: A small amount of lithium, which gives a distinct flame reaction, and a minute trace of which can be detected with the spectroscope, is placed in the cesspool, and after a short time a lithium reaction is secured from the well water.

Rain water is relied upon in some localities for drinking purposes. That collected in cities and in the vicinity of barns and dwellings contains appreciable amounts of organic impurities. The brown colour is due to the impurities, ammonium carbonate being one of these. There are also traces of nitrates and nitrites obtained from the air. When used for drinking, rain water should be boiled.

Improvement of Waters:—Waters are improved by: (1) boiling, which destroys the disease-producing organisms; (2) filtration, which removes the materials mechanically suspended in the water; and (3) distillation, which eliminates the impurities in suspension and solution, as well as destroys all germ life.

Boiling Water:—In order to destroy the bacteria that may be in drinking water, it is not sufficient to heat the water or merely let it come to a boil. It has been found that if water is only partially sterilized and then cooled in the open air, the bacteria develop more rapidly than if the water had not been heated at all. It should boil vigorously five to ten minutes; cholera and typhoid bacteria succumb in five minutes or less. Care should be taken in cooling that the water is not exposed to dust particles from the air nor placed in open vessels in a dirty refrigerator. It should be kept in perfectly clean, tight-stoppered bottles. These bottles should be frequently scalded. Great reliance may be placed upon this method of water purification when properly carried out.

Filtration:—Among the most efficient forms of water filters are the Berkefeld and Pasteur. The Pasteur filter is made of unglazed porcelain, and the Berkefeld of fine infusorial earth (finely divided SiO_2). Both are porous and allow a moderately rapid flow of water. The flow from the Berkefeld filter is more rapid than from the Pasteur. The mechanical impurities of the water are deposited upon the filtering surface, due to the attraction which the material has for particles in suspension. These particles usually are the sources of contamination and carry bacteria. When first used, filters are satisfactory, but unless carefully looked after they soon lose their ability to remove germs from the water and may increase the impurity by accumulation. Small faucet filters are made of porous stone, asbestos, charcoal, etc. Many of them are of no value whatever or are even worse than valueless. Filters should be frequently cleansed in boiling water or in steam under pressure. Unless this is done, the filters may become incubators for bacteria.

Distillation:—When an unquestionably pure water supply is desired, distillation should be resorted to. There are many forms of stills for domestic use which are easily manipulated and produce distilled water economically. The mineral matter of water is in no way essential for any functional purpose, and hence its removal through distillation is not detrimental.

Chemical Purification:—Purification of water by the use of chemicals should not be attempted in the household or by inexperienced persons. When done under supervision of a chemist or bacteriologist, it may be of great value to a community. Turneaure and Russell, in discussing the purification of water by addition of chemicals, state:

> *"There are a considerable number of chemical substances that may be added to water in order to purify it by carrying down the suspended matter as well as bacteria, by sedimentation. Such a process of purification is to be seen in the addition of alum, sulphate of iron, and calcium hydrate to water. Methods of this character are directly dependent upon the flocculating action of the chemical added, and the removal of the bacteria is accomplished by subsidence."*

Ice:—The purity of the ice supply is also of much importance. While freezing reduces the number of organisms and lessens their vitality, it does not make an impure water absolutely wholesome. The way, too, in which ice is often handled and stored subjects it to contamination, and foods which are placed in direct contact with it mechanically absorb the impurities which it contains. For cooling water, ice should be placed around rather than in it. Diseases have frequently been traced to impure ice. The only absolutely pure ice is that made from distilled water.

Mineral Waters:—When water is charged with carbonic acid gas under pressure, carbonated water results, and when minerals, as salts of sodium, potassium, or lithium, are added, artificial mineral waters are produced. Natural mineral waters are placed on the market to some extent, but most mineral waters are artificial products and they are sometimes prepared from water of low sanitary character. Mineral waters should not be used extensively except under medical direction, as many have pronounced medicinal properties. Some of the constituents are bicarbonates of sodium, potassium, and lithium; sulphates of magnesium (Epsom salts) and calcium; and chloride of sodium. The sweetened mineral waters, as lemonade, orangeade, ginger ale, and beer, contain sugar and organic acids, as citric and tartaric, and are flavored with natural or artificial products. Most of them are prepared without either fruit or ginger. Natural mineral waters used under the direction of a physician are often beneficial in cases of chronic digestion disorders or other diseases.

Economic Value of a Pure Water Supply:—From a financial point of view, the money spent in securing pure water is one of the best investments a community can make. Statisticians estimate the death of an adult results in a loss to the state of from $1000 to $5000; and to the losses sustained by death must be added those incurred by sickness and by lessened quality and quantity of work through impaired vitality,—all caused by using poor drinking water. Wherever plants have been installed for improving the sanitary condition of the water supply, the death rate has been lowered and the returns to the community have been far greater than the cost of the plant. Impure water is the most expensive food that can be consumed.

4

Laws Related to Food Products

Prevention of Food Adulteration Act, 1954 and Exchange, Act 1955

To make, complete healthy and safe food products available to the common public, our Legislature has amended many rules and regulations which are applicable in our country. These can be divided into two parts, compulsory or regulatory and voluntary.

Food Adulteration Prevention Act, 1954 is a compulsory or regulatory rule. These types of rules which are drawn by the Parliament for the fulfillment of the food aim, and the right of which is given to the government and governing body, and in connection with these rules proper usage is made compulsory to be followed and this is called an Act.

Through this Act conformity with law has been established. Within this framework the government and governing body has the right to prohibit the production storage, distribution, sale and import, on adulterated & contaminated food products and to keep a restraint and take action against the parties concerned. This is such a complete Act, in which the norms of control, of quality and purity of nearly all the food products have been included. In this way its chief aim is to prevent adulteration of food products.

Food adulteration or mixing cheap harmful chemicals in food products or extracting the essential healthy nutrients, is a crime within this Act. This Act came into existence in 1954 and was further amended in 1976. If any person is found adulterating food products with harmful chemicals, he will be punished with an imprisonment of 6 months and a fine of Rs.1000. If the adulteration endangers a person's life causing an adverse effect on health or any serious illness, he will be punished with life imprisonment and a minimum of Rs. 5000 as fine.

The management of rules and provisions of this Act is vested with the institutions of health services, by the power of the Central Government and is implemented through the State Government. Within this Act, the Director of the State Government is the controller of public health and preventive medicine of the State Government, and he is in charge of and responsible for its implementation, execution and control. According to the provisions of this Act, a chief policy determinant group of Central Standard Food Societies is formed. These organizations advise the Government on this issue. In this Act appropriate standards have been set for the desirable quality and protective use of various food products, through discussions held with specialists and sub organizations, based on the submission of their reports.

Every State Government appoints food inspectors and analysts, who readily help the consumers. We can find out about them through the related area's health officers or directors, health services, state government or food and medicine department. The food inspector collects the samples. One sample is sent to the public analyst and two are sent to the area officer. The public analyst sends his investigation report to the health officer. If the sample tests positive, then the health officer files a complaint against the concerned shopkeeper/businessman/producer/distributor or any other person connected to it, and needful action is taken against him. The accused can express his wish to have the sample tested by the State Food Test Laboratory. In this situation the health officer hands over the sample to the court within five days and the test report is received within 30 days. Excluding the food inspector, the consumer also has the right to have the food substance tested by the analyst for a fixed amount of fee. If the sample is found to be adulterated or contaminated, then the fee is reimbursed. Whenever the consumer has his doubts about the adulteration of the food substance, he should immediately inform the food inspector, hygiene inspector or the area health officer.

Packed/Canned Food Products

With the development of the markets, the consumers have begun giving priority to packed/canned food products, which is easy to handle and can be bought according to a desirable amount, quality and cost. Because of the packing, it is impossible for the consumer to know the quality of the product. The misrepresentation of packed products misguides the consumers in their sale and purchase and this is a common phenomenon. To prevent these types of misleading ideas, the Standard of Weights and Measures (package) Commodities Rule, 1977 was enacted. According to these rules, certain set standards and norms, as to the packing, measurement and weight have to be followed, against which suitable punishment is given.

Main Features of the Rules and Regulations:-

1. The definition of adulterated food products, inferior substances or misbranded substances has been given.
2. The work responsibility and duty of the officer appointed to implement these laws has been clearly mentioned.
3. The import, production, storage and sale of inferior substances, used to adulterate food products have been prohibited and banned.
4. The buyer has been given the right to have the food tested.
5. The procedures of investigating the samples of various food products and giving information, have been clearly mentioned. The persons involved with adulteration of food and the persons supporting or cooperating with him and the persons selling the products (adulterated) and the punishment related with these offences has been explained in great detail.
6. In relation with food substances, special weights and standards have been fixed.
7. Verification by the ISI has been made compulsory for food substances and co-substances used, by which its purity and protection can be determined.
8. To prevent serious health hazards and to determine, the protectiveness of the food products, metallic substances, crop infestation, pesticides and the amount of maximum protection on nature's subjects have been determined and explained.
9. It has been ruled out in such a way so that the consumer has complete information on packed / canned food products printed in detail, for this the label on the package

should have some specific compulsory details. Any false information or misguided theory or confusing designs, could lead to punishment.

10. Strict steps have been taken so that no co-substance is used in food products, about which there is no mention in the act, or has not been permitted.
11. The terms and conditions for sale and license have also been clarified.
12. The officer for food and health is responsible and has been given complete right to stop or prevent food products which are sold after the expiry period.
13. It has been ruled out, that the accused businessman and shopkeepers are subject to severe punishment. A minimum of 6 months imprisonment has been fixed.

Mixed Substances and Adulterated Food

Any substance with the aim to be mixed in food products will be labelled as Mixed Substances, it is clearly stated in the act that the food will be declared as Adulterated.

1. If it is sold by the shopkeeper and is not up to the standard.
2. If a certain substance present in the food product or produced in this way which affects its quality.
3. If the food product is inferior or cheap substance is mixed completely or partially and thus affects the quality of the product.
4. If a factor has been removed completely or partially.
5. If the food product is stored packed or produced, which is injurious to health or where it can get contaminated and therefore possibility of endangering health.
6. If the food product is infected by insects then it is deemed unfit for consumption by humans.
7. Incase the food is acquired by a sick animal.
8. If the food product is mixed with a poisonous chemical or factor, which is dangerous for health.
9. If the food product is mixed with colour or some preservative, the mixing of which, is barred by the act.
10. If the co-substance exceeds the fixed amount, or

11. If the quality and the purity of the food product does not lie within required standard mentioned and can be injurious to health.

Falsely Marked Edible Foods

In the Act the falsely marked edible foods are defined in detail. This is mostly in connection with violating the rules and regulations of the Act. Any food product will be marked falsely as follows:-

1. If any name of the label or design is imitated or is a look alike.
2. If the label gives you a false idea, of the production being of a foreign company.
3. If it is being sold by the name of some other already existing food product.
4. If, to make it look attractive have used colour or perfume, polished or is being sold in the form of powder.
5. If any false claims are mentioned on the label or anywhere else on the package.
6. If the label has any misguiding theory or rumour, picture or design is printed on it.
7. If clear and correct details are not given on the label of the represented product.
8. If the label is not according to the rules or are misguiding.

Examples of Falsely Marked Edible Foods

Selling Guava bark by the assertion of Cinnamon Stick, chicory in the form of coffee, colouring old lentils/pulses with Tar-coal, to hide its deformities and to make it attractive etc. for sale in the market are some of the examples of falsely marked adulterated food.

Essential Commodities Act, 1954

According to this Act, its main aim is to provide the public with the essential commodities through correct rules and regulations. Apart from this, rules regarding profits through illegal hoarding, selling banned commodities without permission and black marketing have been provided in this Act. Within this Act, orders for control have been formed. Some of these are mentioned below:-

- Fruit Production Act, 1955
- Sugar Control Act, 1966
- Vegetable-Oil Production Control Act, 1976
- Meat Production Control Ac, 1955
- Fruit Production Act, 1955.

Within this Act, the Food Resource Council, through the Food and Nutrition Board, for regulation of all kinds of fruit and vegetable products, sweet carbonated water, vinegar, synthetic drinks, have adopted provisions for correct health standards.

Any production and labelling of fruit and vegetable products cannot be done without proper license and permission. Before giving license or permission to the concerned producers, he has to be satisfied, if the quality and standard of the product, hygienic production are being followed. Besides this he will also look into matters relating to the hired staff, given machinery and equipment and work station etc. is according to the law or not. With this permission the producer will be able to mark the products with an F.P.O Standard mark.

Voluntary Standards and Verification System

This system works on voluntary basis. Through the competitive business practice, the high producing quality standard food is made available and is verified and permitted by it. Two organizations are formed in the food producing units for voluntary standards and verification system. The first one is ISI, and the second is Institute for Marketing and Detection.

Establishment of Laboratories for 'Agmark' Classification

'Agmark' has played a major role for the last six years in the quality of food production, verification and protection of consumer rights. In the voluntary programme of the government of India, the food products of daily use are being included in the 'Agmark' Stamped Quality Check. Interested producers are to obtain a license (Govt. Certificate). For the quality check within 'Agmark', the producers adopt special constitutional methods for manufacture of products. This work is being done by the Institute for Marketing Detection, within the parliament Acts of Agricultural Production (classification & marking) Act, 1937 and Amendment of 1986. Though the 'Agmark' classification is a voluntary programme, but the growing public awareness towards the quality of the food products and due to the increasing competition in the market of products like, vegetable oil, spices, flour, fine flour, semolina, gram flour, pulses, Ghee, butter, honey, asafoetida, etc-the producers are feeling the necessity and importance of 'Agmark' guaranteed, quality products.

The method of manufacturing of 'Agmark' products are-Firstly, carefully cleaned and sieved raw materials, secondly, cleaning of raw materials through scientific methods and is formed within favourable conditions. After this, the lot is tested by a suitable chemist and when the quality of the product is found to be according to the specified requirements from the scientific point of view, and then the food products are packed and marked with the 'Agmark' label or 'Agmark' replica.

The products which have been standardized within 'Agmark', they have to go through various laboratory tests to maintain their quality and purity. Thus, to fulfill this aim, the Institute for Marketing & Detection has accordingly established 'Agmark' laboratories in various parts of the country. The main laboratory of the Institute "Central 'Agmark' Laboratory" is based in Nagpur.

The important functions of the laboratory are as follows:-

1. To standardize the agricultural products, the first step is to specify the class and standards for products. The "Central 'Agmark' Laboratory" helps the institute in this process, makes suitable changes in the standards from time to time and also tests the various product samples brought from different places.
2. The "Central 'Agmark' Laboratory" is the apex organization, which makes technical developments in the testing methods.
3. The main function of the laboratory is to impart 'Agmark' quality related necessary training.
4. In the field of standardization and quality control, the "Central 'Agmark' Laboratory" takes support from and maintains relations with existing National and International organization.
5. The "Central 'Agmark' Laboratory" does research work and gives necessary advice.

The "Central 'Agmark' Laboratory" has established 22 area 'Agmark' laboratories, within this quality control programme, in various states. The main functions of these laboratories are given below:-

1. To test the duplicate samples sent by the attached chemists of the packers/producers.
2. To have the checked samples, tested by the Institutes appointed officers and state marketing officers.
3. To test samples of products for export purpose.
4. To do research on the work given by the department.
5. To impart necessary training to state, co-operative or commercial laboratories and packing laboratories.

The function of the packer/producer is to maintain the quality of the product and to determine complete laboratory tests. Therefore, it is necessary for each packer/producer to have their own laboratories, so that they can continuously test the quality of the products. The governments and packers/producers do not have the capacity to setup their laboratories. For these packers/producers, the state government and co-operative societies help in the establishment of laboratories. The packers/producers can attach itself to any one of the laboratories. Then this laboratory makes arrangement for the packer, of the looking after of their production and refinement and also takes the required samples for analysis. In this manner, the packer/producer acquires the opportunity for convenient testing at low cost.

Apart from the state government and co-operative laboratories, a large number of private laboratories have come into existence Packer/producer laboratories are of two types-packers own laboratories and commercial laboratories. Some big packers/producers establish their own laboratories themselves. The government imparts training to the chemists of these laboratories and also has approved Institutes for Marketing and Detection. In India there are 652 laboratories of this kind. The function of the private laboratories is the same as the state classified and co-operative laboratories. These laboratories also provide testing facilities to these packers, who are unable to setup, their own laboratories. The chemists of these laboratories are approved by the Institute.

I.S.I. (Certified Mark) ACT, 1952 and B.I. ACT, 1952

The I.S.I. functions within the Certificate Plan Act, 1896. It has arrangement for 450 edible food products. Under this plan, when the industrialist applies for the above, the Institute will analyse and investigate the process of the industry, and gives the certification mark against this rule. But they can also make an analysis and investigation at ant point of time and if the standards are not as per required, the certification mark of the industry will be retrieved. Under the Institute's certification with the P.F.A Act, some of the products are given below:-

- Food colour and their production method.
- Natural food colour.
- Milk products.
- Milk powder.
- Condensed milk etc.

Food Safety Objectives

The Codex Committee for General Principles (CCGP) at its 15th Session (2000) considered the general aspects of the development and application of food safety objectives, following discussions at the 7th Session of the Codex Committee on Food Import and Export Inspection and Certification Systems (CCFICS) (1999) and 45th Session of the Executive Committee. CCFICS had requested approval of the Commission to undertake the elaboration of Guidelines for the Judgement of Equivalence of Sanitary Measures associated with Food Inspection and Certification System. The proposal included consideration of the concept of Food Safety Objectives.

The CCGP, at its 15th Session, discussed whether there was a need to define 'Food safety objectives' and was of the opinion that the concept was technical in nature and it was premature to generalize the concept with a specific definition. It agreed that the concept could be further developed by other relevant Committees in order to identify how it could be applied to specific food safety issues, and that the Committee would continue to oversee the consistency in definition and application of the concept.

The Codex Committee for Food Hygiene initiated work on Proposed Draft Guidelines for Microbiological Risk Assessment at its 31st Session (1998) and introduced and discussed the concept of Food Safety Objectives. It was advanced to Step 3 for comments at the 32nd Session (1999) and a restructured and revised draft was placed at the 33rd Session (1999) which discussed, among other issues, 'Food Safety Objectives (FSOs), ' changed to 'Microbiological Food Safety Objectives (MFSOs)'. The draft was returned to Step 3 for revision by the drafting group.

At the 34th Session of CCFH (2000) a revised draft was discussed. The concept of Food Safety Objectives was supported by the Committee and the importance of clearly defining the term, so that it was understandable and could be used in a transparent manner, was noted.

Food Safety Objective-Salient Features Identified by CCFH

A Food Safety Objective (FSO) or a Micro biological Food Safety Objective (MFSO) can be a useful tool in [microbiological] risk management.

The function of a FSO is to express the level of a hazard in a food that is tolerable in relation to an appropriate level of consumer protection. This is reflected in the following working definition:

A FSO is a statement based on a risk analysis process, which expresses the level of a hazard in a food that is tolerable in relation to an appropriate level of protection.

An alternate definition proposed by the International Commission for Microbiological Specifications in Foods but not yet accepted is:

The maximum frequency and/or concentration of a [microbiological] hazard in a food at the time of consumption that provides the appropriate level of health protection [(ALOP)].

When justified by the risk assessment, the FSO should express the level of the hazard as its maximum tolerable frequency and/or concentration. The FSO must be technically achievable, practicable and quantifiable. Whilst decisions on acceptable levels of risk should be determined primarily by human health considerations, and arbitrary or unjustified differences in the risk levels should be avoided. Consideration of other factors (e.g. economic costs, benefits, technical feasibility, and societal preferences) may be appropriate in some risk management contexts, particularly in the determination of measures to be taken. These considerations should not be arbitrary and should be made explicit.

FSOs should contain three components:

- food of concern,

- hazard of concern and
- the appropriate level of consumer protection.

The statement of appropriate level of sanitary protection in the WTO SPS Agreement is "The level of protection deemed appropriate by the Member establishing a sanitary measure to protect human health.

Note-Many Members otherwise refer to this concept as the acceptable level of risk."

The appropriate level of consumer protection is a reflection of a particular country's public health goals relative to the application of sanitary measures. For foods in international commerce, it represents a consensus of what participating countries or governments are willing to tolerate in relation to their food supplies.

Once a consensus has been reached on what is considered appropriate, it should be incorporated into an FSO for communication to all affected parties. Industry and regulatory authorities should then adjust their control and inspection systems to meet the FSO.

FSOs are food safety management tools, which can provide a number of functions. A few examples are:

- FSOs provide a reference for the overall design of good hygienic practices and HACCP based food control systems;
- FSOs provide a target for the validation of sanitary measures for segments of food production systems, or for food production systems in their entirety;
- FSOs may form the basis for derivation of performance and hazard criteria for steps in a food production system.

Because significant differences in the occurrence of food borne pathogens can be found between different countries regions, FSOs in general and more specifically sampling plans, criteria etc, should not be considered universally common but should take into account national and regional situations.

Primary users of FSOs are governments and the food industry.

- *By governments to:* communicate the expected level of food safety to the food industry and the consumers.
- *By the food industry to:* show that their products meet the established tolerable level of risk for the specified hazard.

At the international level, FSOs can be used in the determination of equivalence by showing that different sets of control measures meet the same level of protection. FSOs do not prescribe how the expected level of food safety can be achieved, leaving the food industry to select the appropriate technology including the establishment of process and performance criteria.

Because significant differences in the occurrence of food borne pathogens can be found between different countries or regions FSOs in general, and more specially sampling plans, criteria, etc., should not be universally common but should take into account national and regional situations.

Economic Development in India, India's Economic Progress, Achievements

Evolution of Policy-India

The British colonial government of India did not pursue an active policy of agricultural development despite modest efforts to formulate a policy. One such effort was the appointment in 1926 of the Royal Commission on Agriculture, which made some recommendations for improving agriculture and promoting the welfare of the rural population. Most of the commission's recommendations were deferred because of the Great Depression of the 1930s. One outcome, however, was the establishment of the Imperial (later Indian) Council of Agricultural Research in 1929. During World War II, disruptions in international trade also led the government to initiate the Grow More Food Campaign. The government adopted its first agricultural policy statement in the wake of famine in Bengal in 1943. The policy objectives included increased production of food grains, use of better methods of production, improved marketing, better prices for the producers, fair wages for agricultural labour, fair distribution of food, increased production of raw materials, and improvements in research and education. This statement was the basis of many of the policies adopted soon after independence, especially in the First Five-Year Plan, when the central government was committed to giving priority to agricultural production to increase the food supply in the country.

The prolonged neglect of agriculture in India meant that there was almost no growth in the agricultural sector. From 1891 to

1946, output of all crops grew at 0.4 percent a year; the rate for food grains was only 0.1 percent per year. The land tenure system led to exploitative agrarian relations and stagnation. Farmers had little incentive to invest, and despite great strides in foreign agricultural technology, Indian agricultural technology stagnated. Specifically, there were few improvements in seeds, agricultural implements, machines, or chemical fertilizers.

At the time of independence in 1947, agriculture and allied sectors provided well over 70 percent of the country's employment and more than 50 percent of the gross national product. Agricultural development was a key to a number of national goals, such as reducing rural poverty, providing an adequate diet for all citizens, supplying agricultural raw materials for the textile industry and other industries, and expanding exports. In the mid-1960s, the goal of self-reliance was added to this list. The central government has played a progressively more important role on the agricultural front by providing overall leadership and coordination, as well as by providing a significant part of the financing for agricultural programs. However, the primary responsibility for the design and implementation of agricultural programs, in accordance with the constitution, remained with the states in the late twentieth century.

India's agricultural growth strategy after independence evolved over three distinct phases. In the first phase, roughly covering the period through the Second Five-Year Plan, agricultural growth rested on removing basic socioeconomic constraints through land reform, change in the village power structure, reorganization of the rural poor into cooperatives, and better citizen participation in planning. The initial assumption was that changing the land tenure system by abolishing the zamindar system—a method of revenue collecting and landholding developed during the Mughal and British colonial periods—would stimulate agricultural output.

The second phase occurred during the Third Five-Year Plan (FY 1961-65). The continuing shortages of food in the 1960s and the consequent crises convinced planners that raising agricultural output, especially food grains, was essential for political stability and independence from foreign food aid. Self-sufficiency in food-grain production and development of an adequate buffer stock through procurement became clearly defined goals in the mid-1960s. Keeping in mind the variety of socioeconomic and agroclimatic differences, the government adopted an area-specific approach, and emphasized programs such as the Intensive Area Agricultural Programme and the Intensive Agricultural District Programme.

The third phase in India's economic development is identified predominantly as the Green Revolution. This phase relied on better seeds, more water via irrigation, and improved quantity and quality of fertilizer during the Fourth Five-Year Plan (FY 1969-73), the Fifth Five-Year Plan (FY 1974-78), and the Sixth Five-Year Plan (FY 1980-84). The Green Revolution was successful in meeting the goals of self-sufficiency in food-grain production and adequate buffer stocks by the end of the 1970s. Production was more than 100 million tons in 1978 and 1979. Imports were negligible, and the year-end buffer stocks from 1976-79 averaged more than 17 million tons. After 1980 buffer stocks fell below 10 millions tons only once, in 1988.

In the mid-1990s, the major goals of agricultural policy continued to be self-sufficiency in food staples and adequate food supplies at affordable prices for consumers. Expanding cereal production continued to be a major objective because of the population growth rate of almost 2 percent per year. The budgetary share of agriculture, together with irrigation and flood control projects, remained almost constant in the first six plans, varying between 21 percent and 24 percent.

The Eighth Five-Year Plan (FY 1992-96), as conceived in the early 1990s, not only aimed at continued self-sufficiency in food production, but also included plans to generate surpluses of some agricultural commodities for export. It also aimed at spreading the Green Revolution to more regions of the country with an emphasis on dryland farming.

5

Contemporary Food Marketing-Challenges & Ethical Issues

Today's consumers are more flirtatious gazing for an increasing level of fun and variety. Anything that surrounds them for too long jades them. With the dawn of every fresh day, these modern day customers demand for quality and healthy food that is offered as per their convenience and changing cultural needs. The survival of any food outlet or the industry is also highly dependent on them – their palate can either make or break the existence of these companies. This has wrought a great challenge on the marketers of the food industry who intentionally resort to unethical practices that had sourced many lively international debates on ethical and marketing practices of the food industry besides the intervention of regulatory authorities to implement necessary legislation wherever required to reduce the ill-effects on the society.

There has been an increase in the number of tourists (both in-bound and outbound) due to the boost in tourism resulting in the exchange of cultural and traditional ideas among different countries; the development of communication, infrastructure, and information technology due to the liberalization, globalization and various other good reasons has turned the world into a global village; the spending capacity of the middle-class people has also risen due to availability of highly disposable income and increasing economy of the country for the past few years. All these reasons were enough for the food industry to bring into the country a multitude of different gastronomy from across the globe – like the pastas & spaghettis from Italy, the ever-popular chowmein from China, the tacos and enchiladas from Mexico, the Continental pizzas and burgers, the French flambe etc., to name a popular few which were normally ever heard of and were limited within the precincts of star hotels and among those people who could afford them. But of late, there have been a slew of contemporary foods pouring into the market at affordable prices that are targeted at the growing numbers of fashionable consumers. Some of the latest additions to the already existing modern foods include –

- the ready instant mixes that consumes less cooking time (like the idli mix, dosa mix, sambar powder and so on that are added with preservatives to increase their shelf life),
- the ready-to-eat foods like ITCs paneer butter masala, nav ratan kurma, dal makhani and so on (under the Aashirvaad's ReadyMeal brand), that just requires pre-heating through a baine-marie,
- the fusion of cuisines customizing to Indian palate-Italian pizza in the form of Indian Tandoor pizza.

With increasing demands largely from the perpetually growing niche segment – the children and the young adults, there is also rigorous sale of junk foods that mainly includes energy-dense fast foods like the puff pastries and burgers containing large quantity of margarine, mayonnaise, butter or cheese; carbonated soft drinks with high calorie content like Pepsi or Coke; sugary breakfast cereals like the Kelloggs Choco Pops; salty snacks like Haldirams or Leher namkeens; and other baked goods like patties, cookies, doughnuts etc.,

Though these food products are claimed to be manufactured using the best technology under most hygienic standards by trained professionals, they generally tend to be nutrient-poor and High in Fats, Sugars and Salt (HFSS foods) contributing to an environment of more obese people with diet-related non-communicable diseases like the cardiovascular diseases, diabetes, osteoporosis, certain forms of cancer, and high blood pressure.

The Pill with a Sugar Coat

The marketers exploit many innovative practices and use wide unethical deeds and techniques to promote their products to capture the gullible segment. Though most of the practices used by the food marketers seem upright and lawful, it would be found to be immoral only when appropriately examined where it becomes difficult for one to judge and draw a clear line between normal marketing practice and unethical behavior of the marketer. All of us have encountered the marketing gimmicks of many companies in some form or the other – like the buy two get one free; the offer is only for employees of certain organizations; some pop-ups sprouting on the screen when browsing the Internet informing that we have won a prize; or a banner of some sponsor placed at the venue during an event attended, etc. Once the consumer gets attracted by this publicity stunt, he is further lured to become a customer and then a permanent customer. As Vikram Bakshi, MD, McDonald's puts it in one of his recent interviews-

"McDonald's is a family restaurant. We believe that we are here to make our customers feel at home and enjoy their time out with their family when they are at McDonald's. Extra care has been taken to make our restaurants child friendly, by providing play areas wherever possible so that the parents can relax and have a good time when they are visiting McDonald's. Our tables are rounded so that a child does not hurt himself while in the restaurant, our counters are low and the menu pictorially depicted so that a child can order a meal for himself very easily and his parents don't have to bother. At McDonald's, customer always comes first. Every employee strives to provide 100 percent customer satisfaction – for every customer – for every visit. This includes friendly and attentive service, accuracy in order taking, and anticipation of customer's needs. We have hostesses who keep circulating in the lobby helping children and adults alike with straws, napkins, souffle cups, sauce sachets etc., and any other assistance that they may require".

Anyone would hardly resist such royal treatment. These food outlets take into concern not only the comfort and convenience of their guests, but also to convert their first time visitors into repeat business. Meticulous plan is done as per the behavioural patterns and feedback from the target consumers – like from "McDonald's mein hai kuch baat" caption when it first started operations ten years back in India to "Toh aaj McDonald's ho jaye" after getting established properly in the market. Notice the change of talk from the experience of a first time visit to about an everyday experience i.e. the customers are encouraged to visit more often with their family and enjoy their time out. And the segment that wishes to have the food delivered at its place, then there is Domino's Pizza at the neighborhood, a global 'Pizza Delivery Expert' known world over for providing freshly baked pizzas topped with quality ingredients and cheese. This was the first pizza chain in the world committed to the promise of delivering pizzas in 30 minutes or less and most of their outlets in India are delivery-based with only about 25% being both delivery and "sit-down" outlets.

None would get misled or infer anything wrong with the above points against the food industry or its strategies used. As already stated, it is very difficult to draw a clear line between normal marketing practice and unethical behavior. But how far it is ethical on the part of the food companies to offer junk and unhealthy food to its valued customers and again chase them to visit almost daily? Mind you, there is nothing to criticize the food industry here as such with regard to its quality of products or services offered or even doubt on its credibility. It is only on the type of food that they offer that is having its negative impact on the society.

It is agreed that there is nothing called bad food as such, but it is mainly the kind of food that does not add any value or significance to the health of the people. It rather acts as nutrition-less junk food showing its ill effects on the health that affects the mortality rate of the civilization. Again concurring that the modern day consumer is too busy and insists on such kind of food, but how far is it good on the part of the marketer to lure and tempt these innocent gullible with attractive offers and promotions who are unaware or limitedly aware of the consequences. The insistence from the consumer to provide such food does not come on its own unless shaped by the industry in order to survive and earn huge profits. This is created through the heavy dose of advertisements and promotions, the peer pressure, and with the rapid expansion and opening of new branches even in smaller towns of the country.

Ethical Challenges

Naturally, a company will exist and grow in the market by expecting repeat business only when it satisfies its customers' needs i.e. it understands what its customer wants. But, there are some instances where the customers' wants are not good for him or her. Like a child buying a cigarette for his father but smoking himself or an obese patient having more of sweets, oily food. Similarly, it may also happen that some demands of the customers may be good for them but are not good for the society or the environment like the recent killings of the extinct, endangered species to celebrate a high profile dinner, a premarital abortion, etc.

Examining these points from different perspectives i.e.

a) interests and behaviors of the marketers,
b) the extent of consumers' concern to reduce the negative side effects of the products they buy and
c) the steps to be taken to reduce the consumption of products that have ill-effects on the general public at large and the appropriate intervention.

Interests and Behaviors of the Marketers

Any food manufacturer will always strive to increase the sale of his product or service to the maximum extent and leave the negative consequences to be the result of the free choice of consumers – a natural phenomenon. Some food products like burgers, sweets, and carbonated soft drinks are not so harmful as compared to alcoholic drinks, cigarettes or drugs etc., but as mentioned are poor in nutrients with rich fat, sugar and salts content causing obesity and other diseases. Most people especially the young children and the teenage group get addicted to them quickly mainly due to reasons like emulating of Western culture, the environment of nuclear family with sometimes both the parents working, peer coercion in the school/college/office etc. These addicted categories are the company's treasures who later become heavy users as the days pass by accounting for their high profits. Let us understand this with an example:

Presume a teenager is addictive of eating a cheese pizza daily. This promises the company a patron for life and each such new addict expectedly generates a 25-year to 30-year profit stream for the pizza company if the consumer continues to favour the same brand. Suppose the teenager starts eating at the age of 15, eats for 25 years and stops further consumption due to obesity and doctor's advice. If she spends an average of Rs. 10,000/-a year on the pizza, she will spend Rs. 2,50,000/-till she reaches 40. If the company's profit rate is 20%, she is worth Rs. 50,000/-to the company. Which company will not try to attract such a heavy user who is contributing Rs. 50,000/-to its profits? And this profit is the minimum as the lady stopped eating at 40. What if the addiction continued and she consumed the same for another few years neglecting its ill effects? This is the thing that generally happens, as most of the people are unable to control themselves due to the temptations created by these food marketers with their innovative methods.

Are you aware that Coca-Cola is aiming to get people to start drinking Coca-Cola for breakfast instead of orange juice?

Then, McDonald's is encouraging customers to choose a larger hamburger, a larger order of French fries, and a larger cola drink.

And with best of the marketers working for them, it is just a cakewalk to transform the consumer eating habits.

Consumers' Concern to Reduce the Negative Side Effects

Would anybody be ready to reduce their sales or restrain consumption of their products? Never. Hence, there should be at least some kind of pressure from the government or the public. Recently, in the interest of the consumer, the Cola companies were directed by Supreme Court to list the composition of contents on all bottles including the pesticide residues but the company is utilizing the opportunity of time given to approach the High Court on the phraseology. Surrogate advertising though banned is still observed and continued on television, generally seen at places like sports stadiums, art exhibitions in the form of sponsorships of the event. Some of them under close scrutiny of the regulations are McDowell's Mera Number One, Gilbey's Green Label ads, Bagpiper soda water, Kingfisher mineral water, 8PM apple juice, ITC-GTD's (greeting cards division) Expression Greeting Cards, Red & White Bravery Awards and Wills sportswear as they are the titanic advertisers under this category.

Most of the companies, as part of their Corporate Social Responsibility give a statutory warning on their products. For example, like the statutory warning on the cigarette packs, some of the food companies also warn in similar way – on products that contains Monosodium Glutamate (MSG) i.e. Ajinomoto. MSG if consumed in large quantities causes migraines, hormonal disorders and Chinese restaurant syndrome. But still people keep continue to buy such product and the companies who just try to behave in a socially responsible manner know this and are aware that the sales loss resulting from their CSR 'cooperation' is very slight.

On the other hand, there is sometimes resistance from the consumers themselves when the companies genuinely struggle to find avenues to reduce the ill effects of too much consumption of their products. When Mc. Donald's offered a reduced-fat hamburger or salad, consumers rejected it. Keeping the calorie conscious people in mind, Coca-Cola and Pepsi introduced the Diet Coke and Pepsi One brand with low calorie content. Coca-Cola also recently announced the launch of Coca-Cola Zero, a new, zero-calorie cola drink sweetened with a blend of aspartame and acesulfame potassium.

All these modifications and new product development from the company are the results of feedback and behavior from the consumers themselves as well as the pressures from the Government.

Right to Intervene and Reduce the Consumption

Infinite numbers of debates ensued with regard to the right to intrude by the government or any public interest groups in the free choices of individuals whether to reduce or ban the consumption of foods that show their ill effects on the health of the people in due course. On one end, it is detested with remarks like the job of marketer is not to make society a better place or to save the world. He is mainly there to sell more and earn good profits for the shareholders in a legal way. On the other side, there are few people concerned with the personal and societal costs of unregulated consumption. Very sensitive issues are created on certain food products and statistics are developed on the heavy health costs of various diseases caused because of failure to reduce the consumption of such kind of products. These costs affect everyone as they lead to higher medical costs and taxes. Thus, even those who don't consume such products are harmed because of unenlightened behavior of others.

The Finale Act

What legislations have to be brought out by the regulatory authority that would create a check on the marketers while promoting and selling of their products? What ethical practices does the marketer need to carry out in order to create a good image among his customers and also to develop a healthy society? Let us look at this issue from both the perspective.

Promotional Regulations

The regulatory authority of various countries have brought into force various regulations and restrictions with regard to the promotional activities of the food marketers in order to reduce its usage and avoid the related ill effects on the society. As the marketers particularly target the children and the young adults who are found to be the most influential decision makers during any purchases, their promotional activities have created a very high impact on the society that have shown more of negative results. Let us observe few of the strategies of the marketers and the legislations put upon them by the legal authorities.

1. *Television :* The strongest of all the media in the modern world, television is highly used by food marketers to advertise their products with particular target on children. Breakfast cereals, soft drinks, snacks, and fast foods are the common food products advertised frequently through this medium. The effect has been so great over the past few years that there have been strong proposals to restrict television advertising, particularly to children in many countries including India, Australia, Brazil, Germany, United Kingdom, Ireland, Italy, New Zealand, Poland and France. Television ads carried various clauses emphasizing companies not to exploit the credulity of people; be harmful to their physical, mental or moral health; make them feel inferior to others who possess the products; or induce them to unduly pressurize their parents/guardians into purchasing the product.
2. *In-premises marketing:* The food marketer visits the place of customer like schools, colleges, offices or homes and promotes the products. This strategy is used to target all categories of people as all of them would gather together at their respective places. This strategy is found to be second best to television advertising as it has also attached lot of controversy and debate in recent years. The techniques used are direct advertising (e.g. Signage in canteens), indirect advertising (eg. Sponsorship of events) and product sales. Most of the items like soft drinks, confectionary, snacks, ice-creams, instant noodles, etc., which do not even contain the minimum nutritional value (MNV) required are usually sold. Some of the restrictions used especially in schools are prohibiting commercial solicitation, non-distribution of advertisements and other marketing material without the consent of the parents in

advance, not allowing the marketing activities unless the head teacher believes it has an educational objective. In Japan, the meal provided under the school lunch program is the only food to be eaten within school premises.

3. *Sponsorship:* In sponsorship, the food companies provide funds and other resources to an event or activity in return for access to the exploitable commercial potential associated with that event. Sponsorship has the benefits of reaching globally at less cost than conventional advertising when the event sponsored is broadcast worldwide. Food companies sponsor wide range of activities like sporting events, television programs and musical events. The main advantage to the marketer under this strategy is that being a sponsor, he may have influence on the program content and cause program dilution where much publicity for his company and products would be demanded and created among the audience. Some of the regulations under sponsorship include banning sponsorship of children's program, not encouraging purchase or rental of the products or services of the sponsor, etc.
4. *Product Placement:* Under product placement, a visual or graphic uses the message, logo, or object of the food company in exchange for payment. It is found in many forms of visual entertainment like films, television programs, music videos, computer games, etc. This powerful marketing tool of 'surreptitious advertising' and indirect or non-regular advertising is widely used to market food and beverage products. It is a cost-effective technique when compared with the purchase of normal airtime, it is less disruptive than commercial breaks as the viewer is held captive, giving the product his undivided attention because it is part of the program. It is explicitly banned in countries like Austria, Belgium, UK, Norway and is used with restricted time in Philippines.
5. *Internet marketing:* Consumers at present are widely targeted with this new but rapidly expanding strategy with a range of internet-based marketing techniques. The cross-border marketing is especially changing the entire world into a global village. The ideal target group under

this strategy is mainly young people, as they tend to browse the net for longer durations. The strategies used are interactive games and activities, competitions, attractive sites with flashy graphics, chat and e-mail facilities. Keeping the children and teenagers in mind, the website is made more interactive, providing free downloadable games & general information. Subsequently, personal data of the visitors are collected for future promotions and sale of database. There are statutory guidelines and restrictions with self-regulatory codes specific to Internet marketing, e-commerce, data collection, consumer protection, broadcast advertising, link to other websites which are still in the budding stages.

6. *Sales promotion:* Under the sales promotion technique, the marketer creates an incentive scheme to make the consumer buy a product or service at the point-of-sale. Door-to-door selling, ballyhoo, prizes, hawking, price discounts all come under sales promotion. With regard to sales promotion, there are very general regulations like sales promotion must be fair and sometimes are very specific like not allowing any sweepstakes, etc.

Likewise, the food companies may reflect on the following few brief opinions that would act as guidelines for meeting their challenges without foregoing the ethical values. Some of the international food marketers may be already treading on them while some may make use of these for exercising in their organizations.

1. *Following the basic ethical norms and values:* The first and foremost being marketers must do no harm and work for which they are appropriately trained for by adhering to applicable laws and regulations. This will automatically make them actively add value to their organizations and customers. The products should be appropriate for their intended and promoted uses for which intentionally deceptive or misleading communication should be avoided. The ethical values should be embraced, communicated and practiced so as to improve the consumer confidence; they should show honesty by being truthful or forthright in their dealings with customers, employees, investors, Government and other stakeholders.

They should be responsible and accept the consequences of any marketing decisions and strategies, should be fair by trying to balance justly the needs of the buyer with the interests of the seller, respect the basic human dignity of all stakeholders, be open by creating transparency in their marketing operations and finally fulfill the economic, legal, philanthropic and societal responsibilities that serve the stakeholders in a strategic manner.

2. *Using appropriate and ethical marketing strategies:* The ethical and appropriate marketing strategies include the packaging or serving the food in reasonable portion sizes without encouraging overeating that generally food marketers do to increase their product sale. The products also should be reformulated to reduce the size of the portions, the amount of calories, the sodium content along with refined sugars and saturated fats. Emphasis should be to improve the nutritional value of the food by concentrating more on fruits, vegetables, whole grains and low-fat milk contents in the food products. There should be strenuous efforts to promote healthy eating habits by portraying healthful foods in a positive way. The advertisements should not focus on nutritionally poor food products especially on those channels that are particularly watched by children.
3. *Concentration on some specific issues:* Marketers should concentrate on some specific issues as given below particularly in case of marketing the food products for children –
   a. Not to mislead the child regarding the emotional, social or health benefits of a product.
   b. Not to market any food by negatively portraying the parents, teachers or any other popular personalities.
   c. Not to suggest that a person who buys a certain product for the child is better than the person who does not.
   d. Not to link the child's self-image to consumption of his company's food, use any peer pressure or arouse any kind of unrealistic expectations in relation to consuming his company's food (like a child will be more fit physically, will be more happy or popular if he eats a particular food).

   e. Not to use pictures of healthful foods like fruits or vegetables to market the low-nutrition foods.

4. *Making safer products:* The foods to be manufactured and marketed to the consumers should be lighter with minimum quantities of fat and calories. This can be done alternatively by means of selling more of salads and healthy sandwiches. The beverage companies can think of producing nonalcoholic beer in huge quantities as the young population largely consumes it, soft drinks companies can focus on increasing their packaged drinking water that are healthier than carbonated soft drinks. The soft drinks that are sold in underdeveloped countries can be added with nutrients and vitamins so as to deliver better health benefits to the deprived people there.
5. *Support the efforts to foster healthy eating habits:* As most of the people have limited proficiency in nutritional aspects of any food, the companies who have extensive expertise in persuasive techniques should make it a point to support the Government in communicating the effects of various foods on the health of a person. Hence, communicating with the target audience by means of effective media like television through cartoon characters, celebrities, contests etc., about the low-nutrition foods that does not benefit in any way and rather harm their health, along with discouraging them from buying cigarettes, drugs or alcoholic beverages etc., will indirectly help the society to improve itself.
6. *Restrict the sale or use of certain products:* Whenever a product is of any harm to the consumer, such items should be either restricted or totally banned from the market. There have been successful and unsuccessful attempts of frequent prohibitions of alcoholic beverages in different states of the country at different times. Such products should also neither be advertised nor promoted to prevent any illegal usages. This could be effective only with the adequate support of the companies who should take responsibility and show more concern for the society than on its own profit motive. Of course, equal support is required from the society as well to make it a successful accomplishment.

The regulatory authority has put itself on the static end by turning a Nelson's eye simply ignoring the misdeeds of the marketers and giving them more opportunity and space to create a situation which has an unbearable effect on the society. The marketers, being the responsible citizens should be concerned more about the civilization and the environment instead of focused concentration on their company's bottom-line. To conclude, it is not only in the hands of the food companies or the Government or the interested groups at large to create a healthy society but a more patronage and sustaining is required from the consumers themselves to make the world a better place to lead a quality life.

Food & Beverage

The food and beverage industry faces many challenges as companies struggle to keep up with changing consumer tastes and demographics. Today's consumers demand bolder flavours, timesaving conveniences and tempting service options. They understand food safety and environmental issues and are concerned with supply chain protection and whether an operation has gone green. Moreover, current and future consumers embrace technology, an area in which the food and beverage industry has historically lagged.

Consumer lifestyle changes also add new complexity. The days of the three-martini lunch are long gone. New data shows that 50 percent of employees take 30 minutes or less for lunch, and 58 percent eat at their desk. These hurried lunch breaks equate to lost revenue for contract and self-operated dining facilitics, making it morc difficult for food and beverage businesses to remain profitable.

As investors and private equity firms increase their holdings in the food and beverage industry, it is important for them to understand a company's true potential and the trends affecting each segment.

If this is Your Situation

- You want to identify ways to increase revenues and improve profitability in your geographically dispersed restaurant portfolio.
- You want to understand your brand's ability to grow in a variety of markets.

- Your company needs to reduce the cost of your contract-managed foodservice operations while keeping your employees and guests satisfied.
- You want to invest in or purchase a food and beverage company or ready your own company for sale.
- You are a hotel or residential facility and want to determine the best blend and use of food and beverage facility offerings.
- You need to assess your internal controls to improve accountability.
- You want to mitigate the risk of a supply chain breach or a food-borne illness outbreak.

How Pricewaterhouse Coopers can help You

Pricewaterhouse Coopers' (PwC's) hospitality and leisure practice includes food and beverage specialists with extensive knowledge and global experience in all aspects and segments of the industry. Our team works closely with clients to identify and analyse issues, implement innovative solutions, and build strong, trusting relationships. Because we understand that each business has unique needs, we design custom solutions for each client. Clients have relied on PwC to help them grow brand concepts, increase profitability of brands, ready their companies for sale, provide potential buyers with the insight they needed to make sound investment decisions, and identify significant savings. Our team has also worked with companies responding to food-borne illness outbreaks to help them implement proactive strategies to reduce the potential of an outbreak and assess supply chain risk. PwC's extensive food and beverage advisory services include:

Asset analysis and monitoring: We work as an independent third party to inform companies of potential risks and opportunities that may affect operational performance and profitability.

Operational and financial assessments: We conduct four-wall evaluations to analyse infrastructure, labour models, procurement/ supply chain practices, internal controls, current appeal of menu selection, quality of operations, dining experience and historical financial results. Through these evaluations, we provide clients with independent observations and actionable recommendations to mitigate risk, increase revenues and improve profitability.

Self-operating and contract dining foodservice assessment and development: Our experienced team can assess clients' current contract foodservice environment and identify areas of potential improvement and savings. We also work with companies to define and articulate programmatic needs and financial goals to design a relevant foodservice strategy that meets the needs of both the company and its employees. We assist in creating targeted requests for proposal, identify potential contractors and evaluate responses.

Transaction services/strategic assessment: We identify the core financial and operational strengths and weaknesses of a business: assess segment-specific industry trends and evaluate the competitive environment to identify barriers to entry/growth and market appeal. Our multilayered approach, which often includes four-wall analysis of multiple locations, allows us to provide clients with a clear picture of a brand's internal strengths and external opportunities for growth, increased revenues and potential savings.

Market research: The PwC team gathers primary and secondary data and uses advanced analytical techniques to provide clients with recommendations to enhance their business. Our research includes location and industry-specific demographic, sociographic and competitor data.

Infrastructure enhancement: We analyse current strategies and recommend a focused, disciplined model to build a sound infrastructure and organization that increases brand equity and profitability.

Restaurant concept creation/readying concept for franchising: Our specialists recommend compelling, differentiated concepts that will allow growth for independent, multi-unit and franchise clients. We take existing brands and develop the operational support materials needed to ready the concept for franchising.

Profile of Key Responsibilities

Our department is responsible for food safety control, import control on live food animals, management of food incidents and environmental hygiene services and facilities. We have two major areas of responsibilities: environmental hygiene services and food and public health services.

Environmental Hygiene Services

We strive to provide and maintain a clean and hygienic living environment for the people of Hong Kong through organizing and delivering high standard environmental hygiene services in the following major areas-

- Public cleansing services;
- Licensing and control of food businesses;
- Provision and management of environmental hygiene facilities; and
- Control of street trading activities.

Public Cleansing Services

We are committed to keeping public places clean, tidy and free of litter. Direct public cleansing services range from street sweeping and washing, collection of household waste and on-street litter, gully emptying, desludging, to providing toilets for public convenience. These services are provided by our 5 300 cleansing staff or by our private contractors whose services are under our close supervision. We provide more than 16 000 litter containers and 400 dog excreta collection bins throughout Hong Kong. These containers are emptied at least once a day. On household waste, we collect about 5 940 tonnes of household waste daily by a fleet of 387 modern refuse collection vehicles.

Licensing and Control of Food Businesses

We license food businesses to safeguard public health and safety and conduct regular inspections to ensure hygiene standards of licensed food premises are met. We also take law enforcement actions such as prosecutions, summary arrests, imposition of court orders, daily fines and suspension or cancellation of licences against unlicensed and unhygienic premises.

Provision and Management of Environmental Hygiene Facilities

We manage 36 cooked food centers, 24 freestanding cooked food markets and 81 public markets where some 13 000 stalls offer a wide variety of commodities ranging from fresh produce, meat and poultry to household items. We are also responsible for the management of 11 public cemeteries, six crematoria and eight gardens of remembrance.

Control of Street Trading Activities

On-street hawking is an accepted social and economic activity and has become part of Hong Kongs way of life. We are the authority responsible for hawker management. Through licensing and enforcement of legislation, environmental nuisance caused by street trading activities is minimised.

Food and Public Health Services

We monitor the safety of imported and locally produced food to ensure that food available for human consumption is wholesome, unadulterated and properly labelled. We also aim to safeguard public health through testing and control of live food animals; to prevent vector-borne diseases and provide advice to the public on proper food and environmental hygiene practices. The major areas of work include-

- Food surveillance and certification;
- Risk assessment and communication; and
- Pest control.

Food Surveillance and Certification

We take samples at import, wholesale and retail points for chemical, microbiological, radioactivity and toxicological tests to ascertain their fitness for human consumption. Prepackaged food is also checked for compliance with food labelling laws.

Risk Assessment and Communication

We conduct risk assessment on food safety, set food standards and recommend food safety control measures. On risk communication, we introduce and promote the Hazard Analysis Critical Control Point (HACCP) approach to ensure food safety and provide food safety information to the public and the food industry on a regular basis.

Pest Control

We give advice on pest control and prevention to government departments and the general public. Our work includes surveillance and monitoring of pest problems to prevent local transmission and investigation of vector borne diseases. Operational services on pest control are carried out by district pest control sections.

Environmental Policy

Our statement on environmental policy is as follows-

Food and Environmental Hygiene Department is committed to ensuring that all our services are delivered in an environmentally responsible manner, particularly in the collection, recycling and reduction of waste, conservation of energy and water, and prevention of air, noise, water and soil pollution. We will also promote green housekeeping in premises that we manage.

Environmental Objectives and Performance

In line with Governments efforts to protect the environment, we have incorporated environmental considerations in the formulation of our policy and the delivery of our services to ensure that all our operations are conducted in an environmentally responsible manner. The following is an account of our main objectives and performance for our operations and services in 2001.

Objective : To Reduce Waste in our Operations

Our Performance

Waste Recycling in Waste Collection Programme: In support of the Governments Waste Reduction Framework Plan 1998-2007, we have increased the provision of waste separation bins for the collection of waste paper, aluminum cans and plastic bottles from 203 sets in 2000 to 565 sets in 2001. The sets of three waste separation bins are placed at convenient public locations including MTR exits, KCR exits, bus termini, ferry piers and refuse collection points. Our contractors collect and deliver the recyclable waste to recyclers for recycling purpose.

Chemical Waste Recovery and Waste Water Drainage at Vehicle Depots: Waste lubrication oil, spent batteries and air conditioning refrigerants from vehicles are properly recovered and collected by approved contractors. During the year, we have increased the quantity of waste lubrication oil recovered from vehicles to 11 000 litres per annum, compared to 8 000 litres per annum in 2000. Proper drainage systems are also provided for vehicle washing bays to avoid pollution to storm water drainage. All the departmental depots are in compliance with the requirements under the Waste Disposal (Chemical Waste) (General) Regulation and Water Pollution Control Ordinance and are issued with relevant licences by the Environmental Protection Department (EPD).

Food Safety and Control

The amount and the way in which unwholesome food is destroyed is interrelated with the overall environmental objective of producing less waste and mitigating nuisances arising from waste disposal. To this end, we exercise tight control on the import of certain categories of high-risk food including game, meat, poultry, milk and frozen confections. We also conduct food surveillance programme through sampling at different stages of the food supply chain-from import and manufacture to the wholesale and retail stages.

Objective : To Minimise Pollution in the Delivery of our Services

Licensing Control and Enforcement on the Operation of Food Premises.

To ensure that waste generated from the operation of food premises is properly handled, we conduct regular inspections to licensed food premises to check that-

- grease traps installed in food premises are functioning properly to prevent discharge of oil or grease into public drains or sewers;
- plumbing systems in food premises are properly maintained to prevent discharge of offensive or noxious effluents into public places;
- fumes and hot air are discharged in such manner as not to be a nuisance. Metal hood, air-ducts, extraction fans, grease filters/water scrubbers of exhaust systems are maintained in good order;
- waste is properly stored in dustbins for collection; and
- no smoking area together with sufficient and proper no smoking signs are provided in restaurants having more than 200 seats for customers.

Enforcement action will be taken on those food premises not compiling with the licensing conditions. In 2001, we conducted 403 408 inspections to food premises and took 7 229 prosecution actions against food premises.

Cremation Services

To control the quality and volume of emissions generated from cremation services, we

- ensure regular servicing and maintenance of the cremators by Electrical and Mechanical Services Department (EMSD);

- install a Telemetry and Monitoring System with online computerised network supplying information to EPD for monitoring the pollution level. Monitoring system with temperature recorders are installed in major crematoria;
- use the less sulphur content (0.05%) diesel for cremation; and
- enlist the support of the public and funeral service operators to use environmental-friendly coffins through the issue of pamphlets and regular meetings with the funeral trade.

On cremation facilities, the construction of a new crematorium in Kwai Chung with four cremators to replace the existing one has started in early 2001. The works are expected to be completed in late 2002.

Environmental Hygiene Facilities

Efforts are made to improve the drainage systems in our venues including markets, hawker bazaars and refuse collection points (RCPs). All cooked food markets have proper drainage systems with grease traps to prevent the discharge of excessive pollutants into surface channels.

To prevent odour and pollution from RCPs, newly built RCPs will be installed with a water scrubber system, while existing RCPs will be retrofitted with water scrubber system or activated carbon filtration system in phases if circumstances permit.

Objective: To Minimise the Environmental Impact of Pest Control Operations

In the prevention and control of public health pests, we have adopted an Integrated Pest Management approach to rationalise the work to minimise the impact of pest prevention and control on nontarget animals and the environment. It includes finding out the causes of pest infestation and then determining the choice of control method(s). Pest control operations are evaluated regularly and will be terminated if no longer necessary. Advice on environmental improvement for solving pest problems is given to the parties concerned.

Environmental-friendly methodologies, technologies and products are used. Non-chemical means will be considered before adopting the use of pesticides. We are also very cautious in the choice of pesticides so that pest disinfestations are carried out effectively and with the least impact on the environment. Pests and nuisance causing animals are disinfested judiciously to avoid unnecessary disturbance to the ecological system.

Non-chemical Prevention and Control

Mosquito breeding can be forestalled by killing the insect at its adult or/and larval/pupal stages. Application of pesticides has an immediate effect but kills other insects as well. We strive to improve the environment so that it becomes unfavourable for mosquitoes to breed. We shall apply larvicidal oil or pesticide strictly on a need basis and to specific spots only. In 2001, the amount of larvicidal oil applied in streams was 28 421 litres, representing a 34% decrease as compared to the amount used in 2000.

In preventing malaria transmission, an environmental control approach has been adopted and found to be successful. The prevention programme is mainly confined to densely populated areas with a high risk of malaria transmission. In the year, we have put in place a control programme against malaria transmissible mosquitoes, covering a total of 647 streams.

In areas where malaria vector mosquitoes are detected but with a low population, mosquito larvae eating fishes are released to abate mosquito breeding. To further reduce the impact on the environment, *Bacillus thuringiensis israelensis* are used for killing mosquito larvae. *Bacillus thuringiensis israelensis* produce crystal proteins which can be converted into toxins in the gut of the mosquito larva. The toxins act on larvae of limited species including mosquitoes, blackflies and non-biting midges.

Pesticides

The use of pesticides is sometimes unavoidable in pest prevention and disinfestations but they are usually also harmful to nontarget animals and plants. To minimise the detrimental effect to nontarget living organisms, we choose synthetic pyrethroid insecticides which generate less hazards to human beings.

In rodent disinfestations, anticoagulants are used although it takes a longer time to kill the animal. With the right dosage, chosen bait, selected baiting locales and a well-designed baiting programme, the use of anticoagulants is considered much safer than acute rodenticides. Trapping of rodents is preferred to using chemicals. In drawing up rodent disinfestation programmes, we always take into account the environmental concern. During the year, we laid poison baits at 58 724 points and 3 247 traps, disposing of 48 944 rodents.

Judicious Disinfestations

Although some arthropods such as wasps, wild bees, ants, millipedes, motes, etc. are harmful or cause nuisance to human beings, they are not killed unless they pose a threat. When these insects have to be disinfested, non-chemical means will be considered before resorting to pesticides. The control measures include a choice of physical, environmental, biological, legal or chemical methods.

Promotion of Environmental Awareness

To promote a green office environment and to achieve continual improvement in the efficient use of resources, we constantly remind our staff of good green housekeeping measures and organise education programmes and campaigns.

To Promote Green Housekeeping Within the Department

We continue our efforts to use and purchase more green products. In 2001, we have established a list of green products such as recycled photocopying and duplicating papers, recyclable toner cartridges for printers and photocopiers, mercury-free batteries and environmental-friendly soap and liquid detergent as our standard stock items to meet the daily operational requirement.

In the near future, we plan to replace the conventional black lead pencil with green products like Clutch Pencil and Lead Refill. They will become our standard stock range.

To Reduce Consumption of Paper

We constantly remind our staff on paper-saving measures such as-

- keeping photocopying to the minimum;
- sharing copies of circulars, momoranda or publications on a team or division basis instead of making personal copies;
- reviewing distribution lists regularly to keep duplication to the minimum;

- not sending a covering memorandum and fax leading page when forwarding a document without additional message;
- using A5-size paper for short letters and memoranda; and
- using paper on both sides.

In 2001, we have successfully reduced the consumption of paper by 9.6 % when compared with the consumption in 2000.

To Promote the Use of Electronic Communication

We provide PCs and email facilities to all officers with operational needs to promote electronic communications. In 2001, the number of email users has increased to over 1 750. We encourage our staff to communicate through electronic mail as far as practicable. We post notices, circulars, telephone directories and other information that require wide circulation on the department¡¦s electronic bulletin board for sharing.

To Reduce Consumption of Other Stationery

We remind our staff to exercise economy in other stationery such as-

- not using envelopes for unclassified documents;
- reusing envelopes or using transit envelopes;
- monitoring the number of brochures/forms requiring printing or reprinting to keep the requirement to the minimum; and
- encouraging the use of ball pen refills.

In 2001, the number of envelopes used was reduced by 10% when compared with the consumption in 2000.

To Economise on Electricity Consumption

We constantly remind our staff of energy saving practices such as-

- reducing lighting for illumination to the minimum;
- switching off lights when not needed;
- switching off lights/air conditioners, communal facilities (e.g. photocopiers) outside office hours;
- switching on computers only when required;
- using Venetian blinds to reduce direct sun heat;

- closing doors to separate an air-conditioned area from a non-conditioned one;
- controlling the use of personal electrical appliances in the office;
- urging staff to use staircase for inter-floor traffic;
- reducing water consumption as the treatment and distribution of water consume energy; and
- ensuring that the indoor temperature of air conditioned offices and public waiting areas is not lower than 23¢J in the summer months.

To Collect Waste Paper for Recycling

In 2001, we collected 18 372 kg of waste paper in our offices/ venues for recycling, compared to 20 409 kg in 2000. The decrease was probably due to our efforts in reducing paper consumption.

To Maintain No-smoking Workplace Policy

We maintain a smoke-free workplace policy in all offices as well as government vehicles. In 2001, we reissued the circular on smoke-free workplace policy and distributed no-smoking signs to remind all staff to maintain a healthy and smoke-free workplace.

To Incorporate Environmental Considerations in Using Departmental Vehicles

We procure vehicles with engines that meet the latest legislative environmental standard. During the year, we planned for the procurement of vehicles running on cleaner energy. Forty-six light buses using liquefied petroleum gas will be put into service in 2002. Our vehicles are maintained on schedule to minimise the emission of excessive fumes and particles. We participate actively in trials that facilitate assessment of pollutant reduction devices on vehicles, especially those for heavy-duty vehicles like refuse collection vehicles. We will continue to work together with EMSD and Government Land Transport Agency to explore the feasibility of using pollutant reduction devices to protect the environment.

Objective : To Promote Environmental Awareness Through Educational Programmes and Campaigns

Internal : We support green initiatives launched by other government departments and organizations. In 2001, we encouraged our staff to join the "No Plastic Bag, Please" and the

"No Smoking Day in Workplace" Campaigns.

External : The Health Education Exhibition and Resource Centre organises talks for kindergarten and primary school students throughout the year. Apart from messages on personal hygiene, food hygiene and environmental hygiene, the economical use of paper and the reduction of waste are also covered. A total of 100 school talks were organised in 2001.

During the year, in collaboration with other government departments, we organised the "Anti-rodent Campaign" and the "Anti-mosquito Campaign" with the theme of "Lets Remove Stagnant Water, Eliminate Mosquitoes for Healthy Living". The campaigns have enhanced public awareness of the importance of rodent and mosquito control.

The Way Forward

Our senior management places great importance on environmental issues and initiatives and monitors related performance and achievement closely. To strive for continuous improvement, we will-

- monitor the effectiveness of the green measures we have put in place, and modify and improve them as necessary.
- review our environmental objectives regularly and incorporate new techniques that bring about good environmental impact when delivering our services; and
- promote staff awareness and knowledge on environmental issues and support green initiatives and campaigns organised by other organizations.

Future Activities

Looking ahead, we plan to take forward the following environmental initiatives, which will bring about good environmental impact.

Clean Hong Kong Programme : We have launched since December 2000 a three-year Clean Hong Kong Programme with a view to bringing about visible and sustainable improvements on the ground through active cleansing operations, public education and publicity efforts, and to instilling a sense of belonging and pride in the community for the clean environment. In 2002, we will intensify our efforts in Clean Hong Kong and take the following

- implement new action-oriented initiatives addressing district concerns such as cleanup actions all over the territory, face-lifting work to village-type refuse collection points and aqua privies, and public toilet refurbishment programme;
- implement the fixed penalty system against minor cleanliness offences; and
- continue the seasonal thematic activities for cleanup operations (harbour and beaches in summer, country parks and countryside in autumn and year-end operations in winter/spring).

Upgrading of Cremation Facilities : To enhance efficiency and minimise environmental nuisances, we are actively planning for the replacement of cremators at the Fu Shan Crematorium and the Diamond Hill Crematorium, which allow us to increase the capacity and speed for cremation for the provision of a better service.

Improvement of Refuse Collection Points : To further improve waste collection services, we plan to build more off-street RCPs equipped with features to minimise environmental nuisance to nearby residents. New RCPs, which are designed to be visually attractive as well as odourless, are equipped with water scrubber systems, vehicle exhaust extraction systems and high pressure water jet cleaners. In addition to these, upgrading works to another 49 RCPs in the New Territories to enhance pollution control are under active planning.

Using Transport Efficiently : The department is installing electronic vehicle monitoring devices to its special purpose vehicles to monitor the performance of the vehicle fleet. This can help maximise the utilisation of the vehicles and in turn reduce the fuel consumption and pollutants as a result.

Use of Retread Tyres : In support of the Governments initiative on waste reduction and environmental protection, we are exploring the feasibility of using retread tyres for our vehicle fleet. In the initial stage, refuse collection vehicles are selected for trial. If the trial is successful, it will be extended to other types of vehicles.

6

Food Hygiene in Catering Establishments

Legislation and Model Regulations

Food and Agriculture Organization of the United Nations

The World Health Organization, through its Food Safety Programme, which is aimed at ensuring the safety of foods for the consumer, initiated a survey of legislation related to food hygiene in catering establishments. The results of the survey, which are summarized in this publication, and the model food hygiene regulations for catering establishments, also included here, were reviewed by a joint FAO/WHO expert consultation held in Geneva from 28 April to 2 May 1975. This meeting was funded by the United Nations Environment Programme (UNEP) as part of its activity to "support, and accelerate or expand the work of the FAO/WHO Codex Alimentarius Commission on international standards for pollutants in food and strengthening of FAO/WHO capabilities to assist developing countries in food control". In this activity the Food and Agriculture Organization of the United Nations and the World Health Organization are cooperating agencies.

Many of the legislative texts on which this survey was based have been published, in full or in summary, in:

(1) International digest of health legislation. Geneva, World Health Organization (published quarterly); and

(2) Food and agricultural legislation. Rome, Food and Agriculture Organization of the United Nations (published

The survey covers a reasonably representative cross-section of the legislation of Member.

States in all Parts of the World

Food control has two principal objectives: protecting consumers against health risks, fraud, and adulteration of foods and assuring fair practices in the food trade. The survey described here was concerned with the first of these objectives, namely, the safety and cleanliness of food, i.e., food hygiene.

The need for a high standard of food hygiene and for adequate control measures is particularly important in catering^ establishments of all kinds. The fourth report of the WHO Expert Committee on Environmental Sanitation-' points out that:

> *"One careless food handler, or one human carrier of disease, preparing food at home will jeopardize the health of only a small number of persons, mainly members of the family. When one such person works in the kitchen of a restaurant, hospital, factory, canteen, school, or other place where meals are supplied to many people, the number of potential victims is correspondingly greater."*

The present report is therefore concerned essentially with the promotion of food hygiene in catering establishments. Nevertheless, since the basic principles of food hygiene are common to all types of food establishments and food handling activities, the model regulations annexed to this report can be used as the basis for the legal control of all types of food "Food hygiene" has been defined as, "The measures whereby the wholesomeness, soundness and safety for human consumption are secured or increased, covering all facets of food production, harvesting, processing, distribution, preparation and service and of possible causes of toxicity (physical, chemical or microbiological)".

Geneva, World Health Organization

The model code sets out in detail, but in simple terms, the various points which should be legally enforceable in any country and should be embodied in regulations or secondary legislation. It is intended, in particular, for the guidance of developing countries wishing to build up an effective organization for the control of standards of hygiene in catering establishments. In drawing up this code account has been taken of a statement by the Codex

Measures for Promoting Food Hygiene

Effective legislation is essential in any adequate system for promoting food hygiene, but this is only part of such a system. However comprehensive the legislation, it will be ineffective unless it can be enforced. This means that there must be an agency, or agencies, charged with that responsibility. These responsible bodies must in turn employ an adequate number of capable and well trained staff for enforcement duties. Indeed, one of the first steps which developing countries wanting to build up a service to improve standards of food hygiene should take is the development of a trained field staff.

Field staff cannot, however, be engaged solely in law enforcement activities. Their principal role must be to exercise constant surveillance over catering establishments so that they are fully aware of the standards of hygiene being observed and are able to take prompt action to correct any faults that they discover. This work will involve frequent inspections of premises and the collection of samples for bacteriological and chemical analysis, and supporting services such as laboratory facilities will be required. The field staff will also have advisory and educational functions, obtaining improvements in the handling of food through persuasion and consent and the education of managements.

To establish and maintain an adequate field staff with the support services required and to meet related expenditure on, for example, transport, equipment and materials, will require adequate financial resources. Part of the finances required may come from licensing or registration fees or other charges on the catering industry, but the major part will usually have to be obtained from central or local governments, or both. Governments have to decide how the funds are to be provided but it may be necessary to present strong arguments to justify the request, particularly where a country has previously not had a comprehensive food control service. Since the primary object of a food hygiene programme is to protect the health of the public, it is not always easy to present a case on a cost-benefit basis.

It must be recognized that promotion of food hygiene is only one of a number of measures for protecting and improving human health that fall within the scope of environmental health. According to a WHO Expert Committee on National Environmental Health

Programmes: Their Planning, Organization, and Administration, environmental health "refers to the ecological balance that must exist between man and his environment in order to ensure his well-being". Within the field of environmental health, environmental sanitation was defined by a WHO Expert Committee in 1950 as "the control of those factors in man's environment which exercise or may exercise a deleterious effect on his physical, mental, or social well-being".

The report of Joint FAO/WHO Food Standards Programme, Codex Alimentarius Commission. Recommended international code of practice: general principles of food hygiene. Rome, 1969.

WHO Technical Report Series, No. 439, 1970.

Committee on Environmental Sanitation). the WHO Expert Committee on National Environmental Health Programmes lists 17 item considered to be included in, or related to, environmental health. Among those items are water supplies, wastes disposal, vector control, and food hygiene.

Food hygiene, therefore, is an integral part of a health service and it is important to appreciate that it is difficult to develop in isolation a satisfactory programme for raising standards of food hygiene. High priority should be given to achieving proper standards in this particular field, but progress will be made more easily if efforts are also made to improve general environmental health. In other words, a food hygiene programme should be developed within the context of progressive environmental health and personal health programmes. Good food hygiene is impossible without adequate supplies of safe water, proper means for wastes disposal, effective pest control, and reasonable living conditions. It is also difficult to reduce the incidence of food-borne infections where disease is widespread among the population and adequate steps are not taken to reduce sources of infection.

Current Legislation

Registration and Licensing of Premises

To exercise control over premises used for food handling the responsible agency must know the location of the premises, and its task of ensuring that these premises are properly constructed and adequately equipped, and that satisfactory hygienic standards are maintained, is facilitated if a business is not permitted to open until the premises are officially approved. This power of control is strengthened if the agency is able to enforce the closure of unhygienic premises.

Many countries recognize the need to control the opening of catering premises so as to ensure that before business commences they comply with the standards in force. Provision is usually made also for the closure of premises in the event of serious contraventions of the law. The opening of premises is controlled in various ways. Sometimes a permit or licence from the local health department is required, and this may be revoked or suspended if the premises are allowed to fall into an unsatisfactory condition. One large city requires an applicant for a permit to complete successfully a course of instruction in food protection conducted by the health department. Sometimes there is a system requiring premises to be approved before they are opened.

In some countries control is achieved by a requirement that all catering establishments must be registered. For practical purposes no real distinction can be drawn between licensing and registration although licensing is normally for a limited period and implies periodical renewal of licences. However, the health authority will need for its own purposes a recordof the premises for which it is responsible, and a registration scheme therefore seems most appropriate.

WHO Technical Report Series, No. 439, 1970

Registration of food establishments is the process by which food control authorities, local or national, maintain registers in which is entered information that applicants must supply before they may operate. This information should include the name and address of the establishment and other relevant data. The approval of premises may be required before registration; however, this practice is not universal. Registration is usually for an indefinite period of time, subject to cancellation for causes indicated in the law. Licensing of food establishments is the process by which appropriate food control authorities, local or national, issue licences to operators of food establishments that have complied with relevant legal requirements. The licence authorizes the establishment to operate for a specified period of time, after which renewal is required. Licences may be suspended or revoked as provided for in the law.

Where licensing or registration schemes are not operated the task of the health authorities is more difficult, but they could still have power to enforce the closure of premises that present a danger to health. The requirement that premises may not be opened for business until they have been registered or licensed is of value to both the health authorities and the operator of the business. If catering premises may be opened without any prior consultation with the health authority, or without their approval, the operator may be faced subsequently with the need to make substantial alterations at heavy expense in order to comply with the food hygiene regulations. Such expense might be avoided if the operator-is required to consult the health authorities at the outset and accepts guidance from health officers in the design and equipping of the premises. Indeed, the health authorities could warn operators against attempting to use an unsuitable building that could not be. made to comply with the required standards.

Authority to enforce the closure of insanitary premises is most .important. Clearly, there must be a means of speedily closing catering establishments that constitute a danger to public health, but the machinery for doing this requires much consideration.

Construction

Regulations for the construction and equipping of catering premises in force in different countries vary considerably in detail although their basic intention is to provide conditions under which food can be prepared hygienically and without endangering the health of the consumer. There can be little dispute about the basic constructional elements required, or about the essential pieces of equipment necessary for good food hygiene. It is obvious, however, that there is a wide difference of opinion on the extent to which it is necessary to impose on operators of catering businesses detailed legislative requirements concerning the buildings in which they carry on their business and the equipment to be installed.

Regulations may, in addition to specifying some matters in detail, state certain broad principles. For example, one set of national regulations for food premises contains this provision:

"Every food premises shall be so constructed, located and maintained that,

(a) the premises are free from every condition that may,

(i) be dangerous to health,

(ii) injuriously affect the wholesomeness of food prepared, processed, packaged, served or stored therein; ..."

Some other regulations have a similar general requirement worded as follows: "No food business shall be carried on at any insanitary premises or place or at any premises or place the condition, situation or construction of which is such that food is exposed to the risk of contamination."

A Further Example Reads

"Any person who sells, prepares, packages or stores for sale any food under insanitary conditions shall be guilty of an offence." General provisions of this kind are desirable because in legislation it is difficult to specify in detail all conditions which should constitute an offence. The extent to which legislation contains detailed requirements regarding the construction of catering premises varies considerably. The points usually covered are that in rooms where food is stored or prepared the floors must be of smooth, nonabsorbent materials and so constructed as to be easily cleaned; all walls and ceilings in such rooms must be capable of being readily cleaned; all parts of these rooms must be kept in good order, repair and condition so as to enable them to be effectively cleaned. Premises are often required to be of such construction and in such a state of repair as to resist the entry of rats, mice and insects. In some causes, openings to the outer air are required to be effectively protected against the entry of flies and other flying insects.

Lighting and Ventilation

It is usual to require all food preparation and storage rooms to be adequately lighted and ventilated. This is normally stated in general terms but in some areas the degree of illumination is specified in detail. For example, one set of rules prescribes that at least 215 lux (20 foot candles) of light must be provided on all working surfaces and equipment in food preparation, utensil washing, and hand washing areas and in toilet rooms. At least 54 lux (5 foot candles) at a distance of 75 centimetres (30 inches) are required in dining rooms and all other areas during cleaning operations.

Equipment and Utensils

It is usual for food hygiene legislation to contain provisions concerning equipment and utensils. Legislation may require equipment and utensils to be of such materials, workman-ship and design as to be smooth, easily cleaned and resistant to damage. Provisions are sometimes laid down that all surfaces that come into contact with food must be readily accessible for cleansing and inspection. It is quite common to impose an obligation to ensure that all articles, equipment and surfaces must be nontoxic and, as far as possible, nonabsorbent. In one country legislation requires equipment and utensils to be:

(a) of sound and tight construction;

(b) kept in good repair;

(c) of such form and material that it can be cleaned and disinfected;

(d) free from cracks, crevices and open seams; and

(e) corrosion-resistant and nontoxic.

A most important part of the operation of catering establishments is the cleansing of equipment and utensils. The duty of ensuring that these are effectively cleansed after use and maintained in a clean and sanitary condition may be imposed in very general terms, leaving it to the operator of the business to adopt whatever methods he regards as the most effective. In such cases the legislation may simply require facilities for the cleansing of utensils and equipment to be provided and utensils and equipment to be thoroughly cleansed after use and kept clean.

On the other hand, regulations in force in some countries specify in considerable detail how the cleansing of utensils and equipment should be carried out. Sometimes, sinks with two or three compartments must be provided if cleansing is performed manually. Such detailed regulations usually divide cleansing into three operations: prerinsing, cleansing, and disinfecting or sanitizing. The temperature of the water used for cleansing may be laid down, 43.5°C (110°F) being usual. For machine washing, a higher water temperature may be specified.

Use of a Detergent may also be Obligatory

There may be a requirement that after utensils have been washed they should be sanitized by immersion either in hot water or in water containing a sterilizing agent. The temperature of the water used for sanitizing is usually required to be between 76.5°C and 82°C (170°-180°F) with an immersion time of 30 seconds at the lower temperature or 10 seconds at the higher. Where methods of chemical sterilization are specified the required immersion time varies from 45 to 60 seconds. The sterilizing agents allowed are solutions containing 50-100 parts per million of available chlorine, 12.5-25 parts per million of available iodine, or quaternary ammonium compounds at a concentration of not less than 200 parts per million. These solutions are to be used at a temperature of not less than 24°C (75°F).

Rules are also sometimes laid down for the operation of dishwashing machines. Where these are of the immersion type the. requirements are similar to those for manual dishwashing. For spray-type machines the temperature of the rinsing and sanitizing water may be specified. Detailed instructions may be given for cleansing procedures. These may require that, before being washed, articles must be flushed or scraped, and when necessary soaked, to remove large food particles and soil. Effective concentrations of a suitable detergent may be insisted upon for both manual and mechanical dishwashing.

As a check on the efficiency of. dishwashing, utensils may have to meet a prescribed bacterial standard. This is usually a plate count of not more than 100 bacterial colonies per utensil, using the swab technique.

In the design of legislation for the cleansing of utensils and equipment there are clearly two different philosophies. The first is that it is sufficient merely to require the provision of adequate facilities for washing, such as hot and cold water and sinks, and to make it obligatory to cleanse all vessels and other equipment thoroughly after use. The operator of the food business is left to decide for himself the precise methods to be used to achieve a satisfactory standard of cleanliness. The second philosophy is that not only must there be an obligation to provide the necessary cleansing facilities, but the methods to be used must be prescribed in considerable detail including the temperature of the hot water and procedures for sterilization. This philosophy also maintains that visual cleanliness is not enough; after being washed and sterilized, equipment must satisfy a bacteriological test. The need for strict cleanliness is unquestionable and the law should be adequate to enforce this. It is doubtful, however, whether there is really any need to embody in legislation the precise methods and materials to be used. If failure to cleanse equipment adequately is made an offence with an appropriate penalty for noncompliance, this should give the health officer the necessary authority to ensure that proper cleansing procedures are followed. His training should enable him to advise on how the required standards can be maintained.

Washing Facilities for Staff

All food premises need adequate washing facilities for the staff. They must be provided with a sufficient number of suitable wash-hand basins for the use of all persons engaged in the handling of food on or around the premises, and the basins should be conveniently placed in an accessible position. Wash-hand basins should be provided with an adequate supply of hot and cold water or of hot water at a controlled temperature. Soap or other suitable detergent, nailbrushes, and clean towels or other drying facilities must also be supplied. These washing facilities should not be used for any purpose other than personal hygiene. Food hygiene regulations generally contain provisions of this kind. Some insist that signs must be displayed conspicuously, instructing workers to wash their hands after using toilets.

Sanitary Facilities

Satisfactory sanitary facilities are necessary in all food premises for the use of the staff and this is usually legally enforceable. Sometimes, sanitary accommodation is also specifically required in catering establishments for customers' use. This accommodation must be adequately lighted and ventilated and kept clean and in good order.

Sleeping Places

It is usual for food hygiene legislation to prohibit the unhygienic practice of using rooms in which food is prepared, served or stored for sleeping purposes, and in some cases the legislation bans direct communication between sleeping quarters and rooms in which food is handled.

Refuse

Some regulations make it obligatory to provide adequate space, in a suitable situation, for the removal of waste from food, the separation of food fit and unfit for human consumption, and the storage of waste and unfit food before disposal. There must be no avoidable deposit or accumulation of solid or liquid wastes in a food room. Sometimes the law is more precise. It may insist, for example, that all garbage and refuse in kitchen areas should be kept in separate, leakproof, nonabsorbent containers equipped with tight-fitting covers unless otherwise protected from flies and other insects. There may be a specific obligation to maintain refuse storage areas in a clean sanitary condition. Garbage and refuse should be disposed of as often as necessary to prevent decomposition or overflow.

First-aid

The provision of first-aid equipment for food handlers is obligatory in some countries and should be generally compulsory. Storage of clothing It is usual to require lockers to be provided for the outdoor or other clothing and footwear of employees arriving for work in food handling establishments.

Water Supply

An adequate supply of clean and wholesome water is generally stipulated for all food premises. Clearly, this should be a universal requirement.

Food Protection

It is common to embody in food hygiene legislation an obligation to protect food from contamination by insects, rodents, dust, and from all other kinds of contamination. In addition, some countries specifically require the exclusion of domestic animals and birds from premises in which food is handled commercially. In some cases provision is made to avoid contamination of food by toxic materials such as insecticides, rodenticides, and other substances used for the maintenance of hygienic conditions. The points covered are labelling of containers of toxic materials so that the contents may be easily identified, storage of these substances in locked cupboards, and their use in such a manner as not to contaminate food or endanger health.

Food hygiene regulations also often contain obligations concerning the control of the temperature of food in catering establishments. These controls usually apply to perishable or potentially hazardous foods, that is, to foodstuffs that support the growth of pathogenic organisms. The general principle embodied in this legislation is that the foodstuffs concerned should not be kept any longer than is necessary at a temperature favourable to the growth of bacteria. There is some variation in the temperature range specified but the extreme limits are 4.4°C (40°F) and 65.5°C (150°F). This range, with slight variations, is regarded as a danger zone to be avoided as far as possible.

The foods to which temperature control applies are described in different ways. In some cases the legislation refers to "perishable food" or "perishable food of animal or vegetable origin". Sometimes particular foods are referred to, such as "custards, cream fillings or similar products". In one case regulations apply to "infection and toxin prone food" which is defined as "perishable food consisting in whole or in part of milk, milk products, meat, poultry, fish, shellfish or any other ingredient capable of supporting the rapid growth of pathogenic organisms or the production of the toxins of such organisms".

In another case temperature control applies to all food "consisting of meat, fish, gravy, or imitation cream, or prepared from, or containing, any of these substances or any egg or milk". There are, however, exceptions for such articles as bread, biscuits and cakes containing egg or milk as ingredients that were introduced before baking, chocolate or sugar-confectionery, butter and other fats, cheese and uncooked bacon and ham. It is not usual to impose legal requirements for the cooking of food but some regulations provide that pork products must be thoroughly cooked to heat all parts to a minimum temperature of 65.5°C (150°F). Stuffings,-poultry, stuffed meats and stuffed poultry must be heated throughout to a minimum temperature of 74°C (165°F).

Food Handlers

It is a standard requirement of food hygiene legislation that food handlers must be clean and practise hygienic habits. They are generally required to wear clean, washable overclothing and, in some countries, to wear headgear that confines the hair. Smoking in food preparation areas is often prohibited. In some cases food handlers are specifically required to wash their hands after visits to the toilet. One set of regulations requires employees and management to be adequately informed concerning acceptable and sanitary food handling practices. They are expected to attend approved food handler training programmes when these, are available. Another set of regulations requires supervisors of food processing establish-ments, including caterers, restaurants and eating places, to complete a course in food protection. Many countries in their food hygiene legislation try to ensure that persons who become infected and who may transmit infection to food are excluded from handling food while they are in this condition or require all food handlers to undergo periodical medical examinations to determine that they are healthy and-free from infection.

For example, some regulations for restaurants require any restaurant licensee who suspects that an employee has contracted any form of communicable disease, or has become a carrier of such disease, to exclude the employee from the restaurant and notify the local health officer immediately. The health officer has to determine whether the food handler is infected or is a carrier, and laboratory examinations may be required. No persons who have a communicable disease or are carriers of such disease are permitted to work in a restaurant. Restaurants are forbidden to employ such persons or any persons suspected of being so affected. Chest X-ray examinations and/or tuberculin tests are recommended annually for all restaurant personnel. Persons who at any time have had typhoid or paratyphoid fever may not be employed in a restaurant until it has been definitely determined that they are not carriers.

Similar regulations elsewhere provide that every food handler must be free from, and not a carrier of, a disease that could spread through the medium of food, and that food handlers must submit to such medical examinations and tests as the medical officer of health or the minister of health may require. No person who has a communicable skin disease or infection or who resides in a dwelling where there is communicable disease is permitted work as a food handler, unless-he obtains a certificate from the medical officer of health showing that he is free from infection.-The operator of a food business who knows or suspects that an employee is violating these provisions must notify the medical officer of health.

Another example of this kind of legislation is an order prohibiting persons liable to taint or contaminate food from engaging in the handling of food.-This provision applies, inter alia, to persons who:

(1) are suffering, or suspected to be suffering, from typhoid or paratyphoid fever or other Salmonella infections, dysentery, or staphylococcal infections;

(2) are carriers of the microorganisms causing these diseases;
(3) show detectable clinical symptoms of infectious hepatitis;
(4) are suffering, or suspected to, be suffering, from tuberculosis in a communicable state;
(5) are suffering, or suspected to be suffering, from a contagious disease of the skin.

This legislation also requires all persons professionally engaged in the production or distribution of foodstuffs or substances used as food and who are in direct contact with such products to undergo an annual examination to verify that they are free from tuberculosis in a communicable state.

Legislation in another country places an obligation on any person employed as a food handler and who knows that he, a member of his family, or another person who lives in the same dwelling is suffering from a dangerous disease to inform his immediate superior of the facts. The latter must immediately notify the health board.

This legislation also provides that no person who is suffering from boils, a rash or sores, or from a dangerous disease, or from tuberculosis, leprosy or syphilis, may be permitted to engage in the handling of foodstuffs intended for sale. This also applies to carriers of disease. Where necessary, the person concerned must produce a medical certificate proving that the disease from which he is suffering is not contagious or liable to cause food poisoning.

Further, before any person is engaged, or begins to work, as a food handler he must produce a medical certificate to show that he is not suffering from a disease which, having regard to the nature of the work, could involve a danger of contagion or food poisoning through the agency of foodstuffs. The medical certificate must not have been issued more than 30 days previously. It must be kept and, on request, shown to the health and police authorities.

In yet another country, immediately a person engaged in the handling of food becomes aware he is suffering from, or is a carrier of, typhoid or paratyphoid fever or any other Salmonella infection or amoebic or bacillary dysentery or any staphylococcal infection likely to cause food poisoning, he is required to inform his employer who must immediately notify the proper officer of the local authority. Infected persons may be ordered to discontinue or to refrain from engaging in any occupation connected with the preparation and handling of food or drink for human consumption until further notice is given by the local authority that the risk of transmitting infection no longer exists. Food handlers suspected of being carriers of any of the diseases mentioned above may also be required to undergo a medical examination.

One local authority may require food workers, before employment, or at any other time, to undergo a chest X-ray examination or any other test or examination deemed necessary for the protection of the public health. Certification of such examinations may be issued by the local health authority and, when required by the authority, a copy of the certificate for each employee must be in the possession of the management of the food service establishment.

Certificates are not Valid for more than 12 Months from the Date of Issue

Certain countries require food handlers to hold a health booklet or certificate. In one of these countries workers who are to be employed in the food industry are obliged to undergo a pre-employment medical examination. This examination is necessary even for temporary employees, apprentices, and students. The workers covered by this obligation include those employed in the sale of foodstuffs and the provision of meals to the public, as well as in the distribution of snacks and refreshments.

Also in that country, food workers must undergo other preventive medical examinations at times determined by the hygiene services. In addition, they must undergo, without delay, emergency medical examinations:

(a) if they are suffering from diarrhoea, a purulent disease or a fever, or a communicable disease, or if they are suspected or suffering from a communicable disease;

(b) if a communicable disease, or a suspected case of such a disease, occurs in the work-place or at home.

These medical examinations include a detailed clinical examination, a medical history, and a microbiological examination, particularly with a view to the detection of tuberculosis and possible carriers of the pathogens of typhoid and paratyphoid and other salmonelloses and shigelloses.

Workers engaged in the food industry are obliged to hold a health booklet issued by the health community medical officer for the area in which they live or, if they work in a factory having a medical officer, by that officer. In the case of workers employed for short periods a certificate as to their medical fitness is issued in place of the booklet. The booklet (or certificate) is kept by the person in charge of the undertaking, but where workers carry out their work outside the undertaking, they are required to carry the booklet (or certificate) themselves. The person in charge of the undertaking must keep a list of the workers indicating when they were medically examined, the results of the examination, and when the next medical examination should be carried out.

At each medical examination the worker must produce his booklet or certificate. If the physician finds, or suspects, that the worker is suffering from a disease or infection he must take charge of the booklet or certificate and give the worker a written receipt in exchange. The worker is obliged to hand over the receipt, without delay, to the person in charge of the undertaking. Every food establishment must ensure that the handling of food is carried out only by workers holding a booklet or certificate; work may not be commenced before the booklet or certificate has been issued. The establishment must notify the health community medical officer in good time of every worker who is required to undergo a preventive medical examination.

Another country imposes compulsory medical examinations on certain groups of workers including those in catering establishments. In addition to the usual examinations for typhoid, paratyphoid, dysentery and other Salmonella infections, workers in catering establishments are subject to examination for infestation with intestinal parasites. A worker who is transferred to another undertaking, establishment or installation is not subject to a prior medical examination if his health booklet shows that his initial pre-employment examination was satisfactory, that his state of health has been under systematic surveillance, and that during the previous two years, no member of his family or other person living in his household has suffered from an infectious intestinal disease or an intestinal parasitosis. After every absence from work lasting more than one month the person concerned must be examined as if he were beginning work for the first time. Every food handler (i.e., any person who carries out, directly or indirectly, manual activities involving foodstuffs in such a manner as to be able to affect their wholesomeness, quality or hygiene) in another country must undergo the health examinations prescribed by the health authority for the purpose of acquiring a health certificate entitling him to work in that occupation. The certificate must be renewed annually or at more frequent intervals should the health authority consider it necessary. Any person who, while not holding the appropriate health certificate, engages in food handling and the proprietor of the establishment where he works are both liable to penalties.

Another example which may be mentioned is an ordinance concerning hygiene in restaurants and catering establishments. Every worker must undergo a pre-employment medical examination to determine his suitability for the work he will be engaged in. The nature of the examinations required, the classes of workers subject to such examinations, and the frequency of, and procedure for, the medical examinations are prescribed.

A recent piece of legislation on food hygiene states that only persons who provide a medical certificate indicating that they are free from diseases or infections that could be transmitted to other persons by means of foodstuffs may commence work involving the handling of foodstuffs other than pre-packed foodstuffs, or work directly related to hygiene in the handling of foodstuffs, in various types of premises including restaurants and other catering establishments. This legislation also requires persons working in the types of premises to which it applies to undergo at least once a year a medical examination or other health checkup as officially prescribed. Physicians or veterinarians who have good grounds for believing that food poisoning has been caused by a foodstuff contaminated by pathogenic bacteria or extraneous substances during food handling operations are required to notify the local medical officer.

Basic Principles of Food Hygiene Legislation

General

An essential part of the health services of every country must be to ensure that food is safe, wholesome and not injurious to health, and that proper hygienic standards are observed at all stages from production or manufacture until it reaches the consumer. The requirement that food must not be injurious to the consumer means that food traders must be under a legal obligation not to sell food which they know to be unfit for human consumption or could with reasonable diligence ascertain to be unfit. They must also have a duty to take due care to ensure that adequate standards of food hygiene are observed at all times in the conduct of their business.

It is not sufficient merely to place legal obligations on food traders. There must also be official agencies charged with the duty of exercising close surveillance of all types of food premises, including catering establishments. Many environmental factors can influence the maintenance of satisfactory standards of food hygiene and, as indicated on p. 3, progress will be made more easily if a food hygiene programme is developed within a progressive environmental health and personal health programme. Where food hygiene is the responsibility of the agency responsible for general environmental health there should be no problems in securing coordination of effort. Where separate agencies are responsible it is important that there should be close liaison between them. Agencies with the duty of controlling food hygiene should not be regarded merely as law enforcement bodies, though they should possess adequate legal powers to establish and maintain the required standards. Their officers need to have authority to enter food premises during business hours without warning in order to carry out the necessary inspections and investigations, and it should be an offence to obstruct officers who are carrying out these duties.

Effective legislation is necessary to secure the proper observance of hygienic practices. The basic legal requirements should be embodied in national statutes but the more detailed and technical requirements should be contained in regulations which can be readily and quickly changed to keep pace with scientific and technical developments. There is a need also for codes of practice which, while not legally enforceable, give guidance to food traders and the officials responsible for inspection and control of food premises on equipment, materials and practices for maintaining the desired standards.

Although the basic legal requirements embodied in national statutes and the more detailed and technical requirements contained in regulations will cover very many points it is not advisable that legal provisions should be too rigid or too detailed.

Often, the more satisfactory approach is to prescribe the objective to be achieved and to allow some flexibility in the choice of methods to be used to achieve that objective. In any case, it is impracticable for laws to be drafted in sufficient detail to take account of all possible circumstances.

Basic Legal Requirements

The principal points that should be included in the basic legal requirements are as follows :

(a) the authorities responsible for the enforcement of food hygiene legislation should be specified;

(b) it should be an offence to sell food that is diseased, unsound, or unwholesome;

(c) recognized officers of the responsible authorities should be authorized to inspect food intended for sale, to take samples, and to seize and condemn food that appears to be unfit for human consumption;

(d) recognized officers should have power of entry to all food premises;

(e) all food premises of prescribed types should be required to be registered by the responsible authorities before being opened for business and these authorities should be empowered to revoke registration where continued use of the premises constitutes a potential danger to health; particular types of premises would be registered under regulations made in accordance with point (f) below;

(f) authority should be given to the appropriate minister to make regulations containing specific and detailed legal requirements with respect to food hygiene in particular types of premises and different food handling activities; compliance with the appropriate regulations would be a condition for the registration of premises;

(g) physicians who become aware, or suspect, that patients they are attending are suffering from food poisoning should be required to notify the local public health authority;

(h) authority should be given to recognized officers to prohibit the use or removal from the premises of food which they believe is likely to cause food poisoning until investigations have shown whether it may safely be used for human consumption;

(i) persons engaged in the handling of food should be required to notify their employers if they become aware that they are suffering from any condition that might lead to the infection of foods and employers should be under an obligation to inform the local medical officer.

Model Food Hygiene Regulations for Catering Establishments

The basic legal requirements for the control of food hygiene which should be embodied in a national statute have been set out in the preceding section.

As indicated in point (f), detailed legal requirements should be stated in regulations or secondary legislation made under the authority given by the statute. It should be noted that in these model regulations expressions such as "adequate", "suitable", and "sufficient" are frequently used. This is because a legal document of this kind must have sufficient flexibility to meet the varying circumstances found in different types of establishment and in different parts of the world. The interpretation of these terms is left to the discretion of local control authorities. The following Model Code details those matters which it is suggested should be included in the food hygiene regulations for catering establishments.

Registration

(a) No premises shall be used as catering premises unless they are registered for that purpose by the local authority. Any person who uses unregistered premises shall be guilty of an offence.

(b) Application for registration must be made before the premises are opened and the application must be refused if the premises do not comply in all respects with food hygiene regulations for catering premises.

(c) Registration may be revoked if at any time serious breaches of the food hygiene regulations occur.

Where a licensing system is preferred, points (e) and (f) should be amended accordingly.

Where a system of licensing is preferred this section should be amended accordingly.

Construction and Maintenance of Premises

(a) No catering business shall be carried on in any premises in which food is exposed to the risk of contamination.

(b) The premises shall be of adequate size, sound construction and in good repair. Areas used for the handling of food shall be completely separated from any part of the premises used as living quarters.

(c) The internal walls, floors, windows, ceilings, woodwork and all other parts of every room shall be so constructed and maintained in such good order, repair and condition as to enable them to be cleaned effectively and to prevent, as far as practicable, infestation by rats, mice, insects and birds.

(d) The premises must be kept free from rodent and insect pests, and birds, and dogs, cats and other domestic animals must be excluded from areas where food is processed or stored. All rodenticides, insecticides and other toxic substances must be clearly labelled and, when not in use, be kept in separate, locked cupboards.

(e) The premises must be kept in a clean condition and no water must be deposited or allowed to accumulate in rooms in which food is prepared, stored or served, except in so far as this may be unavoidable for the proper conduct of the business.

(f) All rooms in which food is stored, prepared or served, or in which utensils are washed, and all sanitary conveniences shall be well ventilated and well lighted.

(g) No room in which food is stored, prepared or served may be used as a sleeping place or communicate directly with a sleeping place or sanitary convenience.

Water Supply

(a) An ample supply of water of drinking quality must be provided at all premises; where possible this should be from the public supply main but if from any other source it must be approved by the health authority and checked for bacteriological and chemical quality at intervals.

(b) An adequate supply of hot and cold water or of hot water at a suitable controlled temperature shall be provided in all areas where food is prepared and where equipment and utensils are washed.

(c) Water used for making ice shall be of drinking quality.

Drainage

(a) All premises shall be provided with an adequate drainage system which, where practicable, shall be connected to the public sewerage system.

(b) Where connexion to the public sewerage system is not practicable the method of sewage disposal must be approved by the health authority.

Personal Washing Facilities

(a) An adequate number of suitable wash-hand basins shall be provided for the use of all persons engaged in the handling of food. These basins must be conveniently accessible to these persons and in any case must be located in or immediately adjacent to all sanitary conveniences. In all new premises, and where practicable in existing premises, hand-washing facilities must be provided within or immediately adjacent to food preparation areas. All wash-hand basins shall be properly connected to the drainage system and be provided with an adequate supply of hot and cold water or of hot water at a suitable controlled temperature. At each basin shall be provided an adequate supply of soap or other suitable detergent, nail brushes and clean towels or other suitable drying facilities.

(b) Facilities for personal washing must not be used for any other purpose.

Sanitary Facilities

(a) An adequate number of conveniently located sanitary conveniences shall be provided for all employees. Separate conveniences shall be provided for each sex. An adequate supply of toilet paper must be available at all times.

(b) In or near every sanitary convenience a clearly legible notice must be displayed in a prominent position requiring users to wash their hands after using the convenience.

Storage of Clothing

Adequate facilities shall be provided for the storage of employees' clothing and personal belongings not being worn during working hours and such clothing and belongings shall not be kept on the premises other than in the accommodation provided.

First-aid Materials

(a) A sufficient supply of suitable bandages, dressings (including waterproof dressings) and antiseptics shall be provided for the first-aid treatment of persons engaged in the handling of food.

(b) This material must be kept in suitable locations readily accessible to employees and clearly labelled.

Storage of Refuse

(a) A sufficient number of watertight containers of durable and nonabsorbent material with tight-fitting or self-closing lids shall be provided for the storage of food waste and other refuse.

(b) Adequate space shall be provided for the temporary storage of waste; this space must not be in any room where food is stored, prepared or served.

Food

(a) Food, while being stored, prepared, displayed or served, shall be protected from dust, flies, rodents and other pests, and other contamination and all persons engaged in the handling of food shall take all reasonable steps to protect the food from risk of contamination.

(b) Raw meat, poultry, fish, shellfish, milk or uncooked products containing those foodstuffs shall not be permitted to come into contact with any cooked foods. Any persons handling any of these raw or uncooked foodstuffs must, before handling any cooked food, thoroughly wash their hands and carefully cleanse all surfaces, utensils and equipment with which the foodstuffs may have come into contact.

(c) All perishable food consisting in whole or in part of milk or milk products, eggs, meat, poultry, fish, shellfish or other ingredients capable of supporting the rapid growth of pathogenic organisms shall be kept at a temperature that is not within the range from 4.5°C (40°F) to 65.5CC (150°F), except during necessary periods of preparation and service.

(d) Raw, unprocessed fruits and vegetables shall be thoroughly washed in clean drinking-water before use.

(e) All ice used for cooling drinks or food by direct contact shall be made from water of drinking quality.

Equipment

(a) All articles of equipment with which food comes into contact, or may come into contact, must be kept clean, be so constructed, placed, of such materials, and kept in such good order, repair and condition as to:

(i) enable them to be thoroughly cleaned;

(ii) prevent, so far as is reasonably practicable, any matter being absorbed by them; and

(iii) prevent, so far as is reasonably practicable, any risk of contamination of the food.

(b) An adequate number of sinks or other suitable facilities for the washing of food and equipment when necessary shall be provided. These sinks or other facilities shall be provided with an adequate supply of hot and cold water or of hot water at a suitable controlled temperature, or with cold water only where the sink is used only for washing fish, fruit or vegetables. These facilities must not be used for any other purpose.

(c) Equipment shall be so installed as to facilitate its cleaning and the cleaning of adjacent areas.

Personnel

(a) Every person handling or coming into contact with food, or with any equipment or utensil used in its preparation, processing or service shall:

   (i) keep as clean as may be reasonably practicable all parts of his body that are liable to come into contact with the food and, in particular, he shall wash his hands thoroughly before commencing work and after using a sanitary convenience;

   (ii) wear clean, washable outer garments and headgear that confines his hair;

   (iii) keep any open cut or abrasion on any exposed part of his body covered with a suitable waterproof dressing; and

(iv) refrain from spitting and using tobacco in any form while engaged in the handling, preparation or service of food, while handling utensils or equipment, and while he is in any room containing open food.

(b) No person who is affected with any disease in a communicable form may work in any catering premises and the proprietor of any catering establishment shall not permit any such person to work in the establishment. Immediately a person engaged in the handling of food becomes aware, or has reason to suspect, that he is suffering from, or is a carrier of, typhoid, paratyphoid or any other Salmonella infection or amoebic or bacillary dysentery or any staphylococcal infection likely to cause food poisoning he shall immediately inform the person operating the catering premises in which he is employed and that person shall immediately notify the medical officer of the health authority.

Food & Beverage Department-Restaurant Division

Out of the three divisions that the Food & Beverage Department holds, the Restaurant Division is the most popular when it comes to money. Its structure has changed recently, but it's fairly simple and everyone knows who to report to. Described in a simple way, the structure goes like this:

Restaurant Operations Manager

He or she is a three stripe officer and is in charge with the entire restaurant operation. The Windjammer Manager, Portofino Manager and Assistant Dining Room Manager report directly to him or her and, of course, the position is got its own admin now.

The contract length is 4 months with 2 months off and, aside the thousands of dollars salary, he or she is got monthly bonuses from china and linen savings, wine gratuity and the big, fat bonus at the end of the fiscal year.

Windjammer Manager

The Windjammer Manager is a two and a half stripes officer and is in charge with Windjammer Buffet, Johnny Rockets (fast food outlet) and Café Promenade (coffee shop with snacks). Directly to him reports the following positions: Johnny Rockets Supervisor and Windjammer Supervisor.

Just like the Restaurant Operations Manager, the contract length is also 4 months on with 2 months off, and a big, fat bonus included.

Portofino Manager

Portofino Manager is in charge with the Italian specialty restaurant. Is a two stripes officer with a 6 months contract and sharing cabin. From 2 stripes below, no officer is entitled to the yearly bonus, but they got part of the cover charge. The Portofino waiters report directly to him.

Assistant Dining Room Manager

This position was introduced recently. It's a 2 stripe position with a contract length of 6 months and sharing cabin.

Their salary is based on tips, but don't be fooled by it, they make a lot of money. There are 3 Assistant Dining Room Managers, each in charge with one Dining Room deck (our Dining Room has 3 decks/levels). They are responsible with the booking on their respective decks and the Headwaiters working in that deck report directly to them.

Restaurant Operation Admin

The admin reports directly to the Restaurant Operations Manager and basically does everything. He has 2 office boys/girls helping in the morning with paperwork. Is a one stripe officer with 6 months contract and sharing cabin.

Head Waiter

These guys are making more money than a 3 stripe officer because their salary is based on tips. They are one stripe officers, with 6 months contract length and a sharing cabin. Each of them has a station assigned (there are 3 stations on each Dining Room deck) and the waiters and assistant waiters working there report to him/her.

Johnny Rockets Supervisor

He or she is in charge with Café Promenade and Johnny Rockets and reports to the Windjammer Manager. This is a one stripe officer with a 6 months contract and sharing cabin. They get a fix salary with no gratuities. The Café Attendants and Johnny Rockets Attendants report to him/her.

Windjammer Supervisor

There are 2 Windjammer Supervisors onboard, both reporting to the Windjammer Manager. They are in charge with supervising the Windjammer operation and the Assistant Waiters working there are reporting to them. It's a one stripe position, with fix salary, 6 months contract and sharing cabin.

Room Service Supervisor

The Room Service Supervisor reports directly to the Restaurant Operations Manager and is in charge with Room Service operation and Attendants working there. Is a one stripe position, with 6 months contract, fix salary and sharing cabin.

Room Service Operator

The position is pretty much self-explanatory. They are part of the crew with a 6 months contract, fix salary and sharing cabin. The Room Service Operator reports to Room Service Supervisor.

Mess Supervisor

The Mess Supervisor is in charge with both officer and crew messes and directly to him/her are reporting the Mess Attendants. Mess Supervisor is a one stripe position with a 6 months contract, fix salary and sharing cabin. He or she reports to Restaurant Operations Manager.

Room Service Attendant

The above 5 positions are similar; the only difference is the place they work in. Except for the Johnny Rockets who get gratuities from the cover charges in the fast food outlet they work in, the rest have a fix salary and they also get gratuities from the beverages they sell (not too much though). They all have an eight months contract and sharing cabin.

Assistant Waiter

This is a much better position that the ones above because they have a salary based on tips. An average assistant waiter salary can be around $2000 or more a month. Also, the contract length is 6 months and they only work in the Dining Room or Windjammer during the dinner time and in Windjammer (during the day time).

During the diner time, they work 4 weeks in the Dining Room and one week in Windjammer. They get gratuities in the Dining Room, but in Windjammer they get only the gratuities from the beverages they sell. Might not make sense, but this is how the system is set up.

Waiter

Waiter position is a good position as well due to the amount of money they make and the 6 months contract length. An average waiter makes around $3000 and, during the diner time, works only in Dining Room. As a first-timer, this structure might look confusing. Indeed there are a lot of positions in the Restaurant Division, but this is what makes it easier because everyone knows exactly what they are suppose to do.

Food and Beverage Service Occupations

Significant Points

- Most jobs are part time and many opportunities exist for young people—nearly 2 out of 3 food counter and fountain workers are 16-19 years old.
- Job openings are expected to be abundant through 2008, reflecting substantial turnover.
- Tips comprise a major portion of earnings; consequently, keen competition is expected for bartender, waiter and waitress, and other jobs in popular restaurants and fine dining establishments where potential earnings from tips are greatest.

Nature of the Work

Whether they work in small, informal diners or large, elegant restaurants, all food and beverage service workers aim to help customers have a positive dining experience in their establishments. These workers are responsible for greeting customers, taking food and drink orders, serving food, cleaning up after patrons, and preparing tables and dining areas. All of these duties require a high quality of services customers will return.

The largest group of these workers, *waiters* and *waitresses*, take customers' orders, serve food and beverages, prepare itemized checks, and sometimes accept payments. Their specific duties vary considerably, depending on the establishment where they work. In coffee shops, they are expected to provide fast and efficient, yet courteous service. In fine restaurants, where gourmet meals are accompanied by attentive formal service, waiters and waitresses serve meals at a more leisurely pace and offer more personal service to patrons. For example, servers may recommend a certain wine as a complement to a particular entree, explain how various items on the menu are prepared, or complete preparations on a salad or other special dishes at table side. Additionally, waiters and waitresses may check the identification of patrons to ensure they meet the minimum age requirement for the purchase of alcohol and tobacco products.

Depending on the type of restaurant, waiters and waitresses may perform additional duties usually associated with other food and beverage service occupations. These tasks may include escorting guests to tables, serving customers seated at counters, setting up and clearing tables, or operating a cash register. However, formal restaurants frequently hire other staff to perform these duties, allowing their waiters and waitresses to concentrate on customer service.

Bartenders fill drink orders that waiters and waitresses take from customers. They prepare standard mixed drinks and, occasionally, are asked to mix drinks to suit a customer's taste. Most bartenders know dozens of drink recipes and are able to mix drinks accurately, quickly, and without waste, even during the busiest periods. Besides mixing and serving drinks, bartenders collect payment, operate the cash register, clean up after customers leave, and often serve food to customers seated at the bar. Bartenders also check identification of customers seated at the bar, to ensure they meet the minimum age requirement for the purchase of alcohol and tobacco products. Bartenders usually are responsible for ordering and maintaining an inventory of liquor, mixes, and other bar supplies. They often form attractive displays out of bottles and glassware and wash the glassware and utensils after each use.

The majority of bartenders who work in eating and drinking establishments directly serve and interact with patrons. Because customers typically frequent drinking establishments for the friendly atmosphere, most bartenders must be friendly and helpful with customers. Bartenders at service bars, on the other hand, have little contact with customers because they work in small bars in restaurants, hotels, and clubs where only waiters and waitresses serve drinks. Some establishments, especially larger ones, use automatic equipment to mix drinks of varying complexity at the push of a button. Even in these establishments, however, bartenders still must be efficient and knowledgeable in case the device malfunctions or a customer requests a drink not handled by the equipment.

Hosts and *hostesses* try to create a good impression of a restaurant by warmly welcoming guests. Because hosts and hostesses are restaurants' personal representatives, they try to insure that service is prompt and courteous and that the meal meets expectations. They may courteously direct patrons to where coats and other personal items may be left and indicate where patrons can wait until their table is ready. Hosts and hostesses assign guests to tables suitable for the size of their group, escort patrons to their seats, and provide menus. They also schedule dining reservations, arrange parties, and organize any special services that are required. In some restaurants, they also act as cashiers.

Dining room attendants and *bartender helpers* assist waiters, waitresses, and bartenders by cleaning tables, removing dirty dishes, and keeping serving areas stocked with supplies. They replenish the supply of clean linens, dishes, silverware, and glasses in the dining room and keep the bar stocked with glasses, liquor, ice, and drink garnishes. Bartender helpers also keep bar equipment clean and wash glasses. Dining room attendants set tables with clean tablecloths, napkins, silverware, glasses, and dishes and serve ice water, rolls, and butter. At the conclusion of meals, they remove dirty dishes and soiled linens from tables. Cafeteria attendants stock serving tables with food, trays, dishes, and silverware and may carry trays to dining tables for patrons.

Counter attendants take orders and serve food at counters. In cafeterias, they serve food displayed on counters and steam tables, carve meat, dish out vegetables, ladle sauces and soups, and fill beverage glasses. In lunchrooms and coffee shops, counter attendants take orders from customers seated at the counter, transmit orders to the kitchen, and pick up and serve food. They also fill cups with coffee, soda, and other beverages and prepare fountain specialties, such as milkshakes and ice cream sundaes. Counter attendants prepare some short-order items, such as sandwiches and salads, and wrap or place orders in containers for carry out. They also clean counters, write itemized checks, and sometimes accept payment.

Fast-food workers take orders from customers at counters or drive-through windows at fast-food restaurants. They pick up the ordered beverage and food items, serve them to a customer, and accept payment. Many fast-food workers also cook and package food, make coffee, and fill beverage cups using drink-dispensing machines.

Working Conditions

Food and beverage service workers are on their feet most of the time and often carry heavy trays of food, dishes, and glassware. During busy dining periods, they are under pressure to serve customers quickly and efficiently. The work is relatively safe, but care must be taken to avoid slips, falls, and burns.

Part-time work is more common among food and beverage service workers than among workers in almost any other occupation. Those on part-time schedules include half of all waiters and waitresses, and 6 out of 10 food counter and fountain workers, compared to 1 out of 6 workers throughout the economy. Slightly more than half of all bartenders work full-time with 35 percent working part-time and the remainder working a variable schedule.

The wide range in dining hours creates work opportunities attractive to homemakers, students, and other individuals seeking supplemental income. In fact, nearly 2 out of 3 food counter and fountain workers are between 16 and 19 years old. Many food and beverage service workers work evenings, weekends, and holidays. Some work split shifts—that is, they work for several hours during the middle of the day, take a few hours off in the afternoon, and then return to their jobs for evening hours.

Employment

Food and beverage service workers held over 5.4 million jobs in 1998. Waiters and waitresses held about 2,019,000 of these jobs; counter attendants and fast-food workers, 2,025,000; dining room and cafeteria attendants and bartender helpers, 405,000; bartenders, 404,000; hosts and hostesses, 297,000; and all other food preparation and service workers, 280,000.

Restaurants, coffee shops, bars, and other retail eating and drinking places employed the overwhelming majority of food and beverage service workers. Others worked in hotels and other lodging places, bowling alleys, casinos, country clubs, and other membership organizations. Jobs are located throughout the country but are typically plentiful in large cities and tourist areas. Vacation resorts offer seasonal employment, and some workers alternate between summer and winter resorts, instead of remaining in one area the entire year.

Training, Other Qualifications, and Advancement

There are no specific educational requirements for food and beverage service jobs. Although many employers prefer to hire high school graduates for waiter and waitress, bartender, and host and hostess positions, completion of high school is usually not required for fast-food workers, counter attendants, and dining room attendants and bartender helpers. For many people, a job as a food and beverage service worker serves as a source of immediate income, rather than a career. Many entrants to these jobs are in their late teens or early twenties and have a high school education or less. Usually, they have little or no work experience. Many are full-time students or homemakers. Food and beverage service jobs are a major source of part-time employment for high school and college students.

Because maintaining a restaurant's image is important to its success, employers emphasize personal qualities. Food and beverage service workers are in close contact with the public, so these workers should be well-spoken and have a neat, clean appearance. They should enjoy dealing with all kinds of people and possess a pleasant disposition.

Waiters and waitresses need a good memory to avoid confusing customers' orders and to recall faces, names, and preferences of frequent patrons. These workers should also be good at arithmetic so they can total bills without the assistance of a calculator or cash register if necessary. In restaurants specializing in foreign foods, knowledge of a foreign language is helpful. Prior experience waiting on tables is preferred by restaurants and hotels that have rigid table service standards. Jobs at these establishments often have higher earnings, but they may also have higher educational requirements than less demanding establishments.

Usually, bartenders must be at least 21 years of age, but employers prefer to hire people who are 25 or older. Bartenders should be familiar with State and local laws concerning the sale of alcoholic beverages.

Most food and beverage service workers pick up their skills on the job by observing and working with more experienced workers. Some employers, particularly those in fast-food restaurants, use self-instruction programs with audiovisual presentations and instructional booklets to teach new employees food preparation and service skills. Some public and private vocational schools, restaurant associations, and large restaurant chains provide classroom training in a generalized food service curriculum.

Some bartenders acquire their skills by attending a bartending or vocational and technical school. These programs often include instruction on State and local laws and regulations, cocktail recipes, attire and conduct, and stocking a bar. Some of these schools help their graduates find jobs.

Due to the relatively small size of most food-serving establishments, opportunities for promotion are limited. After gaining some experience, some dining room and cafeteria attendants and bartender helpers are able to advance to waiter, waitress, or bartender jobs. For waiters, waitresses, and bartenders, advancement usually is limited to finding a job in a more expensive restaurant or bar where prospects for tip earnings are better. A few bartenders open their own businesses. Some hosts and hostesses and waiters and waitresses advance to supervisory jobs, such as maitre d'hotel, dining room supervisor, or restaurant manager. In larger restaurant chains, food and beverage service workers who excel at their work are often invited to enter the company's formal management training program.

Job Outlook

Job openings are expected to be abundant for food and beverage service workers. Employment of food and beverage service occupations is expected to grow about as fast as the average for all occupations through 2008, stemming from increases in population, personal incomes, and leisure time. While employment growth will produce many new jobs, the overwhelming majority of openings will arise from the need to replace the high proportion of workers who leave this occupation each year. There is substantial movement into and out of the occupation because education and training requirements are minimal, and the predominance of part-time jobs is attractive to people seeking a short-term source of income rather than a career. However, keen competition is expected for bartender, waiter and waitress, and other food and beverage service jobs in popular restaurants and fine dining establishments, where potential earnings from tips are greatest.

Projected employment growth will vary by type of food and beverage service job. Growth in the number of families and the more affluent, 55-and-older population will result in more restaurants that offer table service and more varied menus—requiring waiters and waitresses and hosts and hostesses. Employment of fast-food workers also is expected to increase in response to the continuing fast-paced lifestyle of many Americans and the addition of healthier foods at many of these restaurants. However, little change is expected in the employment of dining room attendants, as waiters and waitresses increasingly assume their duties. Employment of bartenders is expected to decline as drinking of alcoholic beverages outside the home—particularly cocktails—continues to drop.

Earnings

Food and beverage service workers derive their earnings from a combination of hourly wages and customer tips. Earnings vary greatly, depending on the type of job and establishment. For example, fast-food workers and hosts and hostesses usually do not receive tips, so their wage rates may be higher than those of waiters and waitresses and bartenders, who may earn more from tips than from wages. In some restaurants, these workers contribute a portion of their tips to a tip pool, which is distributed among the establishment's other food and beverage service workers and kitchen staff. Tip pools allow workers who normally do not receive tips, such as dining room attendants, to share in the rewards of a well-served meal. In 1998, median hourly earnings (not including tips) of full-time waiters and waitresses were $5.85. The middle 50 percent earned between $5.58 and $6.32; the top 10 percent earned at least $7.83. For most waiters and waitresses, higher earnings are primarily the result of receiving more in tips rather than higher hourly wages. Tips usually average between 10 and 20 percent of guests' checks, so waiters and waitresses working in busy, expensive restaurants earn the most.

Full-time bartenders had median hourly earnings (not including tips) of $6.25 in 1998. The middle 50 percent earned from $5.72 and $7.71; the top 10 percent earned at least $9.19 an hour. Like waiters and waitresses, bartenders employed in public bars may receive more than half of their earnings as tips. Service bartenders are often paid higher hourly wages to offset their lower tip earnings.

Median weekly hourly earnings (not including tips) of full-time dining room attendants and bartender helpers were $6.03 in 1998. The middle 50 percent earned between $5.67 and $7.11; the top 10 percent earned over $8.49 an hour. Most received over half of their earnings as wages; the rest of their income was a share of the proceeds from tip pools.

Full-time counter attendants and fast-food workers, except cooks, had median hourly earnings (not including tips) of $6.06 in 1998. The middle 50 percent earned between $5.67 and $7.14, while the highest 10 percent earned over $8.45 a hour. Although some counter attendants receive part of their earnings as tips, fast-food workers usually do not.

In establishments covered by Federal law, most workers beginning at the minimum wage earned $5.15 an hour in 1998. However, various minimum wage exceptions apply under specific circumstances to disabled workers, full-time students, youth under age 20 in their first 90 days of employment, tipped employees, and student-learners. Employers are also permitted to deduct from wages the cost, or fair value, of any meals or lodging provided. However, many employers provide free meals and furnish uniforms. Food and beverage service workers who work full time often receive typical benefits, while part-time workers usually do not.

In some large restaurants and hotels, food and beverage service workers belong to unions—principally the Hotel Employees and Restaurant Employees International Union and the Service Employees International Union.

Perspectives on Productivity

Most studies of productivity are drawn from manufacturing industries, however, services require an approach that recognises their peculiar characteristics. In the provision of services the processes of production and consumption are often simultaneous or can overlap-generating a specific set of challenges (Johnston & Jones, 2004; Mullins, 1998). Customers are active participants in many service encounters, and therefore an important influence on productivity (Martin et al., 2001).

Quality is so closely entwined with more measurable outcomes in service provision that it becomes very difficult to isolate any one influence on productivity. The intangibility of service, and therefore the importance of psychological outcomes (e.g. comfort and pleasure) in the process of quality creation, represent major challenges in measuring and understanding service sector productivity in general, and the F&B sector in particular.

This section of the report reviews the perspectives held by both employers and employees on productivity in their NZ F&B work-places and the factors that influence it. The thematic areas addressed below reflect the core themes raised by the 20 interviewees and the focus groups employee participants. Survey responses are also reviewed.

What is Productivity and how is it Measured?

The issue of how to measure productivity in the service sector is a critical one for this study. Gummesson (1998) suggests that measurements of service productivity can be 'ambiguous and inadequate', resulting in unhelpful comparisons between industries.

Food and beverage service providers often focus on reducing labour costs while maintaining sales (labour generally comprises around a third of hospitality costs, and food or beverage products, another third) (Reynolds, 2004). Concentrating on the reduction of labour costs as a percentage of sales may achieve short term productivity targets but can also jeopardise long term viability due to the erosion of service standards. Poor service affects customer satisfaction, which in turn influences sales and productivity, thereby creating a cycle of poor productivity.

Some commentators argue that a primary focus in F&B service productivity is quality. Parasuraman (2002) argues that how a company allocates service inputs will directly affect productivity from the customer's perspective. This view is upheld by Bates, Bates and Johnston (2003) who found that providing better service, while labour intensive, yields higher long-term profits per employee. They concluded that better service providers have significantly better return on equity and return on total assets than their counterparts with poorer service levels.

Measuring productivity in hospitality is acknowledged to be particularly difficult (Atkinson & Brown, 2001). David, Grabski and Kasavana (1996) found nine different measurements of productivity alone in their survey of hotel chain bench-marking. Most food service contract companies use sales per labour hour to express productivity (Clark, 1997a), but according to Reynolds, do not measure the cost of food sales, which he views as a 'good measure of labour productivity, but not of operational performance' (1998). The heavy use of part-time and seasonal labour by F&B enterprises adds a further level of complexity to measuring productivity in the sector.

The situation in NZ mirrors the international context quite closely. It is clear that several managers and employees do not have a good understanding of productivity and what it means in the context of their business. As the interviews and focus groups progressed, however, it became obvious that factors related to, and influenced by, productivity were very much in people's minds-its just that productivity was not always the catchall term used to help think about them.

Both the interviews and survey show that managers view customer satisfaction and loyalty rate as the most important factors to use in assessing productivity (74% and 50% of survey respondents), whereas financial measures (meeting budget, costs and balancing, and revenue/sales per person) are 'most important' indicators for under a third of respondents.

Table : Indicators used to assess productivity

	Most important (%)	Least important (%)
Customer Satisfaction	74	11
Return visitation / loyalty	50	12
Volume	30	30
Meeting Budget	27	27
Cost and Balancing	24	45
Revenue / Sales per person	18	41
Number of table turns	13	50
Covers Per Staff	0	67

Larger F&B enterprises (especially those housed in hotels) have fairly sophisticated financial targets on which productivity is measured.

"[Productivity is] the amount of product that gets prepared and cooked and sold in relation to the number of staff I have... how many man hours for our front of house staff measured against revenue for a particular night".

Labour costs and food costs are the most critical and closely reviewed areas underpinning productivity. Fast food/takeaway outlets were found to be acutely aware of the various 'actual' versus 'desired' ratios they are working to.

Nevertheless for most managers (regardless of size or type of enterprise) productivity is defined by customer satisfaction. Favourable feedback from customers through comment cards, tips, and unsolicited remarks are viewed as vital indicators of productivity.

"Productivity is about how customers feel. The quality of the feedback we get from customers in terms of positive comments and tips".

"Communication between customers and staff-observation of their relationships tells me about the level of quality, and therefore, productivity".

Measurement of customer satisfaction ranged from sophisticated feedback forms (larger accommodation based operations) through to the simple observation of client behaviour, responses and tipping (smaller operations). In many cases smaller operators are going by their "gut-feelings" and the number of regulars that return with friends and new clientele are a critical 'measure' of productivity.

Productivity is also correlated with staff being able to meet or exceed expectations in a team setting.

"Defining and measuring productivity must be seen in terms of teamwork. Individual performance leads to team work. And if that works, it flows smoothly. And if it doesn't, we can then isolate with whom the problems lie".

Contented staff and management capability are the two factors management deem to have the most positive influence on productivity, followed by 'internal communication', 'training' and 'employee retention'. The survey results were very much reflecting the information gathered from the interviews-with managers across size and type of enterprise all stressing the importance of staff happiness, communication, and their own ability to manage these situations effectively.

Table : Factors impacting on productivity (% of respondents)

	Negative influence (%)	*Positive influence (%)*	*Mean**
Contented staff	0	85	4.9
Management capability	0	83	4.8
Internal communication	0	62	4.6
Training	2	70	4.5
Employee retention	2	62	4.5
Technology	0	40	4.3
Labour outsourcing	6	9	3.1
Seasonality	15	19	3.1
Employee turnover	27	4	2.2

* *on a scale from negative influence (1) to positive influence (5)*

When asked to comment on what they think would most help improve productivity in their business, managers had a wide range of suggestions which were very similar with those raised in the interviews. Staff attitude to work and ability to work autonomously was the most common factor suggested (22.5%). Staff retention/experience, staff skills/qualifications and training were each commented on by 10% of respondents. Financial considerations at a macro level (e.g. taxation) were raised by 15% of respondents. Communication and networking was also considered important by 15% of respondents. Supply related factors were raised in a further 20% of cases.

Over half of national survey respondents (52.3%) said that the primary barriers to improving their productivity are finding and retaining good staff, lack of qualifications/knowledge/skills, and poor employee attitudes to work. Difficulties with the property/ product upon which the business is based were also a cause for some concern. Interestingly very few workplaces featured productivity incentives with the exception of some of the larger enterprises.

Some comments illustrated the frustrations experienced by some managers:

> *"In my experience, most people will do the least amount of work required until management are forced to make them be*

> *more accountable..." The majority of employees are not given individual productivity-related targets to meet, although non-monetary targets such as quality service are often emphasized. Employees in all focus groups said that general head count, 'table turns', smoothness of daily operations and how much they 'up sold' in a day are good indicators of productivity. Managers were often perceived as "discussing numbers behind closed doors" and targets are not communicated to employees, or the targets do not mean much to the employees.*

Those working in larger organizations are more likely to have financial targets to be met each day and/or each week; and they are also encouraged to up-sell by offering customers drinks with their meals and desserts in order to meet targets. In larger enterprises, there are individual staff incentives for achieving productivity related targets, such as prizes and rewards:

> *"If we sell an extra breakfast we get one point, if we upgrade a room we get two points. When we reach 400 points we can stay for one night in the hotel free. For 20 points we may be able to park our car for one day free".*

Employees said that being efficient at what one does is an indicator of productivity. This includes taking the orders correctly, preparing and serving food quickly, reducing food wastage, and ensuring there are enough resources (i.e. clean glasses and cutlery) to provide to the customers.

Participants across all focus groups said good customer service is an essential indicator of productivity. For them good customer service includes *"being really nice to the guests"*, *"being fast"* but *"not too fast, which can be seen as abrupt"*, having strong abilities for multitasking and *"doing little jobs, which usually don't belong to anyone in particular"*.

The Central Role of Management

The research presented above reveals quite clearly the central importance of effective management in achieving higher productivity in the F&B sector. In an industry as labour-intensive as F&B, people, and their skills, are central to all attempts to enhance productivity (D'Annunzio-Green, Maxwell & Watson, 2000). Research has shown the positive relationship between effective human resource management and superior organisational performance in many different sectors and nations (Drucker, 1994;

Huselid, 1995; Wright and Haggerty, 2005; Neal, West & Patterson, 2005). Such an approach is consistent with current views on the positive role that empowerment and high-involvement work practices can play on productivity improvement.

Such approaches shift the focus from scientific management practices (i.e. task simplification and specialisation) to one that relies more on the intellectual contribution of employees, and emphasises the responsibility for productivity lying at the employee, rather than solely at the management, level. Gavin and Mason (2004) recommend that organisations be designed and managed to promote worker satisfaction, and suggest that healthy and happy employees are more productive. In other research service strategies that took account of the need for employee development and well-being were found to have a positive effect on employee satisfaction and productivity (Goldstein, 2003).

As the Department of Labour (2004) notes in its discussion of productivity drivers, there is a:

> *"need to make sure the activities that create value within a firm are aligned with each other and with the overall business strategy, and that they are functioning effectively."*

This can be aided by employee participation.

> *"It is critical that employees at all levels of a firm have an opportunity to contribute to work organisation and to provide relevant practical advice from their respective positions."*

It is commonly accepted that effective leadership will lead to higher organisational performance and poor leadership will result in poor performance (gaard et al., 2005; Simons 2002). In its discussion of productivity drivers the Department of Labour also notes that:

> *"Leadership by example plays a strong role in creating a positive and productive workplace culture, and inspiring others to pursue those opportunities which have been identified. Leadership depth is important."*

Across all the sectors represented in the interviews, most managers are aware of their role in enhancing productivity.

> *"I am the conductor, I can put my sticks up and down and others have to perform. My performance is determined on good service, standards being met and the financials being sound".*

"No one likes to work for a bad manager. I have learnt from good managers I have had in the past and then applied the good things gained from them. I still watch good managers now and whenever I go into bars and restaurants I watch how their staff work. For a while I did this every month at a cafe in Auckland to learn and observe".

Two management types emerged from the interviews: non-adaptive and adaptive. The former refers to a leadership style underpinned by a more paternalistic philosophy. The adaptive approach, by way of contrast, refers to a leadership style that emphasises things like team tasks and targets, and enhancing employees' readiness to participate in meeting overarching requirements.

It is not easy to generalise which of these approaches is superior in terms of F&B service productivity. The value of each depends on the environment in which the business is operating and the organisational culture and structure it exhibits, along with a range of other variables.

Employee Autonomy and Communication

According to many of managers interviewed, autonomy is important for hospitality employees especially when it comes to the spontaneity involved in the interaction between staff and customers. However, a culture of "controlled autonomy" also exists in some cases-especially in the larger enterprises-and is designed to control the major productivity parameters such as service standards, wastage, human resource costs. Smaller businesses, constrained by heavy and unpredictable workloads and limited resources, tend to give their staff more freedom.

Most of the managers feel that their employees have autonomy in their jobs. The difference lies in the extent to which formal methods are used to enhance communication. The larger organisations-especially hotels-have more formal consultation systems such as 'tea and scone' sessions and regular meetings where staff and management can discuss ideas and performance. As one manager from a larger organisation noted:

"Decision-making in an organisation this size is slower. Roll out of information is slower. No getting away from it, so the key is being smarter about how they make and implement decisions."

Managers were asked in the web survey how they would characterise the level of input their employees have in suggesting how the workplace can be better organised? The majority of the 55 managers who responded feel that their employees have either reasonable (49%) or significant (29%) levels of input into workplace organisation; only 4% believe their employees have no or very limited input.

The ability of staff and management to communicate effectively is vital to the creation of lower-stress workplaces. Stress is associated in a number of studies with reduced work output and poor employee performance (Lo & Lamm, 2005). Although respondents in an Auckland hotel study did not report high levels of work-related stress or stress-induced illness (Lo & Lamm, 2005), other research points to the fact that unpleasant, and stressful conditions in hospitality workplaces will have a negative influence on service quality, employee productivity and business performance.

Most employees feel that their managers rarely if ever discuss productivity concepts with them. Employees of larger organisations said their relationship with their managers is often formal, with some managers being very authoritarian to the point where everything is done as dictated, and no ideas are to be expressed. Participants in the smaller organisations also came across authoritarian managers and were usually disappointed in terms of productivity outcomes:

> *"My manager does not really encourage us to give input she just wants us to do what she asks. We are not encouraged to be creative, just to follow exactly what we are told. Once I put some magazines out for customers but was told to remove them. After that I didn't use my initiative as she didn't want our ideas".*

Some employees, mostly from smaller enterprises, have managers and supervisors who are more open to staff ideas about improving productivity and the work environment:

> *"We can make suggestions to our manager and he will discuss it with people on the same shift. He is willing to try new ideas".*

Those employees in large organisations commented that being casual and/or part time, they don't have much contact with their manager, and thus *"couldn't care less as long as I get paid"*. Quality relationships between staff and management clearly have a bearing on whether the employees feel there is a good climate in which to discuss productivity, and how encouraged they feel to share ideas.

Feedback from managers on employee achievements plays a significant role for some employees in creating job satisfaction. Regular appraisals, pay rises and tips are stated as additional useful monetary indicators of productivity:

> *"One of the main drivers for me to be more productive is recognition, like one of the managers saying thank you at the end of the day."*

Smaller businesses are very positive about seeking staff input, but usually in an informal way with the owners and managers being happy to have staff input or ask staff about how things are going, often through just chatting with employees.

> *"The internal communication among the staff, from me and the staff...keeps the whole thing flowing very well and very productively...."*

The workplace climate both in terms of manager encouragement, as well as other employee attitudes, does not always encourage individuals to improve their work practices, as is illustrated:

> *"From my experience it is more like tall poppy syndrome. If you do something outside the norm everybody else may get niggled because they don't want to push themselves as much. It can be frustrating".*

Participants also admitted that making suggestions sometimes caused unwanted arguments, and organisations (especially larger) often have set ways of doing things making it hard for suggestions to be implemented. Some participants expressed doubt if their suggestions ever *"make it to the head office"*.

Good communication in a team has a significant impact on the efficiency of staff and their ability to perform the *"dance"*, and helps to improve the customer experience. It is especially crucial, but hard to achieve, when there is *"not time to say please and thanks"*. Employees in larger organisations said that communication between staff was better in smaller teams where everyone listened to each other to avoid making mistakes, which helped to reduce conflict at the workplace. These same employees explained how Christmas and social events they have experienced gave them a chance to socialise which enhanced workplace relationships and fostered greater teamwork.

On several occasions focus group participants mentioned that conflict between kitchen staff and wait staff has a significant impact on overall productivity. Wait staff often get caught in the middle when customers are unhappy with their meal and the kitchen does not appreciate the criticism.

Employees think that poor English greatly affects customer service and productivity, especially in the case of phone orders. Chefs with poor English can be a particular cause of conflict among staff, exacerbating the antagonism between front of house and kitchen staff.

"Customers often got annoyed and even 'grumpy' when staff speak poor English, which effectively reduces customer satisfaction".

Quality of Working Life

The majority of managers interviewed said that they feel their jobs could potentially offer a comfortable level of work-life balance, but most choose to work a large number of hours. Many spoke of their passion for what they do, rather than viewing it as work.

"It is full on, it is my fault though. I work 6 days, 60-70 hours a week. I do what I know, and I still really enjoy my job, especially the project work as we have so many resources".

While several managers commented about the fact that they do not demonstrate good work-life balance themselves, they stated that they are highly aware of the importance of it for their staff productivity.

"Work-life balance is very important-they [staff] are rostered off with a weekend off once a month, and are not allowed to come in. We try to roster the days they want off".

The managers who responded to the web survey were asked if they think hospitality is an attractive career. Of the 53 participants who responded, 75% stated that they did feel it is attractive, with only 25% disagreeing.

Employees were less sure about the ability to manage work-life balance in a F&B services role, and less certain about F&B

offering attractive career options. Working too many shifts can be a "novelty" at first, but inevitably results in one being overworked and stressed out. Most employees felt it is harder for permanent employees to achieve work-life balance, making some employees frustrated and leading them to seek less demanding, more motivating, and better paid work.

Employees from a range of organisation types said that hospitality work is *"hard and tiring and poorly paid"*. Negative comments about hospitality work also referred to being paid only minimum wage, working long hours, not getting paid overtime, rarely getting tips and bonuses, stressful work environment, and having to deal with negative customers. Uncertainty over work-flows was often commented on:

"If we are short of staff everyone has to do anything. I have done room service, a la Carte, as well as cashier. When we are not busy it is a totally different pace".

The overwhelming majority of employees say they will not be working in hospitality in the future. Those studying at university plan to quit their hospitality jobs after completing their studies. Among the reasons for quitting are: it's not a *"real"* career; it's not challenging enough; it has negative customers, and low pay. Employee dissatisfaction with high levels of formality at the workplace, as well as their desire to change their job is also apparent in larger enterprises.

"Never took it to be a career, just the hours suited".

There were a number of participants from a range of (mostly small) organisations who genuinely do enjoy working in the industry. These individuals are more likely to be working in establishments where their contribution is sought and valued, and display the attitude and enthusiasm for the industry demonstrated by the managers interviewed. For some employees flexibility in their work environment was also a real positive:

"I have flexibility at work; they are not too strict as long as you do your job properly. The cafe is busy but there are times when there is not too much pressure".

Some employees in larger organisations also believe that hospitality is becoming more professional, offers more opportunities, and people are *"starting to get paid more"*.

Support Networks

As the Department of Labour (2004) notes:

"Firms do not operate in isolation and there are significant productivity gains to be achieved by improving the exchange of knowledge, information and ideas through both formal and informal networks".

Those employers that completed the web survey use a variety of sources to help build managerial capability. The web survey participants were asked where they went to for help as an employer/manager. The two most popular sources are friends and personal networks (73%), followed by accountant or lawyer (45%). The Department of Labour ranks third as a source for those seeking assistance (43%).

Productivity is a topic for discussion for some managers with colleagues in their internal and external networks. External parties were often identified as trustworthy sources with which to discuss productivity, particularly regarding new products and process innovations.

About a third of the managers said that they do not really discuss productivity, especially beyond the walls of their own establishment.

"Productivity is not talked about in NZ like it is overseas-more a cost balancing act here. The industry is not so good at discussing productivity."

For employees networks also play an important role. In many cases ethnic or friendship networks are important in the hiring process-with recommendations for existing staff playing a role in the attraction of new workers. Within firms the 'social capital' associated with close knit work teams was also often mentioned-with effective team work seen a great way to learn new skills and create a more enjoyable work environment.

Hiring & Training

According to Fair and Brook (2001), businesses should "never underestimate the contribution to productivity that ongoing everyday training makes". At the same time the Department of Labour (2004) stresses.

"Skills shortages choke off growth potential. The knowledge, ability and skills of workers contribute to workplace productivity.

Ongoing investment in foundation, technical, supervisory and managerial skills, together with improvements in work organisation, can help improve the productivity and performance of New Zealand firms."

The link between training and productivity is reflected in recent comments by Bruce Robertson, CEO of the Hospitality Association of New Zealand.

"One of the other keys to improved productivity is training. Three trained staff will always outperform four untrained staff and that applies right throughout the industry".

Research has shown that effective hiring and training is linked to a better ability to meet the needs of a target market (Shaw & Patterson, 1995), greater organisation commitment (Roehl & Swerdlow, 1999), more effective use of new technology, and enhanced work outcomes.

A firm can only achieve higher productivity by employing the right individuals with the capacity and desire to contribute to its goals.

"Good hiring creates a team; good communication creates a feeling of involvement, that it's more than just a job..."

Managers were asked in the web survey to identify the key characteristics or skills that they look for when recruiting staff. The two most commonly mentioned characteristics are honesty/ loyalty, and experience (30% each). Personality and ability are sought by 23% and 20% of managers respectively.

Increasingly, these managers are recruiting from international sources and new migrant groups-this can lead to language difficulties. Managers were asked in the web survey about the adequacy of numeracy, literacy and language skills among applicants. Over 80% of managers feel that overall, applicants do have adequate language and literacy skills, although only 66% test language and 59% test literacy skills when hiring. Only a third of managers test for numeracy skills when hiring.

Training can positively impact on employee productivity, promoting customer satisfaction and sustaining competitive advantage. Training is associated with improved job satisfaction and intention to stay, and with reduced workplace problems and staff turnover (Poulston, 2006).

Most managers interviewed for this study believe training has very positive and direct impacts on productivity improvement. Some rank it the number one factor and most of them describe it as having *'important'*, *'crucial'*, *'huge'* and *'massive'* importance. On-the-job, in-house, and self-training are the most common forms of training in the industry. Constrained by cost, many the interviewees from smaller enterprises expressed their inability and reluctance to employ outside trainers, although a couple of them talked about using outside trainers in specialist areas.

These findings are confirmed through the web survey which indicates that 88% of managers say the most common form of training engaged in is informal and on-the-job. This is followed by formal in-house training (40%) and training by an external provider (31%). Over half the managers think the training they are providing to their staff matches their needs. However, constrained by time, money and business pressure, a number of managers expressed their concern about the lack of training they were able to provide.

Tertiary/private training is considered to be too theoretical and as not meeting the industry's requirements well. Most of the managers interviewed, and 60% of web survey participants, feel formal tertiary/private hospitality qualifications do not adequately prepare people to enter employment in their workplace.

"I think on the job training is very important-it is hard to take a student from tech and put them in this environment".

A theme of *"wanting to train them our way"* emerged amongst some of the managers interviewed. Some managers expressed annoyance at needing to at times 'untrain' those that had been trained to do jobs one way.

Employees had generally undergone some type of training when they first started their job; and the majority had on-the-job training provided by other staff and/or the manager. During on-the-job training, participants appreciate the opportunity to see senior staff *"showing tricks of the trade"* in the context of the workplace, and to ask questions. Employees said training provided by the manager rather than senior colleagues was most valuable, as other staff often *"forgot little things"* or deliberately *"withheld information"* on the best ways to do things. Some didn't have either formal or on-the-job training and were forced to follow a *"sink or swim"* approach-*"You are given a till and a bag of money and told to go for it".*

Employees in larger organisations tended to have taken formal induction courses. During induction training, participants watch videos, are given manuals and introduced to key procedures. Research shows that employees of small and medium enterprises are less likely to have the opportunity to take part in this type of training than those working in large organisations Milne et al. (2004).

Employees in the focus groups generally believed that *"training helps to access jobs"*, but were less certain about its ability to provide access directly to managerial level jobs. Those in small organisation focus groups felt that there is a *"gap between education, hospitality and employers' expectations"* and most expressed some scepticism about the ability of tertiary providers to really prepare people for the F&B workforce.

Turnover & Retention

As one F&B manager Interviewed Noted: "Employee retention is important for consistency of products and customer service standards, so customers know what to expect".

Hinkin and Tracey (2000) list the following productivity-related costs of staff turnover: pre-departure productivity loss; learning curve; errors and waste; supervisory and peer disruption. Turnover can also negatively affect productivity within interdependent worker groupings and teams. However not all staff turnover has negative implications. Moderate turnover can help to replace unproductive employees, enable career progression, enhance job and employee matching and is therefore viewed as enhancing productivity by some (Ilmakunnas et al., 2005).

A recent study of Auckland hospitality workers (Poulston, 2006) indicated short lengths of employment are common (87% have been in their current job fewer than five years), and that the majority work part-time. The latest survey conducted by the Restaurant Association (March 2006) indicates an average annual staff turnover of 29%, up from 26% in 2005. A New Zealand study of productivity found that high involvement work practices and employee retention were strongly associated with strong enterprise performance (Guthrie, 2001). While turnover increases exposure to disruptions associated with the loss of employees in high involvement work practices this damage is greater than in settings where processes are more automated, for example the preparation areas of fast food establishments.

Several managers stated in the interviews that they have real problems with staff turnover, tending to attribute much of the problem to the tight labour market rather than to factors that are directly within their control. Of the managers who completed the web survey question asking whether staff turnover affects productivity in their business, 54% feel it does, 29% feel it does not, and 17% responded 'not applicable'. The need for training new staff was seen as having the greatest negative effect on productivity. The time and cost involved are also detrimental effects stemming from staff turnover.

"Turnover is costly and involves extra training-there's also a trust issue with long term staff".

Large hotels are the most proactive in developing strategies to cope with turnover and to increase retention. Such strategies include succession planning, valuing internal communication to develop teams, and offering incentives for staff to stay. Training and flexible hours are also seen to be important in improving retention.

Overall, employees agreed that new staff often reduce productivity, because they are inefficient in their job, and because it is a burden on experienced staff to train someone new. Some employees, however, give new staff credit saying they usually are the most willing to learn.

Longer term staff not only have more industry experience, which helps to increase overall productivity, but also a stronger relationship with the kitchen staff, seen by many as prerequisite for having a *"good night"*.

Technology

In its discussion of productivity drivers the Department of Labour has identified that:

> *"innovation is a key part of raising workplace productivity. The appropriate introduction of advanced technology is linked with higher productivity, greater market share and employment growth".*

The introduction of advanced technology has been cited by several authors as an important and positive influence on productivity. Positive impacts however do not simply 'appear', rather they stem from the competent use and exploitation of IT capabilities (Sigala, 2003). Technology has been found to 'support employees, enhance the quality of service, improve efficiencies, gain competitive advantage, maintain relationships with customers and increase profitability', while poor investment in technology (along with poor training) is likely to reduce profitability.

Several studies have shown that SMEs in the hospitality sector have special difficulties in maximising the productivity potential of information technologies. Such enterprises are more likely to recognise the limitations of technology and emphasise the importance of 'the human touch'. At the same time SME owners and managers are more likely to have to out-source aspects of IT maintenance and may feel more removed from its application to the business setting.

The web survey found that 89% of managers have introduced new technology in the last two years with the view to improving productivity in their workplace. The interviews revealed a similar trend. A range of technologies have been introduced by managers, primarily in the front of house area with computers being the most common purchase. Smaller businesses have a slower uptake of 'cutting edge' ICT devices such as wireless personal digital assistants and text message ordering.

Both managers and employees are divided on the issue of technology and productivity. Some think it enhances staff efficiency, saves time and improves productivity. Others say it in fact creates inefficiencies when it breaks down or requires updating.

While technology was discussed as an important contributor to productivity, most of the technology identified as bringing real efficiency gains is in the front of house environment. In particular, technological innovations are central to streamlining ordering and point of sale processes.

7

Food Hygiene Practices

Food Hygiene Includes all Practices, Precautions and Procedures Involved in:

a. Protecting food from the risk of biological, chemical or physical contamination.

b. Preventing any organisms multiplying to an extent that would expose consumers to risk or result in premature decomposition of food.

c. Destroying any harmful bacteria in food by thorough cooking or processing.

Benefits from high standards of food hygiene include:

a. Reduced risk of food poisoning, foreign body contamination and spoilage.

b. Compliance with MOD and legal requirements.

c. Economic advantages, including increased shelf life and reduction of waste.

d. Consumer satisfaction and enhanced reputation.

e. Increased morale of personnel.

Hazard Analysis

The Food Safety (General Food Hygiene) Regulations 1995 (FS(GFH)R) refer to *Hazard Analysis* (HA). HA is based on five principles, detailed at Annex A to this chapter and are summarised below:

a. Analysis of the potential food hazards in a food operation.

b. Identification of the points in those operations where food hazards may occur.

c. Deciding which of the points identified is critical to food safety ("critical points").
d. Identification and implementation of effective control and monitoring procedures at those critical points.
e. Review of the analysis of food hazards, the critical control points and the control and monitoring procedures periodically and whenever the catering operation changes.

In order to meet the requirements of HA across the MOD, a practical guide for the MOD has been produced, based on the principle that there are four main methods of preparing food. The guide, *Hazard Analysis-The Four Line Method,* is at Annex B to this chapter, which is to be used as a template in all Service establishments. Universally recognised Critical Control Points (CCPs) have been identified, however additional Control Points or Critical Points may be applicable in each case. This will be entirely dependant on the type of catering function and the supporting infrastructure. When preparing individual HA profiles, units are advised to consider the following definitions in order to determine the type of risk that applies at each stage of food preparation:

a. *Control point* – specific stages in those operations where food hazards may occur.
b. *Critical point* – control points which are considered critical points where the hazard must be controlled to ensure that it is eliminated or reduced to a safe level.
c. *Critical control point* – is a critical point in the process where a specific hazard must be controlled on the basis that no further process will adequately eradicate that hazard.

Written records are also important in establishing a Due Diligence defence under the Food Safety Act 1990. HA, as defined in the FS(GFH) R, includes the principles of: Critical Points and the Control of those Critical Points. In this document the term Hazard Analysis (HA) will be used, but this is be taken to be synonymous with HACCP.

Regulation 4(3) of FS(GFH)R states that: "a proprietor of a food business shall identify any step in the activities of the food business which is critical to ensuring food safety and ensure that adequate safety procedures are identified, implemented, maintained and reviewed". This Regulation is designed to make caterers focus on the activities critical to food safety and to find ways of controlling them.

The systematic analysis of each individual food item would result in a heavy burden for most MOD catering operations and would be impractical to implement. An approach, that considers the catering operation step by step, from supply through to consumption, is achievable, effective and forms the basis of food HA in the MOD. The HA approach to ensuring food safety and hygiene is intended to give a clearer focus on the controls that are important to Service caterers to ensure that safe food is provided.

Where catering is provided by contract, the contractor is to use a Hazard Analysis system that meets legislative requirements or adopt the Four-Line Method. Specialist advice, through the Chain of Command may be obtained from DCG Service Support Contracts

Supply of Food and Water

The FS(GFH)R state that no raw materials or ingredients shall be accepted by a food business if they are known to be contaminated with parasites, pathogenic micro organisms, toxic, decomposed or foreign substances and that, after normal sorting and/or preparatory processing procedures, they would still be unfit for human consumption.

Delivery Monitoring Routine checks must be made on deliveries of food for signs of damage, contamination and the presence of pests. The general condition of the food is to be checked, together with more specific checks such as date marks (Best Before and Use By) and temperature. Unfit food or food past its "Use By" date must not be accepted and is to be immediately returned. Temperature monitoring should be conducted at the time of delivery and should form part of the quantity & quality check. For chilled and frozen foods, checks are to be made that the food is delivered at the correct temperature (less than 8oC for chilled and less than –12oC for frozen). The Delivery Monitoring form is no longer required to be completed, the vehicle temperature printed record must now be attached to the Price Advice Note (PAN). For bulk stock "between pack" temperatures are to be taken using an air probe and recorded directly onto the PAN. A note stating "Quality & Date Coding Checked" is to be hand written onto the PAN. A commercially produced ink stamp could also be utilised for this task.

Potable Water Supply. It is essential that galleys and kitchens be supplied with potable water for the purposes of food preparation and cleaning.

Food Storage

The FS(GFH)R requires food products and ingredients to be stored in food premises in appropriate conditions, designed to prevent harmful deterioration and to protect food from contamination.

Dry Provisions Storage. These storerooms are to be kept clean and orderly to minimise the potential hazards from "foreign bodies" and to prevent the harbourage of pests. Where practicable these stores are to be proofed against pest ingress. Part used packs are to be adequately to prevent contamination. High ambient temperatures (above 13oC) and high humidity are to be avoided. Dry goods should be stored on suitable racking raised off the ground.

Chilled Storage (5oC). Cool rooms and refrigerators are to be kept clean and tidy. It is the responsibility of the Catering Manager to raise the appropriate request if refrigerated space is considered inadequate. Best Practice guidance indicates that the ideal operating temperature of a refrigerator is 1-4oC.

Frozen Storage(-18—21oC). Freezers are to be kept clean and tidy at all times. Best Practice guidance indicates that the ideal operating temperature of a freezer is between –18oC to –21oC.

Satisfactory storage is essential if a galley/kitchen/mess is to serve clean and safe food. This should include routine turnover of stock and checks of Best Before Dates. There are four main groups of foods that require differing storage conditions. The groups are as follows:

Where reference is made to a Priced Advice Note; this also means any other form of Invoice or Delivery Note

a. *Fresh Fruit and Vegetables*. These may be contaminated by soil bacteria and are to be stored away from other foods in a cool area, with adequate ventilation, preferably refrigerated at a temperature appropriate to the product.

b. *Dry Foods.* (including Canned Foods, Cereals and Flour). These are to be stored in dry, well-ventilated rooms ideally at 13oC. Food is to be put on racks, shelves or pallets off the floor.

c. *Frozen Foods.* These are to be stored in a freezer as soon as they are delivered. Frozen foods are to be used within 1 month. 'Kitchen prepared' chilled foods that are subsequently frozen are also to be used within 1 month.

d. Perishable Foods. Perishable food temperatures in a refrigerator must not exceed the legal limit of 8oC. Therefore, perishable foods are to be stored in a refrigerator cabinet, set at a target temperature of 5oC. Such food includes chilled dishes, meat, poultry, eggs, cooked meats and vegetable dishes, prepared salads, soft cheeses, sandwiches, fresh pasta, low acid desserts, smoked or cured meats, fish and dairy produce. Best Practice advice, is that chilled foods are to be used within 48hrs. Food that is spoiled or past its "Use By Date" must be removed from food rooms and appropriate action taken prior to disposal. Broken packaging must be avoided.

Food Displays/Serveries. Food displays and serveries should be set at the correct temperature with adequate time allowed for the equipment to achieve target temperatures. It is good practice to have sneeze screens attached to hot and cold food displays to minimise the risk of contamination of food. The handles of utensils should not contact food; this can be achieved by using utensils with longer handles than the service containers.

Cross Contamination

Cross contamination is the process whereby pathogenic bacteria present in raw food, such as meat, poultry, and vegetables, come into contact with ready to eat food, either directly or indirectly, through contact with surfaces, equipment, splashes, drips, utensils, hands and cloths. To prevent cross contamination, raw and ready to eat foods are to be kept apart. Good management planning of workflow through the kitchen can assist in this. The flow of waste is also be considered, along with raw products and prepared food. Additionally, it is to be ensured that:

a. Where possible, there are separate designated preparation areas for raw and cooked foods. If, due to limitation of space, preparation surfaces are used for both high and low risk foods then these activities must be separated by time (ideally low risk foods prepared first). Preparation surfaces must be thoroughly cleaned and disinfected between the two operations.

b. If raw and cooked food is to be stored in the same refrigerator, raw foods are always to be stored (and adequately covered) below cooked or salad foodstuffs.

c. Food handlers always wash their hands between handling raw and cooked foods and change their protective clothing once heavily soiled.

d. Separate colour coded cutting boards (red for raw meat, blue for raw fish, green for fresh fruit, salad and vegetables, white for cooked foods) and colour-coded knives are used (details of NSNs for these items are contained in JSP 308). Always thoroughly wash and disinfect cutting boards and knives in between and after use.

e. Separate machines for raw and cooked food are used, or slicing and mincing machines are thoroughly cleaned and disinfected between raw and cooked food. If separate machines are not available, cooked food must be prepared before raw food.

f. All food is kept in covered, dated and labelled containers during storage and before service.

g. Storing and Cooking with Eggs. Some eggs can contain salmonella bacteria inside or on their shells so care must be taken with their use. They are to be stored in a cool dry place or refrigerated, with exterior packaging removed and kept away from other foods. All egg dishes are to be served immediately or cooled quickly and chilled. Commercially pasteurised egg products should be used in preparation of any recipe that is served uncooked or partially cooked. This includes mayonnaise; bearnaise and hollandaise sauces, some salad dressings, ice-cream, icings and tiramisu.

h. Washing of Fruits and Vegetables. All fruits and vegetables should be washed in potable water before use. In addition fruits and vegetables purchased locally overseas are to be immersed for 30 minutes in water containing either of the agents listed. The items should then be rinsed to remove taste of disinfecting agent:

(i) Calcium hypocholrite granules-one level teaspoon per two gallons of water

(ii) Milton: 5 teaspoons per gallon of water.

Defrosting Food

It is essential that frozen meat and poultry are thoroughly thawed on trivets, or if unavailable in a designated defrosting area, or ideally in a defrosting cabinet. Frozen vegetables must be cooked directly from frozen.

Cooking

It is essential that food is cooked thoroughly to destroy any bacteria on or within it. Food is to be cooked to a core temperature of 75°C, checked with a calibrated digital probe (disinfected with bactericidal wipes). It is important that food such as rolled joints, burgers, and chicken are cooked to 75°C at its thickest part.

Chilling Food

When chilling cooked food for later cold or hot consumption, it is essential that the food be cooled as quickly as possible. In accordance with 'Best Practice' hot food is to be taken through the recognised 'Danger Zone' of 60-10ºC within 4hrs, and subsequently stored in a refrigerator at 8ºC or cooler. (These requirements refer to the temperature of the food, not the air temperature of the equipment). If the target temperatures are not achieved food is to be discarded. The chilling of food to a recognised safe temperature may be achieved using the following methods:

a. Break food down into shallow trays and cover.

b. Cool initially to a low ambient temperature, then refrigerate or blast chill to below 'Danger Zone'.

c. Store in a refrigerator.

Reheating Food

It is advised that the reheating cooked foods is avoided, but if this is not possible it must only be reheated once and the following steps are to be taken:

a. Ensure that the food reaches a core temperature of at least 75°C. (In Scotland it is a legal requirement for the centre of the food being reheated to reach 82°C).

b. Use digital probe thermometers to check the temperature at the centre of the food. (Probes are to be disinfected using bactericidal wipes between each use).

c. The food is to be served and eaten as soon as possible.

d. After reheating, any leftover cooked food is to be thrown away.

Temperature Control and Monitoring

The Food Safety (Temperature Control) Regulations 1995 (FS(TC)R) impose two holding temperatures of below 8ºC or above 63ºC. The purpose of the regulations is to inhibit or prevent harmful micro organisms from multiplying by keeping food outside of the recognised 'Danger Zone' of 60ºC to 10ºC. The FS(TC)R allow limited periods outside temperature control during preparation, display, service, storage or transport, but it is an offence to keep food out of temperature control for so long that it could become unsafe. The requirements do not apply to foods, which by their nature or their packaging (e.g. canned foods) are inherently safe from the growth of such organisms. In such cases the manufacturer's guidelines are to be followed.

Refrigerator and Freezer Temperature Recording. The operating temperature of all appliances should be monitored and recorded thrice daily using either of the templates at Appendices 1 and 4 to Annex B of this Chapter. As a guide, the target operating temperature for a refrigerator is 5°C and for a freezer is-18°to-21°C, but this will depend on the efficiency, age, contents and capacity of the appliance.

Note: The template to be utilised is dependent on establishment size and the number of appliances.

Catering Standing Orders are to specify the corrective action (including Out of Hours/Weekend actions required) to be taken in the event of refrigerators/freezers not achieving recommended operating temperatures or failing completely.

Food Holding Temperatures

Two and Four Hour Rule

Hot food must be kept at 63°C or above. It must either be consumed within 2 hrs from the time the food temperature drops below 63°C, or be disposed of.

Chilled food may be displayed (away from under temperature control) for a maximum period of 4 hours. Only one such period is allowed, no matter how short. If, for example a refrigerated dish has been on display for 1 hour in a non-refrigerated environment, refrigerating it does not mean it can be displayed for a further 3 hours later. Where food is being cooled prior to refrigeration, cooling is to be achieved as quickly as possible as described in paragraph

When hot or cold food is displayed outside a temperature controlled environment, it is to be consumed or discarded.

Target Temperatures

Food Safety legislation and the Dept of Health require that certain temperatures be maintained throughout the food storage and production process.

- Cook
- Temp
- Service
- Temperature
- (At or above)
- Reheat Reheat
- Scotland
- Chilled
- Storage
- Frozen
- Storage
- Legally Required
- Temperature
- 0°C for 2 mins 63°C 75°C 82°C 8°C-18C.

Temperature Measurement and Temperature Probe Calibration

Measurement. A digital thermometer with attached probe is to be used for measuring food temperatures, including final cooking temperatures. The probe is to be disinfected with food safe wipes between measurements. There are also 'Between Pack Probes' are available that are to be used to measure temperatures of frozen and chilled foodstuffs, primarily at the delivery stage. Details of these items can be found in JSP 308.

Numbers of parts as available as follows;

Description	*NSN*	*Remarks*
Wipe Clean Thermometer	7320 99 0173073	
Robust Penetration Probe	7320 99 2154600	
Thermometer Between Pack Probe	6685 99 9906711	6 x 200 pack
Bacterial Probe wipes	7320 99 995890	
Pocket Stick Thermometer	6685 99 0007159	

Calibration: The digital thermometer is to be re-calibrated annually or in accordance with the manufacturer's instructions and warranty. A monthly calibration check is to be undertaken with an appropriate device in accordance with the manufacturer's instructions, and recorded on the template at Annex C to this chapter. The Test Plug is also to be calibrated in accordance with manufacturer's instructions and warranty.

Records

Records. Records are an important aspect of any due diligence defence and are essential in proving that the temperature requirements were being met in the event of any prosecution or food poisoning outbreak. Records (including Calibration records) are to be retained for 6 months. The mandatory records that are to be kept with unit files are listed below:

a. Delivery monitoring records.
b. All refrigerator and freezer temperature monitoring documents.
c. Food temperature monitoring records.
d. Calibration records for temperature probes.

Personal Hygiene

Good personal hygiene is a legislative requirement, ensuring safe food. Induction training must ensure that new staff joining are aware of the required standard Food handlers are a potential source of bacterial and physical contamination of food, and so personal hygiene is a key element in ensuring that food is prepared safely.

Staff training is to include all the basic elements of personal hygiene (including hand washing training) covered in this section and personnel are to understand the relevance of the precautions.

The FS(GFH)R lays down criteria for the personal hygiene of food handlers and the actions to be taken if a food handler is infected. These regulations require every person working in a food handling area to maintain a high degree of personal cleanliness. Any person suffering from a disease that is likely to be transmitted through food must inform the person in charge of the galley/kitchen. A separate regulation states that any such infected person may not be permitted to work in any food handling area, in any capacity, where they might contaminate food.

Specific Requirements

a. *Hand washing.* The hands of food handlers are the principal agents in the transference of bacteria to food. Hand washing facilities (a separate basin that is only to be used for hand washing) in galleys/kitchens and heads/toilets are to include hot and cold running water, soap, nail brush and a suitable means of drying the hands. Regular checks by senior staff are to be made to ensure these facilities are available and are being used effectively. As a minimum, hand washing, is to take place:
   (1) On entering a food room.
   (2) Between handling raw and cooked food.
   (3) After handling waste food or refuse.
   (4) After smoking or eating.
   (5) After visiting the WC.

b. *Cuts.* Open cuts harbour bacteria and must be covered with clean blue waterproof dressing to aid detection. Stocks of these are to be available in food preparation areas and readily accessible to food handlers.

c. *Jewellery.* The wearing of wristwatches, ear rings ('Studs' are acceptable) and other exposed body piercing, bracelets and rings, is not acceptable as they harbour bacteria and there is a risk of physical contamination of food. The wearing of a plain wedding ring is acceptable.

d. *Smoking.* Smoking is not permitted in food areas, as it transfers bacteria from the mouth to hands. Cigarette ends and ash also pose physical contamination risks.

e. *Protective Clothing and Changing Facilities.* Food handlers must wear suitable clean protective clothing (including appropriate footwear and hats) to prevent contamination of food from normal clothing. Such clothing is to be changed at the end of a shift, or sooner if the situation requires, in order to maintain hygienic standards. It is not to be worn outside food areas and associated premises. If necessary, an outer garment is to be worn over protective clothing whilst away from food production environment. Adequate changing facilities must be provided, with locker space for clean and soiled protective clothing. Changing facilities must be kept clean and tidy at all times.

f. *Visitors.* All visitors to a food preparation area are to be viewed as potential sources of contamination. They must therefore be provided with protective clothing and briefed upon good food hygiene practices before entering the food area. Before entering a food preparation area, visitors must confirm that they are not suffering from diarrhoea and/or vomiting, or heavy cold. Individuals who are suffering should not be allowed to proceed.

g. *Eating/drinking.* Food handlers are not to eat or drink in food rooms. It is acceptable for cooks to taste dishes during preparation in a manner that does not contaminate the food i.e. a clean spoon each time.

h. *Toilet Facilities.* Where possible toilets for catering personnel are to be separate from those for non-catering personnel and visitors. Toilets are not to be located directly within a food preparation area. There is to be an intervening ventilated space between toilets and food rooms. Food is not to be stored in that space. Toilets must be ventilated such that associated odours are prevented from permeating into food rooms. They must also be kept clean and tidy, in good repair with adequate supplies of toilet paper, hand washing facilities, nail brushes, soap and hand towels.

Infected Food Handlers

Dispersed Feeding

Dispersed feeding is the production and transportation of food for consumption away from an established unit/galley/kitchen or mess for example to personnel on security duties who are unable to be fed in-mess, non-public section functions, such as barbecues or sports meals. This method of feeding is recognised as high risk, because the majority of foods used require controlled temperatures during transportation in order to comply with Food Safety Legislation. Dispersed feeding should only take place when there is no suitable alternative.

Documentation. Before food leaves the kitchen, the Shift NCO (or equivalent if DEL or contract catering staff) is to ensure the completion (in duplicate) of FCAT 1013.

Dispersed Feeding Record (demanded from DSDC Llangennech)

A copy is to be retained with the food safety records and a copy handed to the person (recipient) taking the food out of the kitchen. The recipient is to be briefed on the following points:

a. Chilled Products. Chilled foods are to be consumed within 4 hours of being removed once cold products leave from a temperature controlled environment i.e. refrigerator or chilled servery and when and the product temperature rises above 8oC, products are to be consumed within 4 hours.

b. Hot Products. Hot foods are to be consumed within 2 hours of being placed into a container. Food is to be served at 63°C. If a hot container meal arrives at its final destination and the product temperature is below 63°C, it is to be consumed as soon as possible (but always within 2 hours from when the product was placed into the container). This time will have been recorded in column (b) of the FCAT 1013.

c. When temperature monitoring is unavailable at a dispersed feeding location, the food is to be consumed within 2 hrs (hot product) or 4 hours (cold product) of being placed in the insulated container or leaving a refrigerated environment. Once again the time of service is to be recorded in column (b) of FCAT 1013.

Transport Of Food

Movement of temperature-controlled foods may include:

a. The collection of food from suppliers and transportation to the main ration stores and messes.

b. The transportation of prepared food from messes to satellite or dispersed feeding facilities.

Transport can include items such as trolleys, bags, boxes, trays and crates. These articles must be kept clean. Where transport is also used for materials other than food, it must be thoroughly cleaned between loads to avoid the risk of cross contamination.

Non-catering personnel collecting foodstuffs from the mess are to be briefed on the importance of maintaining the integrity of the food chain, and how this is achieved.

During transport, all food is to be covered and is to be transported in appropriate insulated containers. High-risk food must be kept separate from anything that could cause contamination. When transporting prepared meals, dispatch and receipt temperature checks are to be recorded in accordance with paragraph.

Cleaning

The FS(GFH)R requires adequate facilities are provided for the cleaning and disinfecting of work utensils and equipment. These facilities must be constructed of materials resistant to corrosion, must be easy to clean and have an adequate supply of hot and cold water.

Equipment items that come into contact with high-risk foods will need to be cleaned and disinfected as necessary. Facilities must be provided to clean and disinfect all tools and equipment, crockery, cutlery, glasses and serving dishes. There are to be sufficient cleaning materials and equipment to match the size of the catering facility. Staff involved in cleaning must wear suitable and adequate protective clothing, which must be changed, at the end of each shift.

Colour coded cleaning equipment, e.g. mops must be cleaned, dried and stored in a designated area once finished with. Drying of equipment must not cause recontamination, e.g. from soiled cloths. A full list of NSNs of colour-coded equipment is shown in JSP 308.

Equipment must be of durable construction and resistant to corrosion, especially items that will come into contact with powerful cleaning chemicals.

Sinks. It is a legal requirement that, where appropriate, adequate provision must be made for any necessary washing of food. Every sink or other facility for the washing of food must have an adequate supply of hot and/or cold potable water as required, and be kept clean. Separate facilities must be provided for hand washing, food preparation and equipment washing if the volume of preparation in the kitchen demands it. In small catering operations, one sink may be used for both equipment and food washing, provided that both activities can be done effectively and without prejudice to food safety, i.e. the sink is to be thoroughly cleaned between each process. It is good practice to have signs above sinks indicating what they can be used for. Hot water supply is not essential if a sink is to be used exclusively for food preparation.

Disinfection. Disinfection is a process that reduces microorganisms to a level that will not lead to harmful contamination or spoilage of food. Sterilisation is a process that destroys all living organisms. The word 'sterilise' is sometimes used in food hygiene literature and in some official publications where the word 'disinfect' would be correct. Cleaning products are often described as 'detergent/sterilise' when 'detergent/disinfectant' would be a more accurate description. The following definitions clarify the relationship between disinfection and cleaning:

a. A disinfectant is a chemical agent used for disinfection after cleaning.
b. Sanitisation is a term used mainly in the food and catering industry. It is a process of both cleaning and disinfecting utensils and equipment.
c. A sanitiser is a chemical agent used for sanitisation.
d. Sterilisation is a process intended to destroy or remove all living organisms. It is not to be confused with disinfection.
e. Cleaning, Heat, and Chemical Disinfectants. Disinfection is essential in food hygiene. It is achieved by:
   (1) Cleaning. This is the most useful and practical method of removing food residues, dirt, grease and other undesirable debris. It can be used alone or in combination with the other two methods. A high proportion of microbial contamination is removed from equipment, food preparation surfaces and hands by thorough cleaning.

(2) Disinfection by Heat. This is considered the most reliable of the three methods of disinfection. Immersion in water at 65ºC for 10 minutes, or at higher temperatures for shorter times can be relied upon to destroy most microorganisms harmful to health, with the exception of bacterial spores. Boiling water is an effective and cheap disinfectant although bacterial spores may survive boiling. The temperature of the washing or rinse cycle in a dishwashing machine can be adjusted to include heat disinfection in the cycle, in accordance with the manufacturer's instruction.

(3) Some chemical disinfectants are active against a wide range of bacteria; others have a narrow range of antibacterial activity. In all circumstances chemical disinfectants must be used in accordance with the manufacturer's instruction. It is military policy to use general-purpose detergent for general cleaning with surface sanitisers. Chemical disinfectants (stored in a designated

Cleaning Procedures

Cleaning of food premises is carried out to remove dirt and grease from all surfaces and equipment, including pathogenic bacteria, that could compromise food safety, as well as food debris. It is imperative that high standards of cleaning are maintained for the following reasons:

a. To comply with the legal requirements of the FS(GFH)R.
b. To reduce the risk of food poisoning by removing food residues, which could contain harmful bacteria.
c. To deny pests harbourage and food.
d. To reduce the risk of foreign objects physically contaminating food.
e. To promote hygiene awareness amongst catering personnel.
f. To provide a pleasant working environment and a favourable image to personnel.

Cleaning Schedule: A planned cleaning schedule programme is important in ensuring that high standards of cleanliness in all food areas are achieved and maintained. This can be achieved by adhering to a written cleaning schedule. Food preparation surfaces must be regularly cleaned whilst in use. This is particularly important where space is limited and the cross contamination risk is increased.

a. Instructions for cleaning specific areas or pieces of equipment are to include the following information relative to the task:
   (1) Job description.
   (2) Cleaning materials and chemicals to be used (in accordance with manufacturer's instruction).
   (3) Safety precautions.
   (4) Job method.

b. The cleaning schedule is to state how often a specific area or piece of equipment is to be cleaned and who is responsible for checking that all cleaning tasks have been completed to a satisfactory standard.

c. General information concerning the cleaning of food equipment, surfaces and the material structures, including a list of cleaning equipment and agents used in food rooms/kitchen/galley/mess, are at Annex D to this chapter.

d. Catering managers are to implement a cleaning schedule that relates to all food areas within their department. A schedule detailing the frequency of routine cleaning tasks should be produced for each catering facility. It is to be contained within Catering Standing Orders and communicated to all personnel (e.g. by displaying the schedule on a notice board). A matrix showing the frequency, details of the task, type of cleaning required and a signature block is considered the most useful layout and should be readily available for operatives to follow and sign off. A signature block should also be included for a supervisory check.

Deep Cleaning: All galleys/kitchens and associated areas are to be deep cleaned in accordance with single Service instructions. Catering managers are to ensure that deep cleaning contracts are adequate to meet the tasks required.

Food Preparation Areas

Surfaces. The FS(GFH)R require that those surfaces which

come into contact with food must be maintained in a sound condition, be easy to clean and, where necessary, disinfect. This requires the use of smooth, washable and nontoxic materials. To comply with this legal requirement, it is important that surfaces that come into contact with high-risk foods must be capable of being disinfected regularly. Examples of such surfaces, assuming that they are properly fixed, applied or installed and maintained, include: stainless steel, ceramics, and food grade plastics. Wooden boards are inappropriate for the preparation of high-risk foods. Food preparation surfaces must either be continuous in their construction or have properly sealed joints.

Design and Layout. The design and layout of food areas are to:

a. Permit adequate cleaning and/or disinfection.
b. Protect against dirt, contact with toxic materials, and formation of condensation and mould.
c. Encourage good food hygiene practices and prevent cross contamination by foodstuffs, equipment, materials, water, air supply or personnel and external sources of contamination such as pests.
d. Where practicable, suitable temperature conditions should be provided for the hygienic preparation of food.

Structural Requirements. In areas where food is prepared, consideration is to be given to floor and wall surfaces, ceilings and overhead fixtures, windows, doors and other openings. There are to be adequate washbasins, sanitary conveniences, ventilation, and drainage. Any maintenance requirements and requests to catering premises are to be recorded in either the Maintenance of Catering Premises – Record of Work Services Template at Annex E to this chapter or the unit works service record. Priority awarded to work service request is entirely dependent on the type of establishment and the impact of the equipment failure. The following priorities are to be applied:

MOD Standards. Defence Estates (DE) Design and Maintenance Guide 18 deals with the design of kitchens and serveries for all ranks, and dining rooms for Junior Ranks. Details of dining rooms for Officers and SNCOs are given in JSP 315 Services Accommodation Code, Scales 29 and 34. The guide is also to be read in conjunction with DE Specification 42 on Catering

Equipment and JSP 315, Scales 01, 39, 40, 45, 47 and 52. For HM Ships and Submarines, the relevant Naval Engineering Standards (NES) publication provides guidance in the design, layout and equipping of Galleys, Storerooms (refrigerated and dry) and associated areas.

Pest Control

Pests are known to carry a number of pathogenic organisms that can be transmitted to humans through contaminated food. In addition, pests will damage food stocks causing financial loss. It is therefore important that food premises are kept pest free. The Prevention of Damage by Pests Act 1949 and the FS(GFH)R impose legal duties on owners and occupiers of buildings to keep their premises free from infestation.

A wide variety of insect and rodent pests will enter food premises for a number of reasons:

a. Food. Even in small quantities, food will enable pests to survive and multiply. Regular and thorough cleaning of spillages is therefore imperative.

b. Warmth. Pests of all types are attracted to buildings, which offer even limited warmth away from outdoor conditions. A few degrees increase in temperature will provide conditions in which breeding is enhanced and proliferation encouraged.

c. Shelter. Almost every building provides a variety of harbourages for pests.

Contrary to common belief, it is the newer buildings with suspended ceilings, panelled walls, service ducts and enclosed electrical trunking, which are more likely to create a problem, than older buildings without such features. Access must be provided to these spaces for the effective control of pests.

Denial of food, warmth or shelter will prevent the survival of pests. This form of control can be termed 'environmental control' and is the first line of defence against possible infestation. Environmental control may be considered as denial of access (proofing), food and harbourage.

Flying Insect Control. Emphasis is to be placed on the environmental and physical control detailed previously to reduce the risk of food contamination. Areas around food premises are to be kept clean and tidy to reduce the number of possible breeding sites.

External refuse containers are to be clean and in good repair, and have tight fitting lids. If skips are used they are to be completely enclosed. Waste food containers must be washed out before being stored outside. Windows and other openings which provide ventilation are to be fitted with close fitting and cleanable fly screens where required. Doors are to be kept closed or fitted with screens or clear plastic heavy-duty strips. Electronic fly killers, where required, are to be installed but must not be sited above food preparation areas. The bulbs within electric fly killers must be changed in accordance with the manufacturer's instructions.

Recording Sightings

All personnel employed in a kitchen/galley have a duty to report to the Head Chef any evidence of pest infestation. Kitchen Managers are to record such sightings in the Pest Management Register at Annex F to this chapter. Under operational conditions or on exercise, trained Service personnel carry out pest and vector or vermin control. In peacetime (except in some overseas Commands and HM Naval Bases where MOD Civilian pest control operators are employed) civilian contractors normally carry out pest control. There are two ways in which a pest control contractor may be used:

a. To deal with and eradicate a single infestation.

b. To act as a long-term contractor who will visit the premises regularly and carry out pest control treatments as necessary. This proactive approach is more suitable and is recommended.

Waste Disposal

The FS(GFH)R require that food waste and other refuse must not be allowed to accumulate in food rooms, except so far as is unavoidable for the proper functioning of the catering department. It is recommended that systems of work are in place to ensure that refuse containers in food rooms are not over filled and are emptied regularly. All waste is to be removed at the end of the working day.

Food waste and other refuse must be deposited in sealed containers which must be of an appropriate construction, kept in sound condition, and, where necessary, be easy to clean and disinfect. Lids are not required on refuse containers used for temporary storage of waste in food preparation areas. They are frequently touched by the hands of food handlers and may be a serious source of contamination. Any refuse containers used for storage of waste awaiting collection and removal are to have a lid and to be constructed of durable material, which makes them easy to clean and disinfect. Refuse containers are to be included in the cleaning schedule.

The FS(GFH)R state that adequate provision must be made for the removal and storage of food waste and other refuse. Refuse stores must be designed and managed in such a way as to enable them to be kept clean, prevent access by pests, and protect against contamination of food, drinking water, equipment or premises. Areas for indoor storage of refuse must be remote from food rooms and not sited near the main delivery entrance. In establishments it is good practice to have a separate area designated for the storage of outdoor waste with well-lit hard standing. A hose is to be provided for cleaning purposes.

Environmental Protection (EP) and Marine Pollution Regulations (MARPOL)

Disposal of food waste must meet the requirements of EP (JSP 418), DEFRA instructions and MARPOL legislation. Revised legislation relating to the disposal of raw meat and fish produced as waste product came into effect 01 Jul 03. Such products can no longer be sent to landfill for disposal. A transitional period until Dec05 has been granted before which DCG will publish policy regarding disposal of such products.

Annex A-The Five Principles of Hazard Analysis

Analysis of the Potential Food Hazards in a Food Business Operation

Food Hazard-A hazard is anything that could cause harm to the consumer. There are three main hazards that may arise with food served in catering premises. These are contamination of food by:

- Bacteria or other microorganisms that cause food poisoning.

- Chemicals, for example by cleaning materials or pest baits.
- Foreign materials such as glass, metal, plastic and so on.

Of these, the most important hazard is likely to be harmful bacteria or other germs that may contaminate and multiply in food. Identification of the Points in those Operations where Food Hazards may occur.

Food passes through many steps; delivery, storage, preparation, cooking, cooling and so on. Hazards can occur at many or all of the steps. For each type of food, the hazards that may occur at each step are to be identified. Mostly these will be steps in the operation where:

- Food can become Contaminated with microorganisms, chemicals or foreign material.
- Bacteria can Multiply if the food is held too long at the wrong temperature.
- Micro organisms Survive a process that should kill them, e.g. when cooking or disinfection of equipment is inadequate.

Deciding which of the critical points identified are critical to ensuring food safety.

Critical Points are steps at which the hazards must be controlled to ensure that a hazard is eliminated or reduced to a safe level.

- Any step where food may be become Contaminated is to be controlled. Controls include clean and disinfected equipment, the personal hygiene of staff, and separation of raw and cooked food. All food is to be protected from contamination by foreign bodies, pests or chemicals.
- Steps where bacteria may be able to Multiply in food must be controlled. The time and temperature at which food is held, stored or displayed are likely to be critical.
- Any cooking or reheating step is to be able to Kill harmful microorganisms. It will be critical that heating is thorough. Cooking is normally the most important control step in most food preparation. Chemical disinfection of equipment is another control point designed to Kill microorganisms.

Identification and implementation of effective control and monitoring procedures at those critical points

Controls must be set for the Critical Points, then Checks Introduced

Controls will either reduce the hazard to an acceptable level or get rid of it completely. The controls are to be precise as possible. For example, it is better to state that certain products will be stored under refrigeration at a set temperature, rather than to simply say that it must be kept in the chiller. A control target is to be set for every critical control point that has been identified. When controls have been set, it is then possible to Monitor the critical points whenever that preparation step is used. The targets can be checked. The frequency of checks is to be set for each control. Checking temperatures does not always involve probing food with a thermometer. Delivery vans or storage chillers may be fitted with temperature monitors and these can be checked. Other critical controls are more difficult to measure, e.g. cleaning & disinfection of equipment or the personal hygiene of staff. They will be often vital to the safety of food, and there are to be regular checks that standards are kept up. Review of the analysis of food hazards, the critical control points and the control and monitoring procedures periodically, and whenever the food business's operations change.

It is not satisfactory to go through this process once and forget about it. Occasionally the system may need to be reviewed and amended, for example:

- If controls or methods of checking are found to be ineffective or impracticable.
- The menu changes. New dishes may have new hazards and controls.
- The method of preparation changes.
- New equipment is introduced.

Annex B-Hazard Analysis

The Four-line Method

This annex contains:

a. Flow Diagram-An Overview of the Four-Lines.
b. Flow Diagram – LINE A – Food/dishes served cold.
c. Flow Diagram – LINE B – Food/dishes served hot.
d. Flow Diagram – LINE C – Food/dishes cooked, chilled and served cold.

e. Flow Diagram – LINE D – Food/dishes cooked. Chilled and reheated.

f. Hazard Analysis Flow Chart – LINE A.

g. Hazard Analysis Flow Chart – LINE B.

h. Hazard Analysis Flow Chart – LINE C.

i. Hazard Analysis Flow Chart – LINE D.

j. Galley/Kitchen/Mess Management Records:

   (1) Daily Food Safety management Record (Template)

   (2) Advance Food Preparation Record (Template)

   (3) Food Time/Temperature Record (Template)

   (4) Galley/Kitchen/Mess Fridge/Freezer/Blast Chiller Daily Monitoring Record (Template)

   (5) Galley/Kitchen/Mess Fridge/Freezer/Blast Chiller Monitoring Record (Template).

Use of the Four-Line Method

All caterers are to use this guide as a reference document. Each catering establishment will have unique hazards, which are to be annotated onto the template as a Control Point, a Critical Point or a Critical Control Point.

The Four-Line Method is to be used as follows:

a. Monitoring and Recording of the HAL's. Record the daily menu on single Service record forms. Determine high-risk menu items and, by referring to the Four-Line method guidance, annotate on the record the relevant Hazard Analysis Line (HAL) to the individual food dish.

b. Whilst the Four-Line method provides a system of HAL within kitchen and provision areas, other factors will need to be considered in ancillary kitchen areas e.g. delivery bays and pot/crock wash.

8

Safe Food Handling

Freezing and Food Safety

Foods in the freezer – are they safe? Every year, thousands of callers to the USDA Meat and Poultry Hotline aren't sure about the safety of items stored in their own home freezers. The confusion seems to be based on the fact that few people understand how freezing protects food. Here is some information on how to freeze food safely and how long to keep it.

What Can You Freeze?

You can freeze almost any food. Some exceptions are canned food or eggs in shells. However, once the food (such as a ham) is out of the can, you may freeze it. Being able to freeze food and being pleased with the quality after defrosting are two different things. Some foods simply don't freeze well. Examples are mayonnaise, cream sauce and lettuce. Raw meat and poultry maintain their quality longer than their cooked counterparts because moisture is lost during cooking.

Is Frozen Food Safe?

Food stored constantly at 0 °F will always be safe. Only the quality suffers with lengthy freezer storage. Freezing keeps food safe by slowing the movement of molecules, causing microbes to enter a dormant stage. Freezing preserves food for extended periods because it prevents the growth of microorganisms that cause both food spoilage and foodborne illness.

Does Freezing Destroy Bacteria & Parasites?

Freezing to 0 °F inactivates any microbes – bacteria, yeasts and molds-present in food. Once thawed, however, these microbes can again become active, multiplying under the right conditions to levels that can lead to foodborne illness. Since they will then grow at about the same rate as microorganisms on fresh food, you must handle thawed items as you would any perishable food.

Trichina and other parasites can be destroyed by subzero freezing temperatures. However, very strict government-supervised conditions must be met. It is not recommended to rely on home freezing to destroy trichina. Thorough cooking will destroy all parasites.

Freshness & Quality

Freshness and quality at the time of freezing affect the condition of frozen foods. If frozen at peak quality, foods emerge tasting better than foods frozen near the end of their useful life. So freeze items you won't use quickly sooner rather than later. Store all foods at 0° F or lower to retain vitamin content, colour, flavour and texture.

Nutrient Retention

The freezing process itself does not destroy nutrients. In meat and poultry products, there is little change in nutrient value during freezer storage.

Enzymes

Enzyme activity can lead to the deterioration of food quality. Enzymes present in animals, vegetables and fruit promote chemical reactions, such as ripening. Freezing only slows the enzyme activity that takes place in foods. It does not halt these reactions which continue after harvesting. Enzyme activity does not harm frozen meats or fish and is neutralized by the acids in frozen fruits. But most vegetables that freeze well are low acid and require a brief, partial cooking to prevent deterioration. This is called "blanching." For successful freezing, blanch or partially cook vegetables in boiling water or in a microwave oven. Then rapidly chill the vegetables prior to freezing and storage. Consult a cookbook for timing.

Packaging

Proper packaging helps maintain quality and prevent "freezer burn." It is safe to freeze meat or poultry directly in its supermarket wrapping but this type of wrap is permeable to air. Unless you will be using the food in a month or two, overwrap these packages as you would any food for long-term storage using airtight heavy-duty foil, (freezer) plastic wrap or freezer paper, or place the package inside a (freezer) plastic bag. Use these materials or airtight freezer containers to repackage family packs into smaller amounts. It is not necessary to rinse meat and poultry before freezing. Freeze unopened vacuum packages as is. If you notice that a package has accidentally been torn or has opened while food is in the freezer, the food is still safe to use; merely overwrap or rewrap it.

Freezer Burn

Freezer burn does not make food unsafe, merely dry in spots. It appears as grayish-brown leathery spots and is caused by air reaching the surface of the food. Cut freezer-burned portions away either before or after cooking the food. Heavily freezer-burned foods may have to be discarded for quality reasons.

Colour Changes

Colour changes can occur in frozen foods. The bright red colour of meat as purchased usually turns dark or pale brown depending on its variety. This may be due to lack of oxygen, freezer burn or abnormally long storage.

Freezing doesn't usually cause colour changes in poultry. However, the bones and the meat near them can become dark. Bone darkening results when pigment seeps through the porous bones of young poultry into the surrounding tissues when the poultry meat is frozen and thawed.

The dulling of colour in frozen vegetables and cooked foods is usually the result of excessive drying due to improper packaging or over-lengthy storage.

Freeze Rapidly

Freeze food as fast as possible to maintain its quality. Rapid freezing prevents undesirable large ice crystals from forming throughout the product because the molecules don't have time to take their positions in the characteristic six-sided snowflake. Slow freezing creates large, disruptive ice crystals. During thawing, they damage the cells and dissolve emulsions. This causes meat to "drip"—lose juiciness. Emulsions such as mayonnaise or cream will separate and appear curdled. Ideally, a food 2-inches thick should freeze completely in about 2 hours. If your home freezer has a "quick-freeze" shelf, use it. Never stack packages to be frozen. Instead, spread them out in one layer on various shelves, stacking them only after frozen solid.

Refrigerator-Freezers

If a refrigerator freezing compartment can't maintain zero degrees or if the door is opened frequently, use it for short-term food storage. Eat those foods as soon as possible for best quality. Use a freestanding freezer set at 0° F or below for long-term storage of frozen foods. Keep a thermometer in your freezing compartment or freezer to check the temperature. This is important if you experience power-out or mechanical problems.

Length of Time

Because freezing keeps food safe almost indefinitely, recommended storage times are for quality only. Refer to the freezer storage chart at the end of this document, which lists optimum freezing times for best quality.

If a food is not listed on the chart, you may determine its quality after defrosting. First check the odor. Some foods will develop a rancid or off odor when frozen too long and should be discarded. Some may not look picture perfect or be of high enough quality to serve alone but may be edible; use them to make soups or stews. Cook raw food and if you like the taste and texture, use it.

Safe Defrosting

Never defrost foods in a garage, basement, car, dishwasher or plastic garbage bag; out on the kitchen counter, outdoors or on the porch. These methods can leave your foods unsafe to eat.

There are three safe ways to defrost food: in the refrigerator, in cold water, or in the microwave. It's best to plan ahead for slow, safe thawing in the refrigerator. Small items may defrost overnight; most foods require a day or two. And large items like turkeys may take longer, approximately one day for each 5 pounds of weight.

For faster defrosting, place food in a leak proof plastic bag and immerse it in cold water. (If the bag leaks, bacteria from the air or surrounding environment could be introduced into the food. Tissues can also absorb water like a sponge, resulting in a watery product.) Check the water frequently to be sure it stays cold. Change the water every 30 minutes. After thawing, cook immediately. When microwave-defrosting food, plan to cook it immediately after thawing because some areas of the food may become warm and begin to cook during microwaving.

Refreezing

Once food is thawed in the refrigerator, it is safe to refreeze it without cooking, although there may be a loss of quality due to the moisture lost through defrosting. After cooking raw foods which were previously frozen, it is safe to freeze the cooked foods. If previously cooked foods are thawed in the refrigerator, you may refreeze the unused portion. If you purchase previously frozen meat, poultry or fish at a retail store, you can refreeze if it has been handled properly.

Cooking Frozen Foods

Raw or cooked meat, poultry or casseroles can be cooked or reheated from the frozen state. However, it will take approximately one and a half times the usual cooking time for food which has been thawed. Remember to discard any wrapping or absorbent paper from meat or poultry.

When cooking whole poultry, remove the giblet pack from the cavity as soon as you can loosen it. Cook the giblets separately. Read the label on USDA-inspected frozen meat and poultry products. Some, such as pre-stuffed whole birds, MUST be cooked from the frozen state to ensure a safely cooked product.

Look for the Usda or State Mark of Inspection

The inspection mark on the packaging tells you the product was prepared in a USDA or State-inspected plant under controlled conditions. Follow the package directions for thawing, reheating, and storing.

Power Outage in Freezer

If there is a power outage, the freezer fails, or if the freezer door has been left ajar by mistake, the food may still be safe to use. As long as a freezer with its door ajar is continuing to cool, the foods should stay safe overnight. If a repairman is on the way or it appears the power will be on soon, just don't open the freezer door.

A freezer full of food will usually keep about 2 days if the door is kept shut; a half-full freezer will last about a day. The freezing compartment in a refrigerator may not keep foods frozen as long. If the freezer is not full, quickly group packages together so they will retain the cold more effectively. Separate meat and poultry items from other foods so if they begin to thaw, their juices won't drip onto other foods. When the power is off, you may want to put dry ice, block ice, or bags of ice in the freezer or transfer foods to a friend's freezer until power is restored. Use an appliance thermometer to monitor the temperature.

When it is freezing outside and there is snow on the ground, it seems like a good place to keep food until the power comes on; however, frozen food can thaw if it is exposed to the sun's rays even when the temperature is very cold. Refrigerated food may become too warm and foodborne bacteria could grow. The outside temperature could vary hour by hour and the temperature outside will not protect refrigerated and frozen food. Additionally, perishable items could be exposed to unsanitary conditions or to animals. Animals may harbour bacteria or disease; never consume food that has come in contact with an animal.

To determine the safety of foods when the power goes on, check their condition and temperature. If food is partly frozen, still has ice crystals, or is as cold as if it were in a refrigerator (40 °F), it is safe to refreeze or use. It's not necessary to cook raw foods before refreezing. Discard foods that have been warmer than 40 °F for more than 2 hours. Discard any foods that have been contaminated by raw meat juices. Dispose of soft or melted ice cream for quality's sake.

Frozen Cans

Accidentally frozen cans, such as those left in a car or basement in subzero temperatures, can present health problems. If the cans are merely swollen – and you are sure the swelling was caused by freezing – the cans may still be usable. Let the can thaw in the refrigerator before opening. If the product doesn't look and/ or smell normal, throw it out. DO NOT TASTE IT! If the seams have rusted or burst, throw the cans out immediately, wrapping the burst can in plastic and disposing the food where no one, including animals can get it.

Frozen Eggs

Shell eggs should not be frozen. If an egg accidentally freezes and the shell cracked during freezing, discard the egg. Keep an uncracked egg frozen until needed; then thaw in the refrigerator. It can be hard cooked successfully but other uses may be limited. That's because freezing causes the yolk to become thick and syrupy so it will not flow like an unfrozen yolk or blend very well with the egg white or other ingredients.

Freezer Storage Chart (0 °F)

Note: Freezer storage is for quality only.)Frozen foods remain safe indefinitely.

Item	Months
Bacon and Sausage	1 to 2
Casseroles	2 to 3
Egg whites or egg substitutes	12
Frozen Dinners and Entrees	3 to 4
Gravy, meat or poultry	2 to 3
Ham, Hotdogs and Lunchmeats	1 to 2
Meat, uncooked roasts	4 to 12
Meat, uncooked steaks or chops	4 to 12
Meat, uncooked ground	3 to 4
Meat, cooked	2 to 3
Poultry, uncooked whole	12
Poultry, uncooked parts	9
Poultry, uncooked giblets	3 to 4
Poultry, cooked	4
Soups and Stews	2 to 3
Wild game, uncooked	8 to 12

Handling Food Safely on the Road

V-A-C-A-T-I-O-N! Oh, how we long for that eight letter word every summer, when millions of us eagerly get away from school and work. We take to the road in cars or recreational vehicles; live on boats; relax in beach or mountain vacation homes; and camp.

No matter where we go or what we do, there is a common denominator that runs through all of our summer travels and relaxation – it's called F-O-O-D!

The "road" to food safety, however, can either be a bumpy one or smooth – depending on what precautions are taken handling meals as we travel this summer.

The U.S. Department of Agriculture's nationwide, toll-free Meat and Poultry Hotline reminds everyone that some simple, common-sense food safety rules can save a vacation from disaster. Following this advice could make the difference between a vacation to remember and one that is remembered because people got sick from improperly handled food. First, some general rules, while travelling this summer:

Remember!

In hot weather (above 90°F), food should never sit out for more than 1 hour. Discard any food left out more than 2 hours (1 hour if temperatures are above 90°F).

Plan Ahead...If you are travelling with perishable food, place it in a cooler with ice or freezer packs. When carrying drinks, consider packing them in a separate cooler so the food cooler is not opened frequently. Have plenty of ice or frozen gel-packs on hand before starting to pack food. If you take perishable foods along for eating on the road or to cook at your vacation spot, plan to keep everything on ice in your cooler.

Pack Safely...Pack perishable foods directly from the refrigerator or freezer into the cooler. Meat and poultry may be packed while it is still frozen; in that way it stays colder longer. Also, a full cooler will maintain its cold temperatures longer than one that is partially filled. Be sure to keep raw meat and poultry wrapped separately from cooked foods, or foods meant to be eaten raw such as fruits.

If the cooler is only partially filled, pack the remaining space with more ice. For long trips to the shore or the mountains, take along two coolers — one for the day's immediate food needs, such as lunch, drinks or snacks, and the other for perishable foods to be used later in the vacation. Limit the times the cooler is opened. Open and close the lid quickly. Now, follow these food safety tips:

When Camping...Remember to keep the cooler in a shady spot. Keep it covered with a blanket, tarp or poncho, preferably one that is light in colour to reflect heat.

Bring along bottled water or other canned or bottled drinks. Always assume that streams and rivers are not safe for drinking. If camping in a remote area, bring along water purification tablets or equipment. These are available at camping supply stores. Keep hands and all utensils clean when preparing food. Use disposable moist towelettes to clean hands. When planning meals, think about buying and using shelf-stable food to ensure food safety.

When Boating...If boating on vacation, or out for the day, make sure the all-important cooler is along. Don't let perishable food sit out while swimming or fishing. Remember, food sitting out for more than 2 hours is not safe. The time frame is reduced to just 1 hour if the outside temperature is above 90 °F.

Now, about that "catch" of fish — assuming the big one did not get away. For fin fish: scale, gut and clean the fish as soon as they are caught. Wrap both whole and cleaned fish in water-tight plastic and store on ice. Keep 3-4 inches of ice on the bottom of the cooler. Alternate layers of fish and ice. Cook the fish in 1-2 days, or freeze. After cooking, eat within 3-4 days. Make sure the raw fish stays separate from cooked foods.

Crabs, lobsters and other shellfish must be kept alive until cooked. Store in a bushel or laundry basket under wet burlap. Crabs and lobsters are best eaten the day they are caught. Live oysters can keep 7-10 days; mussels and clams, 4-5 days.

Caution: Be aware of the potential dangers of eating raw shellfish. This is especially true for persons with liver disorders or weakened immune systems. However, no one should eat raw shellfish.

When at the Beach

Plan ahead. Take along only the amount of food that can be eaten to avoid having leftovers. If grilling, make sure local ordinances allow it. Bring the cooler! Partially bury it in the sand, cover with blankets, and shade with a beach umbrella. Bring along disposable moist towelettes for cleaning hands.

If dining along the boardwalk, make sure the food stands frequented look clean, and that hot foods are served hot and cold foods cold. Don't eat anything that has been sitting out in the hot sun for more than 2 hours (1 hour when the temperature is above 90 °F) — a real invitation for foodborne illness and a spoiled vacation.

When in the Vacation Home or the Recreation Vehicle...If a vacation home or a recreational vehicle has not been used for a while, check leftover canned food from last year. The Meat and Poultry Hotline recommends that canned foods which may have been exposed to freezing and thawing temperatures over the winter be discarded. Also, check the refrigerator. If unplugged from last year, thoroughly clean it before using. Make sure the refrigerator, food preparation areas, and utensils in the vacation home or in the recreational vehicle are thoroughly cleaned with hot soapy water.

Molds On Food: Are They Dangerous?

Some molds cause allergic reactions and respiratory problems. And a few molds, in the right conditions, produce "mycotoxins," poisonous substances that can make people sick. When you see mold on food, is it safe to cut off the moldy part and use the rest? To find the answer to that question, delve beneath the surface of food to where molds take root.

What Are Molds?

Molds are microscopic fungi that live on plant or animal matter. No one knows how many species of fungi exist, but estimates range from tens of thousands to perhaps 300,000 or more. Most are filamentous (threadlike) organisms and the production of spores is characteristic of fungi in general. These spores can be transported by air, water, or insects. Unlike bacteria that are one-celled, molds are made of many cells and can sometimes be seen with the naked eye. Under a microscope, they look like skinny mushrooms. In many molds, the body consists of:

- root threads that invade the food it lives on,
- a stalk rising above the food, and
- spores that form at the ends of the stalks.

The spores give mold the colour you see. When airborne, the spores spread the mold from place to place like dandelion seeds blowing across a meadow. Molds have branches and roots that are like very thin threads. The roots may be difficult to see when the mold is growing on food and may be very deep in the food. Foods that are moldy may also have invisible bacteria growing along with the mold.

Are Some Molds Dangerous?

Yes, some molds cause allergic reactions and respiratory problems. And a few molds, in the right conditions, produce "mycotoxins," poisonous substances that can make you sick.

Are Molds Only on the Surface of Food?

No, you only see part of the mold on the surface of food – gray fur on forgotten bologna, fuzzy green dots on bread, white dust on Cheddar, coin-size velvety circles on fruits, and furry growth on the surface of jellies. When a food shows heavy mold growth, "root" threads have invaded it deeply. In dangerous molds, poisonous substances are often contained in and around these threads. In some cases, toxins may have spread throughout the food.

Where are Molds Found?

Molds are found in virtually every environment and can be detected, both indoors and outdoors, year round. Mold growth is encouraged by warm and humid conditions. Outdoors, they can be found in shady, damp areas or places where leaves or other vegetation are decomposing. Indoors, they can be found where humidity levels are high. Molds form spores which, when dry, float through the air and find suitable conditions where they can start the growth cycle again.

What are Some Common Foodborne Molds?

Molds most often found on meat and poultry are *Alternaria, Aspergillus, Botrytis, Cladosporium, Fusarium, Geotrichum, Monilia, Manoscus, Mortierella, Mucor, Neurospora, Oidium, Oosproa, Penicillium, Rhizopus* and *Thamnidium*. These molds can also be found on many other foods.

What are Mycotoxins?

Mycotoxins are poisonous substances produced by certain molds found primarily in grain and nut crops, but are also known to be on celery, grape juice, apples, and other produce. There are many of them and scientists are continually discovering new ones. The Food and Agriculture Organization (FAO) of the United Nations estimates that 25% of the world's food crops are affected by mycotoxins, of which the most notorious are aflatoxins.

What is Aflatoxin?

Aflatoxin is a cancer-causing poison produced by certain fungi in or on foods and feeds, especially in field corn and peanuts. They are probably the best known and most intensively researched mycotoxins in the world. Aflatoxins have been associated with various diseases, such as aflatoxicosis in livestock, domestic animals, and humans throughout the world. Many countries try to limit exposure to aflatoxin by regulating and monitoring its presence on commodities intended for use as food and feed. The prevention of aflatoxin is one of the most challenging toxicology issues of present time.

How Does the U.S. Government Control Aflatoxins?

Aflatoxins are considered unavoidable contaminants of food and feed, even where good manufacturing practices have been followed. The U.S. Food and Drug Administration and the USDA monitor peanuts and field corn for aflatoxin and can remove any food or feed with unacceptable levels of it.

Is Mushroom Poisoning Caused by Molds?

No, it is due to the toxin produced by the fungi, which are in the same family as molds. Mushroom poisoning is caused by the consumption of raw or cooked mushrooms, which are higher-species of fungi. The term "toadstool" (from the German "Todesstuhl" — death's stool) is commonly given to poisonous mushrooms, but there is no general rule of thumb for distinguishing edible mushrooms from poisonous toadstools. The toxins that cause mushroom poisoning are produced naturally by the fungi. Most mushrooms that cause human poisoning cannot be made safe by cooking, canning, freezing, or any other processing. The only way to avoid poisoning is not to eat poisonous mushrooms.

Are any Food Molds Beneficial?

Yes, molds are used to make certain kinds of cheeses and can be on the surface of cheese or be developed internally. Blue veined cheese such as Roquefort, blue, Gorgonzola, and Stilton are created by the introduction of *P. Roqueforti* or *Penicillium roqueforti* spores. Cheeses such as Brie and Camembert have white surface molds. Other cheeses have both an internal and a surface mold. The molds used to manufacture these cheeses are safe to eat.

Why can Mold Grow in the Refrigerator?

While most molds prefer warmer temperatures, they can grow at refrigerator temperatures, too. Molds also tolerate salt and sugar better than most other food invaders. Therefore, molds can grow in refrigerated jams and jelly and on cured, salty meats — ham, bacon, salami, and bologna.

How can You Minimize Mold Growth?

Cleanliness is vital in controlling mold. Mold spores from affected food can build up in your refrigerator, dishcloths, and other cleaning utensils.

- Clean the inside of the refrigerator every few months with 1 tablespoon of baking soda dissolved in a quart of water. Rinse with clear water and dry. Scrub visible mold (usually black) on rubber casings using 3 teaspoons of bleach in a quart of water.
- Keep dishcloths, towels, sponges, and mops clean and fresh. A musty smell means they're spreading mold around. Discard items you can't clean or launder.
- Keep the humidity level in the house below 40%.

Don't Buy Moldy Foods

Examine food well before you buy it. Check food in glass jars, look at the stem areas on fresh produce, and avoid bruised produce. Notify the store manager about mold on foods!

Fresh meat and poultry are usually mold free, but cured and cooked meats may not be. Examine them carefully. Exceptions: Some salamis — San Francisco, Italian, and Eastern European types — have a characteristic thin, white mold coating which is safe to consume; however, they shouldn't show any other mold. Dry-cured country hams normally have surface mold that must be scrubbed off before cooking.

Must Homemade Shelf-Stable Preserves be Water-Buth Processed?

Yes, molds can thrive in high-acid foods like jams, jellies, pickles, fruit, and tomatoes. But these microscopic fungi are easily destroyed by heat processing high-acid foods at a temperature of 212 °F in a boiling water canner for the recommended length of time.

How Can You Protect Food from Mold?

- When serving food, keep it covered to prevent exposure to mold spores in the air. Use plastic wrap to cover foods you want to stay moist — fresh or cut fruits and vegetables, and green and mixed salads.

- Empty opened cans of perishable foods into clean storage containers and refrigerate them promptly.
- Don't leave any perishables out of the refrigerator more than 2 hours.
- Use leftovers within 3 to 4 days so mold doesn't have a chance to grow.

How Should You Handle Food with Mold on It?

Buying small amounts and using food quickly can help prevent mold growth. But when you see moldy food:

- Don't sniff the moldy item. This can cause respiratory trouble.
- If food is covered with mold, discard it. Put it into a small paper bag or wrap it in plastic and dispose in a covered trash can that children and animals can't get into.
- Clean the refrigerator or pantry at the spot where the food was stored.
- Check nearby items the moldy food might have touched. Mold spreads quickly in fruits and vegetables.
- See the attached chart "Moldy Food: When to Use, When to Discard."

Beef...from Farm to Table

Since 1910, the first year that statistics were compiled, Americans have been eating an average of 60 pounds of beef yearly. About 36 million cattle were inspected in 1997 alone by USDA's Food Safety and Inspection Service. This translates into 64 pounds of beef per person in 1997. In calls to the Hotline, beef is the third food category (behind turkey and chicken) callers most ask about. The following information answers many of their questions.

What is Beef?

The domestication of cattle for food dates to about 6500 B.C. in the Middle East. Cattle were not native to America, but brought to the New World on ships by European colonists. Americans weren't big eaters of fresh beef until about 1870, due to the enormous growth of the cattle industry in the West. The introduction of cattle cars and refrigerated cars on the railroad facilitated distribution of the beef.

"Beef" is meat from full-grown cattle about 2 years old. A live steer weighs about 1,000 pounds and yields about 450 pounds of edible meat. There are at least 50 breeds of beef cattle, but fewer than 10 make up most cattle produced. Some major breeds are Angus, Hereford, Charolais, and Brahman.

"Baby beef" and "calf" are 2 interchangeable terms used to describe young cattle weighing about 700 pounds that have been raised mainly on milk and grass. The meat cuts from baby beef are smaller; the meat is light red and contains less fat than beef. The fat may have a yellow tint due to the vitamin A in grass.

"Veal" is meat from a calf which weighs about 150 pounds. Those that are mainly milk-fed usually are less than 3 months old. The difference between "veal" and "calf" is based on the colour of their meat, which is determined almost entirely by diet. Veal is pale pink and contains more cholesterol than beef.

Note: This information is about whole muscle beef and variety beef. "Focus on Ground Beef" for information about hamburger and ground beef.

How are Cattle Raised?

All cattle start out eating grass; three-fourths of them are "finished" (grown to maturity) in feedlots where they are fed specially formulated feed based on corn or other grains.

Can Hormones & Antibiotics be Used in Cattle Raising?

Antibiotics may be given to prevent or treat disease in cattle. A "withdrawal" period is required from the time antibiotics are administered until it is legal to slaughter the animal. This is so residues can exit the animal's system. FSIS randomly samples cattle at slaughter and tests for residues. Data from this Monitoring Plan have shown a very low percentage of residue violations. Not all antibiotics are approved for use in all classes of cattle. However, if there is a demonstrated therapeutic need, a veterinarian may prescribe an antibiotic that is approved in other classes for an animal in a non-approved class. In this case, no detectable residues of this drug may be present in the edible tissues of the animal at slaughter.

Hormones may be used to promote efficient growth. Estradiol, progesterone, and testosterone (three natural hormones), and zeranol and trenbolone acetate (two synthetic hormones) may be used as an implant on the animal's ear. The hormone is time released, and is effective for 90 to 120 days. In addition, melengesterol acetate, which can be used to suppress estrus, or improve weight gain and feed efficiency, is approved for use as a feed additive. Not all combinations of hormones are approved for use in all classes of cattle. Hormones are approved for specific classes of animals only, and cannot be used in non-approved classes.

How is Beef Inspected?

Inspection is mandatory; grading is voluntary, and a plant pays to have its meat graded. USDA-graded beef sold at the retail level is Prime, Choice, and Select. Lower grades (Standard, Commercial, Utility, Cutter, and Canner) are mainly ground or used in processed meat products. Retail stores may use other terms which must be different from USDA grades.

USDA Prime beef (about two percent of graded beef) has more fat marbling, so it is the most tender and flavourful. However, it is higher in fat content. Most of the graded beef sold in supermarkets is USDA Choice or USDA Select. The protein, vitamin, and mineral content of beef are similar regardless of the grade.

How is Ungraded Beef Different?

All beef is inspected for wholesomeness. The overall quality of ungraded beef may be higher or lower than most government grades found in retail markets.

What is Marbling?

Marbling is white flecks of fat within the meat muscle. The greater amount of marbling in beef, the higher the grade because marbling makes beef more tender, flavourful, and juicy.

Retail Cuts of Fresh Beef

There are four basic major (primal) cuts into which beef is separated: chuck, loin, rib, and round. It is recommended that packages of fresh beef purchased in the supermarket be labelled with the primal cut as well as the product, such as "chuck roast" or "round steak." This helps consumers know what type of heat is best for cooking the product. Generally, chuck and round are less tender and require moist heat such as braising; loin and rib can be cooked by dry heat methods such as broiling or grilling.

Unfortunately, names for various cuts can vary regionally in stores, causing confusion over the choice of cooking method. For example, a boneless top loin steak is variously called: strip steak, Kansas City Steak, N.Y. strip steak, hotel cut strip steak, ambassador steak, or club sirloin steak.

How Much Beef Is Consumed?

Figures from the USDA's Economic Research Service show average annual per capita beef consumption for the following selected periods:

How Much Beef is Consumed?

Year	Weight	Year	Weight
1910-15	51 pounds	1960-65	69 pounds
1920-25	46 pounds	1970-75	85 pounds
1930-35	41 pounds	1980-85	78 pounds
1940-45	45 pounds	1990-95	67 pounds
1950-55	55 pounds	1995-97	64 pounds

Nutrition Labelling

Nutrition claims such as "lean" and "extra lean" are sometimes seen on beef products. Here are their definitions:

"Lean"-100 grams of beef with less than 10 grams of fat, 4.5 grams or less of saturated fat, and less than 95 milligrams of cholesterol. "Extra Lean"-100 grams of beef with less than 5 grams of fat, less than 2 grams of saturated fat, and less than 95 milligrams of cholesterol.

What Does "Natural" Mean?

All fresh meat qualifies as "natural." Products labelled "natural" cannot contain any artificial flavour or flavouring, colouring ingredient, chemical preservative, or any other artificial or synthetic ingredient; and the product and its ingredients are not more than minimally processed (ground, for example). All products claiming to be natural should be accompanied by a brief statement which explains what is meant by the term "natural."

Some companies promote their beef as "natural" because they claim their cattle weren't exposed to antibiotics or hormones and were totally raised on a range instead of being "finished" in a feedlot.

How & Why is some Beef Aged?

Beef is aged to develop additional tenderness and flavour. It is done commercially under controlled temperatures and humidity. Since aging can take from 10 days to 6 weeks, USDA does not recommend aging beef in a home refrigerator.

Why is Beef Called a "Red" Meat?

Oxygen is delivered to muscles by the red cells in the blood. One of the proteins in meat, myoglobin, holds the oxygen in the muscle. The amount of myoglobin in animal muscles determines the colour of meat. Beef is called a "red" meat because it contains more myoglobin than chicken or fish. Other "red" meats are veal, lamb, and pork.

Colour of Beef

Beef muscle meat not exposed to oxygen (in vacuum packaging, for example) is a burgundy or purplish colour. After exposure to the air for 15 minutes or so, the myoglobin receives oxygen and the meat turns bright, cherry red. After beef has been refrigerated about 5 days, it may turn brown due to chemical changes in the myoglobin. Beef that has turned brown during extended storage may be spoiled, have an off-odor, and be tacky to the touch.

Iridescent Colour of Roast Beef

Sliced cooked beef or lunch meat can have an iridescent colour. Meat contains iron, fat, and many other compounds. When light hits a slice of meat, it splits into colours like a rainbow. There are also various pigments in meat compounds which can give it an iridescent or greenish cast when exposed to heat and processing. Iridescent beef isn't spoiled necessarily. Spoiled cooked beef would probably also be slimy or sticky and have an off-odor.

Additives : Additives are not allowed on fresh beef. If beef is processed, additives such as MSG, salt, or sodium erythorbate must be listed on the label.

Dating of Beef Products : Product dating is not required by Federal regulations. However, many stores and processors may voluntarily date packages of raw beef or processed beef products. If a calendar date is shown, there must be a phrase explaining the meaning of the date. Use or freeze products with a "Sell-By" date within 3 to 5 days of purchase. If the manufacturer has determined a "Use-By" date, observe it. This is a quality assurance date after which peak quality begins to lessen but the product may still be used. It's always best to buy a product before its date expires. It's not important if a date expires after freezing beef because all foods stay safe while properly frozen.

What Foodborne Organisms are Associated with Beef?

Escherichia coli can colonize in the intestines of animals, which could contaminate muscle meat at slaughter. *E. Coli* O157:H7 is a rare strain that produces large quantities of a potent toxin that forms in and causes severe damage to the lining of the intestine. The disease produced by it is called Hemorrhagic Colitis and is characterized by bloody diarrhea. *E. coli* O157:H7 is easily destroyed by thorough cooking.

Salmonella may be found in the intestinal tracts of livestock, poultry, dogs, cats, and other warm-blooded animals. There are about 2,000 *Salmonella* bacterial species. Freezing doesn't kill this microorganism, but it is destroyed by thorough cooking. *Salmonella* must be eaten to cause illness. They cannot enter the body through a skin cut. Cross-contamination can occur if raw meat or its juices contact cooked food or foods that will be eaten raw, such as salad.

Staphylococcus aureus can be carried on human hands, nasal passages, or throats. Most foodborne illness outbreaks are a result of contamination from food handlers and production of a heat-stable toxin in the food. Sanitary food handling and proper cooking and refrigerating should prevent staphylococcal foodborne illness.

Listeria monocytogenes is destroyed by cooking, but a cooked product can be recontaminated by poor handling practices and poor sanitation. FSIS has a zero tolerance for *Listeria monocytogenes* in cooked and ready-to-eat products such as beef franks or lunchmeat. Observe handling information such as "Keep Refrigerated" and "Use-By" dates on labels.

Rinsing Beef

It isn't necessary to wash raw beef before cooking it. Any bacteria which might be present on the surface would be destroyed by cooking.

How to Handle Beef Safely

- Raw Beef: Select beef just before checking out at the register. Put packages of raw beef in disposable plastic bags, if available, to contain any leakage which could cross-contaminate cooked foods or produce. Beef, a perishable product, is kept cold during store distribution to retard the growth of bacteria.

Take beef home immediately and refrigerate it at 40 °F; use within 3 to 5 days (1 or 2 days for variety meats such as liver, kidneys, tripe, sweetbreads, or tongue) or freeze (0 °F). If kept frozen continuously, it will be safe indefinitely.

It is safe to freeze beef in its original packaging or repackage it. However, for long-term freezing, overwrap the porous store plastic with aluminum foil, freezer paper, or freezer-weight plastic wrap or bags to prevent "freezer burn," which appears as grayish-brown leathery spots and is caused by air reaching the surface of food. Cut freezer-burned portions away either before or after cooking the beef. Heavily freezer-burned products may have to be discarded for quality reasons. For best quality, use steaks and roasts within 9 to 12 months.

- Ready-Prepared Beef: For fully-cooked, take-out beef dishes such as Chinese food, barbecued ribs, or fast food hamburgers, be sure they are hot at pickup. Use cooked beef within 2 hours (1 hour if the air temperature is above 90 °F) or refrigerate it at 40 °F in shallow, covered containers. Eat within 3 to 4 days, either cold or reheated to 165 °F (hot and steaming). It is safe to freeze ready-prepared beef dishes. For best quality, use within 4 months.

Safe Defrosting

There are three safe ways to defrost beef: in the refrigerator, in cold water, and in the microwave. Never defrost on the counter or in other locations.

- Refrigerator:. It's best to plan ahead for slow, safe thawing in the refrigerator. Ground beef, stew meat, and steaks may defrost within a day. Bone-in parts and whole roasts may take 2 days or longer. Once the raw beef defrosts, it will be safe in the refrigerator for 3 to 5 days before cooking. During this time, if you decide not to use the beef, you can safely refreeze it without cooking it first.
- Cold Water:. To defrost beef in cold water, do not remove packaging. Be sure the package is airtight or put it into a leakproof bag. Submerge the beef in cold water, changing

the water every 30 minutes so that it continues to thaw. Small packages of beef may defrost in an hour or less; a 3-to 4-pound roast may take 2 to 3 hours.

- Microwave:. When microwave defrosting beef, plan to cook it immediately after thawing because some areas of the food may become warm and begin to cook during microwaving. Holding partially-cooked food is not recommended because any bacteria present wouldn't have been destroyed.

Foods defrosted in the microwave or by the cold water method should be cooked before refreezing because they may have been held at temperatures above 40 °F.

It is safe to cook frozen beef in the oven, on the stove, or grill without defrosting it first; the cooking time may be about 50% longer. Do not cook frozen beef in a slow cooker.

Marinating : Marinate beef in the refrigerator up to 5 days. Boil used marinade before brushing on cooked beef. Discard any uncooked leftover marinade.

Partial Cooking : Never brown or partially cook beef to refrigerate and finish cooking later because any bacteria present wouldn't have been destroyed. It is safe to partially pre-cook or microwave beef immediately before transferring it to the hot grill to finish cooking.

Liquid in Package : Many people think the red liquid in packaged fresh beef is blood. However, blood is removed from beef during slaughter and only a small amount remains within the muscle tissue. Since beef is about 3/4 water, this natural moisture combined with protein is the source of the liquid in the package.

Microwave Directions

- When microwaving unequal size pieces of beef, arrange in dish or on rack so thick parts are toward the outside of dish and thin parts are in the centre; cook on medium-high or medium power.
- Place a roast in an oven cooking bag or in a covered pot.
- Refer to the manufacturer's directions that accompany the microwave oven for suggested cooking times.
- Use a meat thermometer to test for doneness in several places to be sure temperatures listed above have been reached.

Storage Times

Since product dates aren't a guide for safe use of a product, how long can the consumer store the food and still use it at top quality? Follow these tips:

- Purchase the product before the date expires.
- Follow handling recommendations on product.
- Keep beef in its package until using.
- It is safe to freeze beef in its original packaging. If freezing longer than 2 months, overwrap these packages with airtight heavy-duty foil, plastic wrap, or freezer paper or place the package inside a plastic bag.
- For storage times, consult the following chart.

Focus on Ground Beef

Questions about "ground meat" or "hamburger" have always been in the top five food topics of calls to the USDA's Meat and Poultry Hotline. Here are the most frequently asked questions.

What's the difference between "hamburger" and "ground beef"?

Beef fat may be added to "hamburger," but not "ground beef," if the meat is ground and packaged at a USDA-inspected plant. A maximum of 30% fat by weight is allowed in either hamburger or ground beef. Both hamburger and ground beef can have seasonings, but no water, phosphates, extenders, or binders added. They must be labelled in accordance with Federal Standards and Labelling Policy and marked with a USDA-inspected label.

Most ground beef is ground and packaged in local stores rather than in food processing plants under USDA inspection. Even so, the Federal labelling laws on fat content apply. Most states and cities set standards for store-packaged ground beef which, by law, cannot be less than Federal standards. If products in retail stores were found to contain more than 30% fat by weight, they would be considered "adulterated" under Federal law.

Is ground beef inspected and graded?

All meat transported and sold in interstate commerce must be federally inspected. The larger cuts are usually shipped to local stores where they are ground. The Food Safety and Inspection Service carries out USDA's responsibilities under the Federal Meat

Inspection Act. These laws protect consumers by ensuring that meat products are wholesome, unadulterated, and properly marked, labelled, and packaged.

For meat being transported and sold within a state, state inspection would apply. State inspection programs must enforce requirements at least equal to those of Federal inspection laws.

Grades are assigned as a standard of quality only. It is voluntary for a company to hire a Federal inspector to certify the quality of its product. Beef grades are USDA Prime, Choice, Select, Standard, Commercial, Utility, Cutter, and Canner. They are set by the USDA Agricultural Marketing Service. Most ground beef is not graded.

From what cuts of beef are ground beef and hamburger made?

Generally, ground beef is made from the less tender and less popular cuts of beef. Trimmings from more tender cuts may also be used. Grinding tenderizes the meat and the fat reduces its dryness and improves flavour.

What is the Significance of the "Sell-By" Date on the Package?

"Sell-By" dates are a guide for retailers. Although many products bear "Sell-By" dates, product dating is not a Federal requirement. While these dates are helpful to the retailer, they are reliable only if the food has been kept at proper temperature during storage and handling. USDA suggests that consumers cook or freeze ground beef within 2 days after purchase for maximum quality.

What is the safe food handling label now on meat and poultry packages?

A safe food handling label should be on all raw or partially precooked (not ready-to-eat) meat and poultry packages. The label tells the consumer how to safely store, prepare, and handle raw meat and poultry products in the home.

What kind of bacteria can be in ground beef? Are they dangerous?

Bacteria are everywhere in our environment. Any food of animal origin can harbour bacteria. Pathogenic bacteria, such as *Salmonella, Escherichia coli* O157:H7, *Campylobacter jejuni, Listeria monocytogenes,* and *Staphylococcus aureus,* cause illness. These harmful bacteria can not be seen or smelled.

When meat is ground, more of the meat is exposed to the harmful bacteria. Bacteria multiply rapidly in the "Danger Zone" —

temperatures between 40 and 140 °F. To keep bacterial levels low, store ground beef at 40 °F or less and use within 2 days, or freeze. To destroy harmful bacteria, cook ground beef to 160 °F.

Other bacteria cause spoilage. Spoilage bacteria are generally not harmful, but they will cause food to deteriorate or lose quality by developing a bad odor or feeling sticky on the outside.

Why is the E. Coli O157:H7 bacterium of special concern in ground beef?

E. Coli O157:H7 can colonize in the intestines of animals, which could contaminate muscle meat at slaughter.

O157:H7 is a strain of *E. Coli* that produces large quantities of a potent toxin that forms in the intestine and causes severe damage to the lining of the intestine. The disease produced by the bacteria is called Hemorrhagic Colitis.

E. Coli O157:H7 survive refrigerator and freezer temperatures. Once they get in food, they can multiply very slowly at temperatures as low as 44 °F. The actual infectious dose is unknown, but most scientists believe it takes only a small number of this strain of *E. Coli* to cause serious illness and even death, especially in children. It is killed by thorough cooking.

Illnesses caused by *E. Coli* O157:H7 have been linked with the consumption of ground beef. Raw milk, apple cider, dry cured sausage, and undercooked roast beef have also been implicated.

Can bacteria spread from one surface to another?

Yes. It is called cross-contamination. Bacteria in raw meat juices can contaminate foods that have been cooked safely or raw foods that won't be cooked, such as salad ingredients. Bacteria can also be present on equipment, hands, and even in the air.

To avoid cross-contamination, wash your hands with soap and hot water before and after handling ground beef to make sure you don't spread bacteria. Don't reuse any packaging materials. Use soap and hot water to wash utensils and surfaces which have come into contact with the raw meat. Don't put cooked hamburgers on the same platter that held the raw patties.

What's the best way to handle raw ground beef when I buy it?

At the store, choose a package that is not torn and feels cold. If possible, enclose it in a plastic bag so leaking juices won't drip on other foods. Make ground beef one of the last items to go into your shopping cart. Separate raw meat from ready-cooked items in your cart. Have the clerk bag raw meat, poultry, and fish separately from other items.

Plan to drive directly home from the grocery store. You may want to take a cooler with ice for perishables.

How should raw ground beef be stored at home?

Refrigerate or freeze ground beef as soon as possible after purchase. This preserves freshness and slows growth of bacteria. It can be refrigerated or frozen in its original packaging if the meat will be used soon.

If refrigerated, keep at 40 °F or below and use within 1 or 2 days.

For longer freezer storage, wrap in heavy duty plastic wrap, aluminum foil, freezer paper, or plastic bags made for freezing. Ground beef is safe indefinitely if kept frozen, but will lose quality over time. It is best if used within 4 months. Mark your packages with the date they were placed in the freezer so you can keep track of storage times.

What is the best way to thaw ground beef?

The best way to safely thaw ground beef is in the refrigerator. Keeping meat cold while it is defrosting is essential to prevent growth of bacteria. Cook or refreeze it within 1 or 2 days.

To defrost ground beef more rapidly, you can defrost in the microwave oven or in cold water. If using the microwave, cook the ground beef immediately because some areas may begin to cook during the defrosting. To defrost in cold water, put the meat in a watertight plastic bag and submerge. Change the water every 30 minutes. Cook immediately. Do not refreeze ground meat thawed in cold water or in the microwave oven.

Never leave ground beef or any perishable food out at room temperature for more than 2 hours.

Is it dangerous to eat raw or undercooked ground beef?

Yes. Raw and undercooked meat may contain harmful bacteria. USDA recommends not eating or tasting raw or undercooked ground beef. To be sure all bacteria are destroyed, cook meat loaf, meatballs, casseroles, and hamburgers to 160 °F. Use a food thermometer to check that they have reached a safe internal temperature.

Are there people who are more at risk from eating ground beef that is undercooked or mishandled?

The very young, the very old, and those with immune systems that have been weakened by cancer, kidney disease, and other illnesses are most at risk and vulnerable to illnesses associated with contaminated food. The symptoms of foodborne illness – such as diarrhea or vomiting, which can cause dehydration – can be very serious. Safe food handling practices at home or anywhere food is served is especially important for those in the "at-risk" group.

Are Microwaved Hamburgers Safe?

Yes, if cooked properly to destroy harmful bacteria. Since microwaves may not cook food as evenly as conventional methods, covering hamburgers while cooking will help them heat more evenly. Turn each pattie over and rotate midway through cooking. Allow patties to stand 1 or 2 minutes to complete cooking. Then use a food thermometer to check that the internal temperature is 160 °F.

Is it safe to partially cook ground beef to use later?

No. Partial cooking of food ahead of time allows harmful bacteria to survive and multiply to the point that subsequent cooking cannot destroy them.

Can I refrigerate or freeze leftover cooked hamburgers? How should they be reheated?

If ground beef is refrigerated promptly after cooking (within 2 hours; 1 hour if the temperature is above 90 °F), it can be safely refrigerated for about 3 or 4 days. If frozen, it should keep its quality for about 4 months.

When reheating fully cooked patties or casseroles containing ground beef, be sure the internal temperature reaches 165 °F or it is hot and steaming.

Why is prepackaged ground beef red on the outside and sometimes dull, grayish-brown inside?

Oxygen from the air reacts with meat pigments to form a bright red colour which is usually seen on the surface of meat purchased in the supermarket. The pigment responsible for the red colour in meat is oxymyoglobin, a substance found in all warm-blooded animals. Fresh cut meat is purplish in colour. The interior of the meat may be grayish brown due to lack of oxygen; however, if all the meat in the package has turned gray or brown, it may be beginning to spoil.

Why does ground beef release a lot of "juice" while cooking?

In making ground beef, some retail stores grind the meat while it is still frozen. Ice crystals in the frozen meat break down the cell walls, permitting the release of meat juices during cooking. The same thing happens after ground meat is frozen at home.

What causes ground beef patties to shrink while cooking?

All meat will shrink in size and weight during cooking. The amount of shrinkage will depend on its fat and moisture content, the temperature at which the meat is cooked, and how long it is cooked. Basically, the higher the cooking temperature, the greater the shrinkage. Cooking ground beef at moderate temperatures will reduce shrinkage and help retain juices and flavour. Overcooking draws out more fat and juices from ground beef, resulting in a dry, less tasty product.

Ham and Food Safety

Hams may be fresh, cured, or cured-and-smoked. Ham is the cured leg of pork. Fresh ham is an uncured leg of pork. Fresh ham will bear the term "fresh" as part of the product name and is an indication that the product is not cured. "Turkey" ham is a ready-to-eat product made from cured thigh meat of turkey. The term "turkey ham" is always followed by the statement "cured turkey thigh meat."

The usual colour for cured ham is deep rose or pink; fresh ham (which is not cured) has the pale pink or beige colour of a fresh pork roast; country hams and prosciutto (which are dry cured) range from pink to a mahogany colour.

Hams are either ready to eat or not. Ready-to-eat hams include prosciutto and cooked hams; they can be eaten right out of the package. Fresh hams and hams that are only trichinae treated (which may include heating, freezing, or curing in the plant) must be cooked by the consumer before eating. Hams that must be cooked will bear cooking instructions and safe handling instructions.

Hams that are not ready to eat, but have the appearance of ready-to-eat products, will bear a prominent statement on the principal display panel indicating the product needs cooking, e.g., "cook thoroughly." In addition, the label must bear cooking directions.

Curing Solutions

Curing is the addition of salt, sodium or potassium nitrate (or saltpeter), nitrites, and sometimes sugar, seasonings, phosphates and cure accelerators, e.g., sodium ascorbate, to pork for preservation, colour development and flavour enhancement.

Nitrate and nitrite contribute to the characteristic cured flavour and reddish-pink colour of cured pork. Nitrite and salt inhibit the growth of *Clostridium botulinum,* a deadly microorganism which can occur in foods under certain situations.

Curing and flavouring solutions are added to pork by injection and by massaging and tumbling the solution into the muscle, both of which produce a more tender product.

Dry Curing

In dry curing, the process used to make country hams and prosciutto, fresh ham is rubbed with a dry-cure mixture of salt and other ingredients. Dry curing produces a salty product. In 1992, FSIS approved a trichinae treatment method that permits substituting up to half of the sodium chloride with potassium chloride to result in lower sodium levels. Since dry curing draws out moisture, it reduces ham weight by at least 18% — usually 20 to 25%; this results in a more concentrated ham flavour.

Dry-cured hams may be aged more than a year. Six months is the traditional process but may be shortened according to aging temperature.

These uncooked hams are safe stored at room temperature because they contain so little water, bacteria can't multiply in them. Dry-cured ham is not injected with a curing solution or processed by immersion in a curing solution, but it may be smoked. Today, dry cured hams may be marketed as items that need preparation on the part of the consumer to make them safe to eat. So, as with all meat products, it is important to read the label of hams to determine the proper preparation needed.

Wet Curing or Brine Cure

Brine curing is the most popular way of producing hams. It is a wet cure whereby fresh meat is injected with a curing solution before cooking. Brining ingredients can include ingredients such as salt, sugar, sodium nitrite, sodium nitrate, sodium erythorbate, sodium phosphate, potassium chloride, water and flavourings. Smoke flavouring (liquid smoke) may also be injected with brine solution. Cooking *may* occur during this process.

Smoking and Smoke Flavouring

After curing, some hams are smoked. Smoking is a process by which ham is hung in a smokehouse and allowed to absorb smoke from smoldering fires, which gives added flavour and colour to meat and slows the development of rancidity. Not all smoked meat is smoked from smoldering fires. A popular process is to heat the ham in a smoke house and generate smoke from atomized smoke flavour.

Foodborne Pathogens

These foodborne pathogens (organisms in food that can cause disease) are associated with ham:

- *Trichinella spiralis* (trichinae)-Parasites are sometimes present in hogs. All hams must be processed according to USDA guidelines to kill trichinae.
- *Staphylococcus aureus* (staph)-Bacteria are destroyed by cooking and processing but can be reintroduced via mishandling. The bacteria can then produce a toxin which is not destroyed by further cooking. Dry curing of hams may or may not destroy *S. Aureus,* but the high salt content on the exterior inhibits these bacteria. When the ham is sliced, the moister interior will permit staphylococcal multiplication. Thus sliced dry-cured hams must be refrigerated.
- *Mold*-Can often be found on country cured ham. Most of these are harmless but some molds can produce mycotoxins. Molds grow on hams during the long curing and drying process because the high salt and low temperatures do not inhibit these robust organisms. DO NOT DISCARD the ham. Wash it with hot water and scrub off the mold with a stiff vegetable brush.

Quantity to Buy

When buying a ham, estimate the size needed according to the number of servings the type of ham should yield:

- 1/4-1/3 lb. per serving of boneless ham
- 1/3-1/2 lb. of meat per serving of bone-in ham.

Cooking or Reheating Hams

Both whole or half, cooked, vacuum-packaged hams packaged in federally inspected plants and canned hams can be eaten cold just as they come from their packaging.

However, if you want to reheat these cooked hams, set the oven no lower than 325 °F and heat to an internal temperature of 140 °F as measured with a food thermometer. Unpackaged, cooked ham is potentially contaminated with pathogens. For cooked hams that have been repackaged in any other location outside the plant or for leftover cooked ham, heat to 165 °F.

Spiral-cut cooked hams are also safe to eat cold. The unique slicing method, invented in 1957, solves any carving difficulties. These hams are best served cold because heating sliced whole or half hams can dry out the meat and cause the glaze to melt and run off the meat. However, if reheating is desired, hams that were packaged in plants under USDA inspection must be heated to 140 °F as measured with a food thermometer (165 °F for leftover spiral-cut hams or ham that has been repackaged in any other location outside the plant). To reheat a spiral-sliced ham in a conventional oven, cover the entire ham or portion with heavy aluminum foil and heat at 325 °F for about 10 minutes per pound. Individual slices may also be warmed in a skillet or microwave.

Cook-before-eating hams or fresh hams must reach 160 °F to be safely cooked before serving. Cook in an oven set no lower than 325 °F. Hams can also be safely cooked in a microwave oven, other countertop appliances and on the stove. Consult a cookbook for specific methods and timing. Country hams can be soaked 4 to 12 hours or longer in the refrigerator to reduce the salt content before cooking. Then they can be cooked by boiling or baking. Follow the manufacturer's cooking instructions.

Timetable for Cooking Ham

Country Ham

Whole or Half. (Soak 4 to 12 hours in refrigerator. Cover with water and boil 20 to 25 minutes per pound. Drain, glaze, and brown at 400 °F for 15 minutes.)

Ham Glossary

Canned Ham: "Canned meat with Natural Juices" is acceptable for product that has been pumped or contains up to 10% of a solution before canning and processing. Processed, canned, uncured meat products (when water or broth is added to the can) may not be called "with natural juices." The acceptable name would be "with juices." Canned hams come in two forms:

- Shelf stable-Can be stored on the shelf up to 2 years at room temperature. Generally not over 3 pounds in size. Processed to kill all spoilage bacteria and pathogenic organisms such as *Clostridium botulinum, Salmonella* and *Trichinella spiralis*. The product is free of microorganisms capable of growing at ordinary room temperature. However, high temperature storage – above 122 °F (50 °C) – may result in harmless thermophylic bacteria multiplying and swelling or souring the product.
- Refrigerated-May be stored in the refrigerator for up to 6 to 9 months. Its weight can be up to 8% more than original uncured weight due to the uptake of water during curing. It need not be labelled "Added water" except for "In Natural Juices." Net Weight is the weight of the actual ham excluding the container. Processed at a time to temperature sufficient to kill infectious organisms (including Trichinae); however, the ham is not sterilized so spoilage bacteria may grow eventually.

Capacollo, Cooked

(Capicola, Capocolla, Capacola, Capicollo, Cappicola, Capacolo– Italian): This product does not meet the definition of ham because it is not from the hind leg of a hog. It is boneless pork shoulder butts which are cured and then cooked. The curing process may be dry curing, immersion curing, or pump curing. The cured product is coated with spices and paprika before cooking. This product shall always be labelled with "Cooked" as part of the product name. Water added is permitted.

Capacolla, Ham, Cooked: Ham that has been cured and then cooked.

Cook Before Eating: Needs cooking or further cooking. Is not cooked in the plant or heat treated in the plant and should be cooked to a safe minimum internal temperature of 160 °F.

Cottage "Ham": A cut from the top end of the shoulder, known as the shoulder butt, which has been cured in brine. Because it is not from the hind leg of the hog, it doesn't meet the definition of ham. The meat is not cooked. Another term for it is "cottage roll."

The uncooked, cured, dried, smoked or unsmoked meat food products made respectively from a single piece of meat conforming to the definition of "ham," or from a single piece of meat from a pork shoulder. They are prepared by the dry application of salt or by salt and one or more optional ingredients: nutritive sweeteners, spices, seasonings, flavorings, sodium or potassium nitrate, and sodium or potassium nitrite. They may not be injected with curing solutions nor placed in curing solutions. The product must be treated for the destruction of possible live trichinae.

Fully Cooked Or Cooked: Needs no further cooking because it is fully cooked at the establishment where it was produced and packaged. Product can be eaten directly as it comes from its packaging or reheated. Fully cooked is synonymous with cooked.

Gelatin: Gelatin is a binder/extender and is only permitted in a few meat and poultry products like sausage, luncheon meat, and meat loaves. About 1/4 ounce of dry gelatin is often added before a canned ham is sealed to cushion the ham during shipment. During processing, natural juices cook out of the ham and combine with the gelatin. When the ham cools, a jell forms. Gelatin is included in the net weight statement on the label and its presence is also qualified in the product name, e.g., Canned Ham, Gelatin Added."

Half Ham: "Half Ham" is permitted on labels for semi-boneless ham products which have had the shank muscles removed during processing. The two halves of the finished product have approximately an equal amount of bone. The term "No Slices Removed" has also been deemed suitable for use with a ham item referred to as "Half Ham."

Ham: Cured leg of pork. In order to be labelled as "Ham," the product must be at least 20.5% protein in lean portion as described in 9 CFR 319.104. Added water is permitted in a product labelled as "Ham." In fact, water will be declared in order of predominance in the ingredients statement. This is how the cure solution is introduced into a ham.

Ham And Water Products X% of Weight is Added Ingredients: Product contains more additives than a "Ham Water Added," but the product name must indicate percent of "added ingredients." For example, "Ham and Water Product 25% of Weight is Added Ingredients" for any canned ham with less than 17.0% protein.

Ham, Boiled: A fully cooked, boneless product which must be cooked in water and may be processed in a casing or can. The product may be of various shapes and may be partially cooked in boiling water.

Ham, Fresh (or uncured): The uncured leg of pork. Since the meat is not cured or smoked, it has the flavour of a fresh pork loin roast or pork chops. Its raw colour is pinkish red and after cooking, grayish white. Ham that does not contain a cure must be labelled either "Fresh" or "Uncured" – prepared without nitrate or nitrite. This also applies to cooked product, and must be labelled cooked product "Cooked Uncured Ham."

Ham Salad: Product must contain at least 35% cooked ham. Chopped ham may be used without it appearing in the product name.

Ham, Scotch Style: A cured, uncooked, boned, and rolled whole ham either tied or in a casing.

Ham Shank End, Ham Shank Half or Ham Shank Portion: The lower, slightly pointed part of the leg. A "portion" has the centre slices removed for separate sale as "ham steaks." A half ham does not have slices removed.

Ham, Skinless, Shankless: A ham with all of the skin and the shank removed. The leg bone and aitch (hip) bone remain.

Ham, Smithfield: This is an aged, dry-cured ham made exclusively in Smithfield, Virginia. The use of the words "brand" or "style," e.g., "Smithfield Brand Ham," "Smithfield Style Ham," does not eliminate this requirement.

Ham Steak: Another name for ham slices.

Ham-Water Added: The product is at least 17.0% protein with 10% added solution.

Ham With Natural Juices: The product is at least 18.5% protein.

Hickory-smoked Ham: A cured ham which has been smoked by hanging over burning hickory wood chips in a smokehouse. May not be labelled "hickory smoked" unless hickory wood has been used. Atomized liquid hickory smoke and heat can combine to produce "hickory smoke."

Honey-cured: May be shown on the labelling of a cured product if (1) the honey used contains at least 80% solids or is U.S. grade C or above; (2) honey is the only sweetening ingredient or when other sweetening ingredients are used in combination with honey, they do not exceed 1/2 the amount of honey used; and (3) honey is used in an amount sufficient to flavour and/or affect the appearance of the finished product.

"Lean" Ham: The term "lean" may be used on a ham's label provided the product contains less than 10 grams fat, 4.5 grams or less of saturated fat, and less than 95 milligrams cholesterol per 100 grams and Reference Amount Customarily Consumed (RACC).

"Extra Lean" Ham: A ham labelled "extra lean" must contain less than 5 grams fat, less than 2 grams saturated fat and the same cholesterol as allowed per the amount of "lean" ham.

Pork Shoulder Picnic: A front shoulder cut of pork. The term "picnic" cannot be used unless accompanied with the primal or subprimal cut. Pork shoulder picnic is not always a cured item. A shoulder "picnic" comes from the lower portion of the shoulder.

Prosciutto: Italian for ham, dry cured. The product name "Prosciutto" is acceptable on labelling to identify a dry-cured ham. An Italian-style dry cured raw ham; not smoked; often coated with pepper. Prosciutto can be eaten raw because the low water content prevents bacterial growth. PARMA HAM is prosciutto from the Parma locale in Italy. These hams tend to be larger than the U.S. produced product, as Italian hogs are larger at slaughter.

Prosciutto, Cooked: The product name "Cooked Prosciutto" is acceptable on labelling to identify a Prosciutto that is cooked.

Sectioned And Formed Ham or Chunked and Formed Ham: A boneless ham that is made from different cuts, tumbled or massaged and reassembled into a casing or mold and cooked. During this process it is usually thoroughly defatted. The qualifying phrase "sectioned and formed" is no longer required on boneless ham products, e.g., "ham" and "ham-water added." The addition of small amounts of ground ham added as a binder to such products may be used without declaration. The amount of ground ham that may be used can represent no more than 15% of the weight of the ham ingredients at the time of formulation. Products containing more than 15% ground ham trimmings must be labelled to indicate the presence of the ground ham, e.g., "a portion of ground ham added."

Sugar Cured: May be used on the labelling of a cured product (1) if the sugar used is cane sugar or beet sugar; (2) sugar is the only sweetening ingredient or when other sweetening ingredients are used in combination with sugar, they do not exceed one-half the amount of sugar used; and (3) sugar is used in an amount sufficient to flavour and/or affect the appearance of the finished product.

Westphalian Ham: A German-style dry-cured ham that is similar to Prosciutto; smoked, sometimes made with juniper berries.

Hot Dogs and Food Safety

Whether you call it a frankfurter, hot dog, wiener, or bologna, it's a cooked sausage and a year-round favourite. They can be made from beef, pork, turkey, chicken, or a combination — the label must state which And there are Federal standards of identity for their content.

Definitions

Frankfurters (a.k.a., hot dogs, wieners, or bologna) are cooked and/or smoked sausages according to the Federal standards of identity. Federal standards of identity describe the requirements for processors to follow in formulating and marketing meat, poultry, and egg products produced in the United States for sale in this country and in foreign commerce. The standard also requires that they be comminuted (reduced to minute particles), semisolid products made from one or more kinds of raw skeletal muscle from livestock (like beef or pork), and may contain poultry meat. Smoking and curing ingredients contribute to flavour, colour, and preservation of the product. They are link-shaped and come in all sizes — short, long, thin, and chubby.

The most popular of all categories, the skinless varieties, have been stripped of their casings after cooking. Water or ice, or both, may be used to facilitate chopping or mixing or to dissolve curing ingredients. The finished products may not contain more than 30% fat or no more than 10% water, or a combination of 40% fat and added water. Up to 3.5% non-meat binders and extenders (such as nonfat dry milk, cereal, or dried whole milk) or 2%

isolated soy protein may be used, but must be shown in the ingredients statement on the product's label by its common name.

Casings

Some hot dogs have a casing, or a thin skin. If the species of the casing is different than that of the hot dog, the label must say so. For example, if a turkey hot dog has a pork casing, the label must list the pork casing on the ingredients list. If the casing is artificially coloured, the label must indicate this as well.

Byproducts, Variety Meats

"Frankfurter, Hot Dog, Wiener, or Bologna With Byproducts" or "With Variety Meats" are made according to the specifications for cooked and/or smoked sausages, except they consist of not less than 15% of one or more kinds of raw skeletal muscle meat with raw meat byproducts. The byproducts (heart, kidney, or liver, for example) must be named with the derived species and be individually named in the ingredients statement.

Species

Beef Franks or Pork Franks are cooked and/or smoked sausage products made according to the specifications above, but with meat from a single species and do not include byproducts.

Turkey Franks or Chicken Franks can contain turkey or chicken and turkey or chicken skin and fat in proportion to a turkey or chicken carcass.

Ingredients Statement

All ingredients in the product must be listed in the ingredients statement in order of predominance, from highest to lowest amounts.

"Meat" Derived By Advanced Meat Bone Separation and Meat Recovery Systems.

The definition of "meat" was amended in December 1994 to include any "meat" product that is produced by advanced meat/bone separation machinery. This meat is comparable in appearance, texture, and composition to meat trimmings and similar meat products derived by hand. This machinery separates meat from bone by scraping, shaving, or pressing the meat from the bone without breaking or grinding the bone. Product produced by advanced meat recovery (AMR) machinery can be labelled using terms associated with hand-deboned product (e.g., "pork trimmings" and "ground pork").

The AMR machinery cannot grind, crush, or pulverize bones to remove edible meat tissue, and bones must emerge essentially intact. The meat produced in this manner can contain no more than 150 milligrams (mg) of calcium per 100 grams product (within a tolerance of 30 mg. of calcium). Products that exceed the calcium content limit must be labelled "mechanically separated pork" in the ingredients statement.

Mechanically Separated Meat (MSM)

Mechanically separated meat is a paste-like and batter-like meat product produced by forcing bones, with attached edible meat, under high pressure through a sieve or similar device to separate the bone from the edible meat tissue.

In 1982, a final rule published by FSIS on mechanically separated meat said it was safe and established a standard of identity for the food product. Some restrictions were made on how much can be used and the type of products in which it can be used. These restrictions were based on concerns for limited intake of certain components in MSM, like calcium.

Due to FSIS regulations enacted in 2004 to protect consumers against Bovine Spongiform Encephalopathy, mechanically separated beef is considered inedible and is prohibited for use as human food. It is not permitted in hot dogs or any other processed product. Mechanically separated pork is permitted and must be labelled as "mechanically separated pork" in the ingredients statement. Hot dogs can contain no more than 20% mechanically separated pork.

Mechanically Separated Poultry (MSP)

Mechanically separated poultry is a paste-like and batter-like poultry product produced by forcing bones, with attached edible tissue, through a sieve or similar device under high pressure to separate bone from the edible tissue. Mechanically separated poultry has been used in poultry products since the late 1960's. In 1995, a final rule on mechanically separated poultry said it was safe and could be used without restrictions. However, it must be labelled as "mechanically separated chicken or turkey" in the product's ingredients statement. The final rule became effective

November 4, 1996. Hot dogs can contain any amount of mechanically separated chicken or turkey.

Food Product Dating Terms

The labelling on a package of hot dogs may contain one of several different types of dates. Product dating is voluntary and not required by Federal regulations. If a date is used, it must also state what the date means.

- "Sell-By" date tells the store how long to display the product for sale. You should buy the product before the date expires.
- "Use-By" date is the last date recommended for use of the product while at peak quality. This date has been determined by the manufacturer of the product.
- "Best if Used By (or Before)" date helps consumers by stating a precise date for best flavour or quality.
- "Expiration Date" helps stores and consumers by stating the shelf-life or the last day product should be used while it is wholesome.

Safety After Date Expires

Except for "Use-By" dates, product dates don't refer to home storage and use after purchase. If a "Sell-By," "Best if Used By (or Before)," or "Expiration Date" date expires during home storage, a product should be safe and wholesome if handled safely and kept at 40 °F or below.

Food Safety Guidelines

The same general food safety guidelines apply to hot dogs as to all perishable products — "Keep hot food hot and cold food cold." Although all hot dogs are fully cooked, always reheat before eating. Use a food thermometer to make sure hot dogs reach 165 °F or are steamy hot throughout. Studies have shown a high level of the harmful bacteria *Listeria* in hot dogs. Thus, for added precaution, persons at risk may choose to avoid eating hot dogs and luncheon meats, such as bologna, unless they are reheated until steamy hot.

When you leave the grocery store with hot dogs, head straight home and refrigerate or freeze them immediately. If there is no product date, hot dogs can be safely stored in the unopened package for 2 weeks in the refrigerator; once opened, only 1 week.

For maximum quality, freeze hot dogs no longer than 1 or 2 months. And, of course, never leave hot dogs at room temperature for more than 2 hours and no more than 1 hour when the temperature goes above 90 °F.

Safety of Fresh Pork...from Farm to Table

Although pork is the number one meat consumed in the world, U.S. consumption dropped during the 1970s, largely because its high fat content caused health-conscious Americans to choose leaner meats. Today's hogs have much less fat due to improved genetics, breeding and feeding. Read on for more information about this red meat.

What is Pork?

Pork is the meat from hogs, or domestic swine. The domestication of "pigs" (immature hogs) for food dates back to about 7000 B.C. in the Middle East. However, evidence shows that Stone Age man ate wild boar, the hog's ancestor, and the earliest surviving pork recipe is Chinese, at least 2000 years old.

Hogs were brought to Florida by Hernando de Soto in 1525, and soon was America's most popular meat. In the 19th century — as America urbanized and people began living away from the farm, "salt pork" — pork that is prepared with a high level of salt to preserve it — became the staple food. Pork has continued to be an important part of our diet since that time.

Pork is generally produced from young animals (6 to 7 months old) that weigh from 175 to 240 pounds. Much of a hog is cured and made into ham, bacon and sausage. Uncured meat is called "fresh pork."

Can Antibiotics and Hormones Be Used in Pork Raising?

Antibiotics may be given to prevent or treat disease in hogs. A "withdrawal" period is required from the time antibiotics are administered until it is legal to slaughter the animal. This is so residues can exit the animal's system and won't be in the meat.

FSIS randomly samples pork at slaughter and tests for residues. Data from this monitoring program have shown a very low percentage of residue violations.

How is Pork Inspected?

All pork found in retail stores is either USDA inspected for wholesomeness or inspected by state systems which have standards equal to the federal government. Each animal and its internal organs are inspected for signs of disease. The "Passed and Inspected by USDA" seal insures the pork is wholesome and free from disease.

Is Pork Graded?

Although inspection is mandatory, its grading for quality is voluntary, and a plant pays to have its pork graded. USDA grades for pork reflect only two levels: "Acceptable" grade and "Utility" grade. Pork sold as Acceptable quality pork is the only fresh pork sold in supermarkets. It should have a high proportion of lean meat to fat and bone. Pork graded as Utility is mainly used in processed products and is not available in supermarkets for consumers to purchase.

What to Look For When Buying Pork

When buying pork, look for cuts with a relatively small amount of fat over the outside and with meat that is firm and a grayish pink colour. For best flavour and tenderness, meat should have a small amount of marbling.

Retail Cuts of Fresh Pork

There are four basic (primal) cuts into which pork is separated: shoulder, loin, side and leg.

Shoulder

- Shoulder Butt, Roast or Steak
- Blade Steak
- Boneless Blade Boston Roast
- Smoked Arm Picnic
- Smoked Hock
- Ground Pork for Sausage.

Side

- Spare Ribs/Back Ribs
- Bacon.

Loin

- Boneless Whole Loin (Butterfly Chop)
- Loin Roast
- Tenderloin

- Sirloin Roast
- Country Style Ribs
- Chops.

Leg

- Ham/Fresh or Smoked and Cured.

How much Pork is Consumed in America?

Figures from the USDA's Economic Research Service show average annual per capita pork consumption for the following selected periods:

- 1970: 48 pounds
- 1975: 39 pounds
- 1980: 52 pounds
- 1985: 48 pounds
- 1990: 46 pounds
- 1994: 50 pounds.

What does "Natural" Mean?

All fresh meat qualifies as "natural." Products labelled "natural" cannot contain any artificial flavour or flavouring, colouring ingredient, chemical preservative or any other artificial or synthetic ingredient; and the product and its ingredients are not more than minimally processed (ground, for example). All products claiming to be natural should be accompanied by a brief statement which explains what is meant by the term "natural."

Why is Pork a "Red" Meat?

Oxygen is delivered to muscles by the red cells in the blood. One of the proteins in meat, myoglobin, holds the oxygen in the muscle. The amount of myoglobin in animal muscles determines the colour of meat. Pork is classified a "red" meat because it contains more myoglobin than chicken or fish. When fresh pork is cooked, it becomes lighter in colour, but it is still a red meat. Pork is classed as "livestock" along with veal, lamb and beef. All livestock are considered "red meat."

Dating of Pork

Product dating (i.e. applying "sell by" or "use by" dates) is not required by Federal regulations. However, many stores and processors may voluntarily choose to date packages of raw pork.

Use or freeze products with a "sell-by" date within 3 to 5 days of *purchase*. If the manufacturer has determined a "use-by" date, observe it. It's always best to buy a product before its date expires. *It's not important if a date expires after freezing pork because all foods stay safe while properly frozen.*

What Foodborne Organisms are Associated with Pork?

Pork must be adequately cooked to eliminate disease-causing parasites and bacteria that may be present. Humans may contract trichinosis (caused by the parasite, *Trichinella spiralis*) by eating undercooked pork. Much progress has been made in reducing trichinosis in grain-fed hogs and human cases have greatly declined since 1950. Today's pork can be enjoyed when cooked to an internal temperature of 160 °F. Some other foodborne microorganisms that can be found in pork, as well as other meats and poultry, are *Escherichia coli, Salmonella, Staphylococcus aureus* and *Listeria monocytogenes*. They are all destroyed by proper handling and thorough cooking to an internal temperature of 160 °F.

Rinsing Pork

It isn't necessary to wash raw pork before cooking it. Any bacteria which might be present on the surface would be destroyed by cooking.

How to Handle Pork Safely

Raw Pork. Select pork just before checking out at the supermarket register. Put packages of raw pork in disposable plastic bags (if available) to contain any leakage which could cross contaminate cooked foods or produce. Take pork home immediately and refrigerate it at 40 °F; use within 3 to 5 days or freeze (0 °F).

Ready-Prepared Pork. For fully cooked take-out pork dishes such as Chinese food or barbecued ribs, be sure they are hot at pick-up. Use cooked pork within two hours (one hour if air temperature is above 90 °F) or refrigerate it at 40 °F or less in shallow, covered containers. Eat within 3 to 4 days, either cold or reheated to 165 °F (hot and steaming). It is safe to freeze ready prepared pork dishes. For best quality, use within 3 months.

Safe Defrosting

There are three safe ways to defrost pork: in the refrigerator, in cold water (in an airtight or leak-proof bag) and in the microwave.

Never defrost on the counter or in other locations. It's best to plan ahead for slow, safe thawing in the refrigerator. After defrosting raw pork by this method, it will be safe in the refrigerator 3 to 5 days before cooking. During this time, if you decide not to use the pork, *you can safely refreeze it without cooking it first.*

When microwave-defrosting pork, plan to cook it immediately after thawing because some areas of the food may become warm and begin to cook during microwaving. Holding partially cooked food is not recommended because any bacteria present wouldn't have been destroyed. *Foods defrosted in the microwave or by the cold water method should be cooked before refreezing because they potentially may have been held at temperatures above 40 °F.*

It is safe to cook frozen pork in the oven, on the stove or grill without defrosting it first; the cooking time may be about 50% longer. Use a meat thermometer to check for doneness. Do not cook frozen pork in a slow cooker.

Marinating

Marinate pork in the refrigerator in a covered container up to 5 days. Boil used marinade before brushing on cooked pork. Discard any uncooked leftover marinade.

Irradiation

Irradiation has been approved for use on pork by FDA and USDA/FSIS in low-doses (to control trichina). Treated pork would not be sterile and would still need to be handled safely. *Trichinella* could be alive but would be unable to reproduce. Packages of irradiated pork must be labelled with the irradiation logo as well as the words "Treated with Irradiation" or "Treated by Irradiation" so they would be easily recognizable at the store.

Partial Cooking

Never brown or partially cook pork, then refrigerate and finish cooking later, because any bacteria present wouldn't have been destroyed. It is safe to partially pre-cook or microwave pork *immediately* before transferring it to the hot grill to finish cooking.

Safe Cooking

For safety, the USDA recommends cooking ground pork patties and ground pork mixtures such as meat loaf to 160 °F. Whole muscle meats such as chops and roasts should be cooked to 160 °F.

For approximate cooking times for use in meal planning, see the attached chart compiled from various resources. Times are based on pork at refrigerator temperature (40 °F). Remember that appliances and outdoor grills can vary in heat. Use a meat thermometer to check for safe cooking and doneness of pork.

Can Safely Cooked Pork Be Pink?

Cooked muscle meats can be pink even when the meat has reached a safe internal temperature. If fresh pork has reached 160 °F throughout, even though it may still be pink in the centre, it should be safe. The pink colour can be due to the cooking method or added ingredients.

Chicken Grading

Inspection is mandatory but grading is voluntary. Chickens are graded according to USDA Agricultural Marketing Service regulations and standards for meatiness, appearance and freedom from defects. Grade A chickens have plump, meaty bodies and clean skin, free of bruises, broken bones, feathers, cuts and discoloration.

Fresh or Frozen

The term *fresh* on a poultry label refers to any raw poultry product that has never been below 26 °F. Raw poultry held at 0 °F or below must be labelled *frozen* or *previously frozen*. No specific labelling is required on raw poultry stored at temperatures between 0-25 °F.

Dating of Chicken Products

Product dating is not required by Federal regulations, but many stores and processors voluntarily date packages of chicken or chicken products. If a calendar date is shown, immediately adjacent to the date there must be a phrase explaining the meaning of that date such as *sell by* or *use before.*

The use-by date is for quality assurance; after the date, peak quality begins to lessen but the product may still be used. It's always best to buy a product before the date expires. If a use-by date expires while the chicken is frozen, the food can still be used.

Index

E

F

G

H

I

L

M

N

O

P.

❑❑❑